FOREIGN INFLUENCES
IN AMERICAN LIFE

PRINCETON STUDIES

IN AMERICAN CIVILIZATION

———

The Constitution and World Organization

By Edward S. Corwin

Foreign Influences in American Life

Edited by David F. Bowers

Evolutionary Ideas in the United States

Edited by Stow Persons

(In Preparation)

This series is published under the auspices of
the Program of Study in American Civilization,
Princeton University, and is designed to foster
research in the humanistic, social, and technological aspects of American civilization as they affect
one another; to promote an understanding of
civilization in America in relation to other civilizations; and to encourage both lay and scholarly interest in American
studies.

FOREIGN INFLUENCES IN AMERICAN LIFE

ESSAYS AND CRITICAL BIBLIOGRAPHIES

EDITED FOR THE PRINCETON
PROGRAM OF STUDY IN AMERICAN CIVILIZATION

By DAVID F. BOWERS

NEW YORK
PETER SMITH
1952

Printed in the United States of America

FOREWORD

As a field for exploitation, as a haven for nonconform-
ism, and most recently as the single safe refuge for the
intellectual life of the western world, America has
ever been the focus of competing interests from abroad, and
has registered the effect of these interests at all levels of the
national culture. With no sense of confusion it early became
and has since remained a sphere which could as easily accommodate the experimentation of a Robert Owen or a Joseph
Priestley as the spirit of Calvin or the rapacity of English,
Dutch, and Spanish entrepreneurs.

And this is only half the story. For if Europe, Asia, and
Africa have sought America, it is also true that America has
sought them. As a young people, we have ever been engrossed
with the moment of our own origins, seeking in the circumstance of early settlement and revolt a special competence and
prerogative denied to others. But we have also envisaged
that prerogative as a natural growth whose seeds were first
planted long ago and among other peoples. Far from regarding ourselves as innovators, we have conceived our task as
mainly one of refinement, development, and implementation,
with the result that we have never ceased to be conscious of
comparative national achievements. What we have refused
to imitate we have not ignored but have sought to surpass;
and where we could not legitimately despise we have stopped
to admire. In this way, our people and institutions, our art,
our literature, our religion, and our philosophy have always
been apprised of and therefore also conditioned by the course
of events elsewhere.

Yet such influences, whether avoided or sought, have
never been transmitted without modification. In the beginning, even the physical environment itself exhibited a peculiar
capacity to resist and transmute, confronting old aptitudes
with new exigencies and forcing new forms of expression upon
previously received opinions. Nor has this quality since been

lost. Rather, it has been intensified and confirmed as the distinctive pattern of American life has emerged and become more fixed. Thus, in absorbing we have always refashioned, and in swallowing we have, for the most part, digested.

For this reason, the fact of foreign influence in America constitutes a problem of special difficulty and one whose study has scarcely yet begun. The present volume, therefore, makes no pretense of finality. In a rough sense, its essays and critical bibliographies seek merely to define the problem: to describe the basic forms of cultural impact and assimilation, to trace something of their history in American life, and to survey or illustrate their more manifest effects upon our economic, political, artistic, religious, and philosophic institutions. In covering such a large subject within so brief a compass the procedure inevitably becomes selective and in some measure arbitrary; but an effort has been made to compensate by selecting for discussion only topics of a representative character.

It remains only to say a word about the sponsorship of the volume and the contributors who have made it possible. The volume is issued under the auspices of the Program of Study in American Civilization at Princeton University and represents material developed and presented in connection with the regular undergraduate conference of the Program held during 1942-1943. This explains the emphasis placed upon the bibliographical essays and the particular form these essays have assumed. Since the plan of the conference called for full undergraduate participation in the shape of discussion and reports, each bibliography was accompanied by a statement of the problem, a list of general reference works, and a group of titles dealing with special topics. This form has been preserved in the present volume for whatever worth it may have. For readers interested in the mechanics of the conference itself, a description and an appraisal of its operation have been published separately, and may be had upon request to the Program of Study in American Civilization, Princeton University, Princeton, New Jersey.

As editor, I wish to thank publicly all those who have collaborated in the volume either directly or indirectly. I am particularly indebted to my Princeton colleagues: Dr. Stow Persons of the Department of History, Professor Frank D. Graham of the Department of Economics, Professor D. D. Egbert of the Department of Art and Archaeology, as well as to Mr. R. P. Blackmur of the Princeton Program in Creative Writing, Professor J. G. Leyburn of Yale and Dr. Oscar Handlin of Harvard, all of whom have contributed essays. To these and others, I am also indebted in various degrees for assistance in the preparation of the bibliographies: to Dr. Persons for the bibliographical material on the history of immigration, on cultural and social assimilation and on the religious and philosophic impact; to Professors Graham and Egbert for material on the economic and artistic impact respectively; to Professor Edward S. Corwin of the Princeton Department of Politics for material on the political impact, and to Professor Willard Thorp of the Princeton Department of English for material on the literary impact. I should like to acknowledge especially, however, the help of Dr. Persons and Professor Egbert who not only contributed when questions relating to their own fields of specialization were in point, but aided materially in planning the structure and format of the project as a whole. I am also particularly grateful to Mrs. L. J. Lee for her accurate and painstaking correction of proof.

Last but not least, I wish to thank the Princeton seniors who participated in the conference from which the volume is derived, and whose patience and interest were ultimately responsible for the successful completion of both enterprises. Expressed as this interest was in the midst of preparing themselves for war, their ready cooperation in what was then an untried experiment proves a rare devotion to the idea of education. And it is to these men, accordingly, now all in the service of their country, that the present volume should be considered inscribed.

January 2, 1944.

D. F. B.

CONTENTS

CONTENTS

PART II. CRITICAL BIBLIOGRAPHIES

[x]

PART I · ESSAYS

I · THE PROBLEM OF
SOCIAL AND CULTURAL IMPACT

By DAVID F. BOWERS

THE origin and growth of the United States represents one chapter in the history of a great migration. This migration, which was initiated by the people of Europe in the sixteenth century and which has involved the movement of ideas and institutions as well as of men, is one of the largest and most important in world history. Extending over a period of four hundred years, it has consisted of a continuous, and even accelerating, dislocation of previously stable populations and their dispersion, often at the rate of a million persons a year, over every continent of the globe.

The resulting change in the pattern of human relationships has been tremendous. Europe has been forced to adjust to the exodus of these groups, primitive peoples everywhere to their influx; and, in consequence, totally new institutional complexes, totally new social attitudes, and even totally new modes of thought have been gradually evolved all over the globe. To find a movement comparable in magnitude, velocity, and social profundity, it is necessary to go back to the barbarian invasions of Rome, and beyond these to the wanderings of primitive tribes in prehistoric times.

Of the nations affected by this migration of men, institutions, and ideas, the United States has probably been influenced most. In the first place, it was among the earliest of the new nations to be colonized and, therefore, one of those affected longest. In the second place, it has been the most important of the immigrant-receiving countries, admitting between 1820 and 1930 no less than 38 million immigrants, or about sixty per cent of the total number estimated for the period. And, in the third place, as a growing culture with few traditions of its own, it has always been alert to discover and to seize upon the arts and beliefs of other peoples. Although early in our history we strove for a political, economic, and general cultural independence of the old world, there has always been a sizable group of Americans who have looked back to the older cultures for their inspiration and ideals.

But although foreign influence has thus been very great, our civilization is not wholly a derivative one, not a mere transplantation persisting unchanged except for environment. For the most part, we have absorbed as well as admitted these influences: their transformation has been chemical as well as mechanical in nature. Placed in the American context, they have acquired new forms, new accents, new meanings, totally different from those previously manifested.

For this reason if no other, the study of foreign influence is as difficult as it is important. To understand it fully (and no one does) would require, among other things, an exact knowledge of the character and historical background of each belief, each attitude, almost each individual, which has ever been imported into the American scene; a detailed grasp of the existing state of American culture and society at the moment of importation; and a careful tracing of the effect of this importation both upon the invading element itself and upon the subsequent course of American life. Only by some exhaustive procedure such as this could we hope to grasp clearly the precise character and force of the impact.

In view of this complexity, it is clearly desirable both that we limit the scope of our inquiry, and that we have some conception to begin with of the kind of analysis foreign impact requires. Unless the problem is definitely limited at the outset and our investigation guided by a clear sense of what the problem involves, the inquiry can easily grow unmanageable and become lost in the mere accumulation of unrelated details.

The present essay attempts such a limitation of the subject and such an analysis. It is not suggested, however, that the limitation and the analysis proposed are definitive or even the most adequate available. They are offered as merely one approach among many and as a means of focusing the present discussion of the problem more sharply.

I

Foreign influences in America have poured in through many different channels, have affected in one way or another almost every phase of our national life, and have operated continuously throughout our history.

Many factors in American society have served to mediate foreign influence. The most obvious and important of these has consisted of the "alien in our midst": the foreign-born colonizer, immigrant, or slave, who, although physically present in, and interactive with, the American scene, embodies attitudes and tendencies which have been molded elsewhere. A second and equally familiar agent, however, is found in the native American who, having become aware of foreign developments in art, politics, religion, business methods, or the like, has been moved to appropriate them for his use either by direct imitation or with modifications. Still a third agency is represented in our diplomatic and foreign relations in so far as these have affected the national life.

Moreover, there has been no period in our history in which such agencies have not been active. We have always had, for example, "the alien in our midst." In colonial times, he was the native Indian coming upon a white settlement for the first time, or the newly imported Negro, or the recently arrived British, German, or Dutch settler. In the nineteenth century, he was the disembarking immigrant from southern, eastern, or central Europe. And in the twentieth century, to continue the catalogue, he has been the foreign-born Jap, Chinaman, Mexican, or Filipino, trying to adjust himself to the conditions of American life.

Being a young people, we have also always been strongly disposed to admit and imitate foreign ideas and practices. These have differed in character and source with different periods, but the tendency itself has always been present. Thus, in the colonial period, it was the British whom we imitated and admired the most; in the early national period, the French; and, in the late nineteenth century the Germans; while today, under the pressure of international affairs, it is the culture and institutions of Latin America which occupy the focus of our interest.

Finally, there has also been continuously present an influence mediated through our foreign policy. We have never, for example, been a people long at peace. In our 400 years of history as a colony and nation, we have fought no less than nine formally declared wars, none of which were spaced more than a single generation apart, and all of which have had repercussions upon our domestic economy. And this is to say nothing of the effect of our foreign policy generally.

From all this, it should be clear that an adequate treatment of the problem of impact would involve an investigation of: (a) all the dates and places at which influences were felt; (b) all the agencies through which these influences were introduced; (c) all foreign groups represented by the agencies; and (d) all the phases or parts of American life affected by them. But it should also be clear that in the time at our disposal this is utterly impossible. Accordingly, it will be well to restrict the inquiry, at least so far as the present study is concerned, in the following ways:

(1) *That it be limited historically to the period between 1800 and 1941.* This restriction has many advantages and may be justified on a variety of grounds. In the first place, owing to the national isolation consequent upon the Revolution, American society had, by 1800, developed a relatively stable and distinctive institutional pattern of its own. In the second place, it was not until the early years of the nineteenth century that foreign immigration, one of the most important channels of influence, began to assume the proportions of a mass movement. And in the third place, it was not until 1820 that reliable census statistics on immigration became available. For our purposes here, therefore, the year 1800 provides an

excellent date at which to begin. This restriction does not signify that we can dispense entirely with the history of America prior to 1800. It means only that we shall be interested in the earlier period merely as a background and not for its own sake. The terminating date of 1941 is convenient since it coincides with the entry of America into the second World War.

(2) *That not all types of agents of impact be investigated.* It is difficult to impose this kind of limitation rigidly without excluding important sources of influence. But it seems possible to concentrate, without undue distortion, upon two types of influence: those arising from immigration, and those arising from widely circularized foreign ideas, works of art, inventions, and the like. Influences occasioned by war and diplomatic exchange, by the tourist, student, and businessman traffic in general, and by the circulation of unpublicized foreign cultural products are normally too difficult to trace, and, in any case, do not seem to rank in importance with the type of agency just mentioned. This holds good, however, only as a general rule, and there will be occasions, therefore, when this particular limitation must be disregarded.

(3) *That the study be limited to certain selected ethnic and national groups and to certain selected phases of American life.* Even if we confine the inquiry to a relatively short segment of American history, and to a few channels of influence, our task would still be impossibly difficult if we were to attempt to canvass the influence of *all* foreign groups or even the influence of any one of them on *all* phases of American life. It is desirable, therefore, that we restrict the scope of our study still further, and be concerned with only such groups as have affected the national life in a decisive way and with only such of their effects as fall within one or more of the following fields: literature, the major and minor arts, economic institutions and theory, political institutions and theory, religious dogma and practice, and philosophic doctrine. This means that certain groups and certain phases of American

culture will not be touched on at all, or, at most, only incidentally, but within the limits indicated representative conclusions should be possible.

II

The study of impact frequently constitutes a complex problem. As noted above, an impact may extend over a long period of time, may be transmitted through many different channels, and may end by affecting group life in a number of different ways. It will be of some help, therefore, to concentrate upon the nature of impact as such. Although any given instance of impact presents features peculiar to itself alone, it is sufficiently like other instances to render such an inquiry both possible and useful.

In this section, accordingly, we shall be concerned with four problems: (1) the definition of certain basic terms; (2) the description of the processes through which ethnic and national impacts are usually transmitted; (3) the description of certain characteristic effects of impact; and (4) the definition of the norms available for its evaluation.

1. Basic Terms

Certain terms, such as "ethnic group," "national group," "culture," and the like, are crucial in the present type of inquiry, and it is essential that we come to some agreement on how they shall be used. In defining these terms, it will be legitimate to consult only our own convenience since none of them has a fixed, definite meaning.

Ethnic Group or Race. By an "ethnic group" or "race" we shall mean any group of people belonging to a common biological stock and sharing a common biological ancestry. The two terms will thus be used interchangeably to refer to any "family" of peoples—such as the European, the North American Indian and the Negro—and to any sub-grouping of these—e.g., the Teuton, the Celt, and the Scandinavian. Few racial families can be defined sharply, and it is difficult to determine with accuracy the family or race to which any given people ultimately belongs. But if we do not attempt to push the classification too far—particularly too far into the remote past—it remains valid of the more recent biological groupings, and is therefore of some use.

National Group. By a "national group" we shall mean all the individuals belonging by birth or citizenship (a) to a single nation or (b) to a single confederation of nations, where "nation" is construed to mean an independent political unit. The French, the Italians, and the Japanese may be considered examples of the former; the British (as comprising the English, the Scotch, and the North Irelanders) may be taken to exemplify the latter.

National groupings cut across racial groupings in a bewildering fashion, but it is convenient to retain both as principles of classification. In the study of impact, sometimes the one, sometimes the other, will be the more significant. Thus, a study of the "Negro impact" is likely to prove more useful than a study of "the impact of French Equatorial Africa," if only because the slave status of the Negro tended to obliterate all tribal differences immediately upon arrival in this country. On the other hand, where national differences have survived migration and have made a difference in the resulting impact, it will be better to stress nationality rather than race. Thus, we shall probably learn more from a study of "the French impact" and "the Italian impact" taken separately than from a study of them as parts of "the Latin impact." In general, we may proceed upon the principle of employing that type of grouping whose presence and effect are most visible in the total effect upon American life.

Culture and Civilization. We shall use "culture" and "civilization" as related terms: the first as equivalent to the "ethos" or "spiritual" attitude of a people, its basic beliefs, preferences, ideals, etc.; the second as equivalent to the complex of institutions and practices in which that ethos has been overtly expressed.

This is not the only way in which these terms may be defined, but it is the usage we shall adopt here. As we go on, we shall discover it is extremely helpful to be able to distinguish between the "inner" and "outer" aspects of group life. We shall find, for example, that it has always been easier for the immigrant to bring along the dominant attitudes of his group than it has been to transport its institutions, and that this is a fact of great importance in the transmission of impact. It is essential therefore that we be able to express this kind of distinction clearly.

Ethnic and National Impact. An ethnic or national "impact" may be defined most simply as the sum total of all the effects registered upon a racial or national group as a result of interacting with the people, civilization, or culture of a different race or nation. It will thus include all changes whatsoever, whether direct or indirect, immediate or remote, which can be traced specifically to contact with the affecting group.

In the present context, however, this definition must be somewhat modified. Since we have agreed to include in our study only those foreign influences which have been specifically mediated through immigration or through the general interchange of ideas, it is only the latter type of impact which will be relevant to the present inquiry.

2. The Process of Impact

Ethnic and national impacts are always transmitted through highly complex processes. Once the immigrant has disembarked or the alien idea been introduced, he or it begins immediately to interact with members and elements of the invaded society. Conflicts are generated, efforts at adjustment begun, and the entire social organism is forced into a series of compensating changes which it would not otherwise have had to undergo.

This process, which continues until all sense of conflict has been removed, is flexible in character. It may vary in course and duration, in the type and degree of adjustment achieved, and in its ultimate effects upon both the invading and invaded groups. To see all this clearly, however, it is necessary to examine each of these factors in more detail.

Role of Conflict. Group impact is not always the result of conflict. Group interplay may spring from a mutual recognition of common needs, and be guided by a rational decision to cooperate in their pursuit. This happens, for example, when nations ally themselves in war, and when they arrange trade pacts and treaties in time of peace.

But in the type of interaction with which we are concerned here—that between a society and the foreign groups or ideologies invading it—the situation is apt to be different. Without the neutralizing and restraining influence of diplomatic protocol, racial and cultural differences are thrown into vivid relief. Inconsistencies in attitude and ideals seem more glaring, diversity of purpose and interest more sharply incompatible, and conflict in some form or another almost inevitably results. This is why, for example, the presence of immigrants and of alien ideas is normally regarded by the native born as a "problem," and why the special agencies created to meet this problem often try to solve it by deliberately minimizing differences: by trying to "Americanize" the immigrant or idea on the one hand, or by teaching the native born to tolerate their peculiarities on the other. The role of conflict in the transmission of impact may, therefore, be very great. But it enters into that transmission in two different ways which it is important to distinguish.

In the first place, it functions as the primary cause and condition of the process of adjustment. When the foreign element first appears in the environment, the normal reaction is one of fear and uneasiness. The mere presence of an individual who dresses, speaks, and acts in ways different from ourselves, or the mere expression of a belief or art form to which we are unaccustomed, arouses in most of us a sense of insecurity and instability, a feeling that "something is wrong" and that "something must be done about it"; and when this reaction is intensified (as is often the case) by the failure to establish a quick and easy means of communication with the offending element, or by the discovery that its presence constitutes an active threat to our own vested interests, our initial attitude tends to be hostile. And it is this hostility which generates the effort at adjustment. The fear and hate which normally accompany conflict are in and of themselves unpleasant and automatically become the occasion of activity designed to eliminate their cause.

In the second place, conflict may also figure as an *effect* of the effort at adjustment. This happens in two ways. First, conflict may be occasioned by the sheer novelty of the form the adjustment seeks to take. Whatever agency is employed for this purpose, it itself will often constitute a new thing in the environment, a novel fact which it is just as difficult to accept and adjust to as the foreign element itself. This is shown, for example, in the frequent criticisms of the settlement house and of the adult education movement which are agencies of this sort.

Second, conflict may also be occasioned by disputes and disagreement as to the proper method of adjustment. Not all efforts at adjustment are effective, and no rule can be laid down as to which will guarantee success. There usually exists, accordingly, no obvious policy on which all interested parties can agree, and so a new source of conflict may arise. How violent this type of conflict can become is illustrated in the emotional tension created by the mid-nineteenth century argument over whether the Negro should be repatriated to Africa or allowed to remain in America.

The transmission of impact involves, thus, two types of conflict; a primary conflict between the native and the foreign which instigates and sustains the process of adjustment until complete adjustment is effected; and a secondary type of conflict incident to the process of adjustment itself. Both are equally important in the study of impact since each may be productive of far-reaching social change.

Factors Affecting Adjustment. The effort of a group to overcome the conflicts generated by an invading element will continue, as was already remarked, until a satisfactory adjustment has been made. But the period of time required for this varies considerably, depending upon attendant circumstances. These special circumstances are too numerous to list here, but we may note certain ones of them as being more important than others:

(a) One such is the degree in which the conflicting groups or ideas resemble or differ from each other. All else being equal, the less differences there are in physique, language, cultural ideals, and the like, the fewer the opportunities for conflict and the less time required for effecting adjustment. This is shown by the fact that in America the German immigrant and German ideas have been more easily assimilated than the Slavic, and the Slavic more readily than the Oriental.

(b) Another important factor is the invaded group's opinion, at the moment of impact, of the country or race of the invader. This will depend upon similarity of stock and culture, upon how well the alien country or race is known, and upon the current state of international affairs, but in any case the influence of this opinion may be decisive. Again, all else being equal, the more favorable this opinion is, the more tolerant will the invaded group be of the invasion, and the more easily, accordingly, will basic differences be adjudicated and overcome. This is illustrated by our contrasting reception, at the turn of the present century, of the German and the Italian, when the latter was referred to contemptuously as "spaghetti eater" and the former welcomed as the representative of a nation then greatly admired.

(c) A third factor, when the invading element is a person, is the attitude of the invader himself. Each immigrant brings with him or acquires in due course, a definite opinion of his adopted country, and this often governs his relation to it.

This opinion, for example, may be one of whole-hearted approval, leading to a complete break of all ties with the homeland and to an identification of personal welfare with the welfare of the adopted country. At the opposite extreme, however, this opinion may be one of contempt or distrust, and eventuate in a decision on the part of the immigrant either to exploit the adopted country for purely personal ends, or to abandon it altogether and to return to the land of his birth. But, whatever the attitude, it will figure actively in the creation and adjustment of conflict. It is clear that an attitude of the first type, for example, is more likely to promote social harmony than is one of the second type, and that the period of adjustment in the one case is apt to be shorter than that in the other.

(d) Further factors affecting the duration and adjustment of conflict are the numerical proportion of the invading elements relative to the invaded, and the location of the area, physical or mental, in which the conflict arises. Up to a certain point, the greater the number of invading elements present in a community the more time is apt to be required for resolving the conflicts they create. This is true not only because more conflicts are thereby likely to occur, but also because the greater number of elements favors a greater diversity in type of conflict and thus precludes the use of simple schemes of adjustment.

Beyond a certain point, however, this generalization will not hold. When the invading elements greatly outnumber the native elements, there is a tendency for the latter to be quickly dominated or to abandon the field altogether, thus terminating the struggle at an early stage. This is illustrated, for example, in the growth of immigrant residential areas from which the native-born inhabitants have voluntarily withdrawn, and in the temporary ascendancy alien art forms or styles will sometimes obtain among native artists.

In America, this phenomenon has scarcely, if ever, occurred on a national scale. Our people have never been so outnumbered by foreigners or our culture so flooded by foreign ideas that it has been easier to give in at once than to continue the struggle for modes of adjustment more favorable to the native element. Hence, increases in immigrant traffic and in the influx of foreign ideas have usually tended to delay adjustment rather than to accelerate it.

Again, the location of the conflict may be important. This is clearly evident in the case of the immigrant. In rural areas which are sparsely settled and where the new immigrant is rarely thrown into highly intimate association with the native born, there is less need or occasion for adjustment and greater opportunity for retaining old customs. The result is a less intense form of conflict but at the same time a more protracted one. Group differences under such circumstances will remain submerged and therefore less inciting, but they will continue to exist and from time to time require adjustment. This has happened, for example, in the case of the Pennsylvania Germans. Maintaining a highly insulated community life from the beginning, this group has never violently quarreled with surrounding groups. Indeed, on many counts, they are held in high respect by their neighbors. But after 150 years of contact some conflict is still going on, as is evident in the group's continued struggle against the use of English in the public schools.

In urban districts, on the contrary, where the immigrant has from the beginning been thrown into immediate and vital contact with American life, the period required for adjustment is usually shorter, and will often be encompassed in the space of a single generation. This is not true of all alien groups, however, and notably untrue of Negroes and Jews. In these and other cases, the institution of the "ghetto" has often intervened and served to nullify the more normal effects of urban association.

The factor of location also affects the duration of conflict when the invading element is an idea or a cultural form. In this case, however, "location" must be defined not geographically but in terms of area of interest. Thus, if the invading idea obviously contradicts something held sacred or important by the invaded group, conflict will break out immediately but will usually be of short duration, since under such circumstances the normal course is to reject the new idea at once. On the other hand, if the novel idea deals with matters held to be trivial or of little moment, or if it is concerned with important matters but fails to make this clear, the result is apt to be different. In both cases the conflict may never become intense, and in the latter it may be protracted indefinitely, operating as a submerged inconsistency in group thought or practice.

(e) A final factor worthy of mention consists of the agencies purposely set up to overcome conflict. These agencies may be established either by the invaded or the invader and may differ widely in type. In some instances they will be eleemosynary in character, in others, educational, and in still others will consist merely of various legal contrivances. The American people themselves have been particularly active in creating agencies of this type. We have, for example, legally forbidden certain kinds of immigration—notably that from the Orient —and have legally prohibited, on occasion, the circulation of certain foreign political doctrines. On the other hand, we have also from time to time instituted programs designed to encourage alien influence. Most prominent among these have been: (1) the agencies that once existed to promote immigration; (2) such more recent ventures as the settlement house, the International House, and others which have been designed to foster interracial tolerance; and finally (3) the various business and technological "institutes" which now seek to keep American manufacturers abreast of technical improvements abroad. Even the international cartel functions in this way whenever it reserves portions of the American market for European goods. But native-born Americans have not been alone in these endeavors. Instances may be multiplied of similar activities among the foreign groups themselves. This may be seen in their many and varied efforts to "sell" America on the importance of their "contributions" and in their frequent attempts at helping their own members become Americanized as quickly as possible.

All formal efforts of this sort will affect the duration and intensity of group conflict in one way or another, but not all with equally desirable results. Certain types of endeavor, in fact, tend to prolong rather than shorten conflict. This is particularly true of those which rely mainly on methods of segregation and elimination, as may be seen in the failure of our immigration policy with respect to China and Japan. The refusal to admit citizens from these two countries on an equal basis with other countries has not only failed in its main purpose of curbing the flow of Chinese and Japanese immigration entirely, but, through its tacit encouragement of racial prejudice, has obstructed the peaceful assimilation of the Chinese and Japanese already here. In general, it has only been the more positive types of agency, those promoting complete assimilation, and full understanding and sympathy which have succeeded in avoiding this danger.

These, then, are some of the factors affecting the duration and adjustment of group conflict. It should be noted in conclusion, however, that no one of them alone can guarantee completeness of adjustment or, conversely, postpone it indefinitely. Failure or success in adjustment will depend, usually, upon the operation of many independent factors acting concurrently, and there is no assurance, in any given case, that the positive or negative influence of any single factor will be enough to offset the influence of all the others present. Each factor, in other words, represents merely one out of many prevailing influences in the total situation.

Conscious and Unconscious Adjustment. As may be seen from the preceding section, the effort at group adjustment is often a matter of deliberate policy and control. But this is not always the case. Much, and perhaps most of it, is carried on unconsciously.

Immediately upon contact with one another, individual

representatives of conflicting groups tend to enter upon processes of adjustment. This, in fact, is almost an automatic procedure. But unless special circumstances dictate otherwise, these processes may never rise above the unconscious level. Once the initial, startling effect of the other's presence has worn off, there is a disposition on the part of each to take the other for granted, and, in a manner of which they are often totally unaware, to imitate and appropriate features of each other's behavior and attitude. The same is true in the reception of a foreign idea. Unless we reject or forget it immediately, it will soon insinuate itself into our stock of accepted beliefs and its foreign origin come to be forgotten. Thus without the intervention of an explicit group policy (and often in spite of such a policy), a fusion of the foreign and native may go steadily and automatically forward, and, freed, in this manner, of reflective control, produce profound and unpredictable changes in group character and attitude.

It is important to note the fact of unconscious adjustment for several reasons: In the first place, since it goes on independently of formal programs of adjustment and may remain undetected in so doing, it will often succeed in nullifying such programs. This is illustrated by the friendliness which sometimes develops between alien and native born even where the definite policy in their locality is one of segregation. In the second place, it is the more painless and more peaceful method of adjustment. Unlike conscious efforts at adjustment, which are apt to be unbending and to insist that all adjusting be done by the other party, it will often assume the form of a compromise in which each will, in some measure, accommodate itself to the demands of the other. For this reason, finally, unconscious adjustment is responsible for the most subtle and revolutionary forms of group impact. Since it is both unconscious and compromising in tendency, it is able to insinuate radical and far-reaching changes into patterns of group behavior without arousing active suspicion or resistance.

The Primary Forms of Adjustment. Whether it be consciously or unconsciously guided, every process of adjustment assumes a certain definite pattern or character. These patterns, of which there are only a few basic types, differ principally in their methods for achieving adjustment and in the extent to which they produce socially satisfactory results.

Certain of these primary forms are listed below, together with their special methods and effects. But before describing them it is necessary to explain what is meant here by "socially satisfactory results." Any form of adjustment will be socially satisfactory in the extent to which it fulfills the following three conditions: (a) the eradication of all diversity which is injurious; (b) the preservation of all diversity which enriches; and (c) the accomplishment of both these objectives without social or individual distress. Some types of diversity are bad, as when, for example, two different group attitudes or two different ideas existing in juxtaposition possess less intrinsic value than would result if one or the other were to exist alone. Similarly, some diversity is good, as when the continuing juxtaposition of two diverse elements—say two interpretations of Hamlet—manifests a greater value conjointly than either one separately.

It is virtually certain that no form of adjustment will ever be able to fulfill all three requirements perfectly. The enriching and the injurious types of diversity are frequently too intricately interconnected to be separated, and almost any process of adjustment is bound to involve pain for someone. But some forms of adjustment will approximate this ideal more closely than others, and this enables us to scale them in terms of their social value.

(a) *Annihilation, Exile, and Segregation.* The least satisfactory forms of adjustment are those which depend upon annihilating, exiling, or segregating one of the conflicting elements. Annihilation consists in literal destruction: in murder when the opposition is a person; in total suppression when it is an idea. Exile and segregation are less extreme in character, but achieve similar results. Exile consists in expulsion and exclusion from the group territory, or mind, and segregation in rigidly confining the alien elements to certain functional, social, or geographic areas within the group life. Thus the denial of entry to an immigrant Chinaman and the prohibition of polygamy would be examples of exile, while the institution of the ghetto and the banning of left-wing orators to Union Square would be examples of segregation.

But while all three of these may be properly termed forms of adjustment, since they serve to remove sources of conflict, it is clear that their social consequences are anything but satisfactory. Each imposes great hardship upon minority groups and unnatural restriction upon the expression of ideas, and rules out from the start the possibility of preserving whatever is of value in the alien element.

Such methods, however, have been used by almost all countries at some time or another, and America offers no exception to the rule. We have rarely engaged in the mass murder of dissidents, but we have, often enough, suppressed their opinions. This happened, for example, in the persecution of Abolitionism before the Civil War, in the suppression of Mormonism during the same period, and in the "Red" purges of the last twenty years. We have also used the method of exile, as in our former efforts to repatriate the Negro, and in our policy of deporting "undesirable" aliens. But of the three methods mentioned, we have probably resorted most often to segregation. This is shown by our confinement of the Indian to reservations, by our exclusion of the Jew from certain recreational centers and facilities, and by our elimination of the Negro from all but the most menial and unskilled type of employment. We may not have relied on these methods as frequently and on the same scale as other nations, but that we have resorted to them frequently enough there can be no doubt.

(*b*) *Tolerance*. Midway in character between the negative, eliminative types of adjustment just described and the more positive types, yet to be mentioned, there exists a highly unstable form of adjustment which can be described simply as "tolerance." Tolerance comes into play whenever our attitude toward minorities or differing opinions is neither friendly nor unfriendly, and when, although we are not disposed to deny them full participation or expression in group life and do nothing to prevent either, we are indifferent as to whether they participate or are expressed or not. This is a purely neutral and passive form of adjustment, since it consists essentially in stopping conflicts by refusing to become excited about their causes.

The practice of tolerance is obviously a more satisfactory form of adjustment than those so far mentioned. Unlike them, it is peaceful in character, not permitting diversity as such to become a source of conflict, and does not rule out therefore the possibility of social enrichment through foreign contributions. But it is also an extremely unstable form. Since it does nothing to remove diversities actually or potentially dangerous, these, if present, may flare into conflict at any time, and the attitude of indifference felt originally may be supplanted by a desire to repress or persecute. On the other hand, even if conflict does *not* eventuate, there is nothing inherent in this neutral attitude itself to prevent its developing into a positive, friendly interest. And this often happens. In either case, however, tolerance itself will have given way to another type of adjustment altogether.

(c) *Assimilation by Absorption, Fusion, and Imitation.* "Assimilation" is the name for any process of adjustment which has as its end result the initiation of the alien element into full-fledged membership in the community life or mind. It may, therefore, assume many different forms. Of these, however, the three most important are assimilation by absorption, by fusion, and by imitation.

Assimilation through absorption consists, ideally, in so reconditioning the alien element that he or it loses all traces of former identity and becomes wholly indistinguishable from elements which were native to begin with. A case in point is the immigrant who has been so thoroughly "Americanized" that he looks, thinks, and acts exactly like a native-born American. Another case in point is the foreign doctrine which in being translated or popularized loses its original and essential point entirely and is interpreted to be a mere variant of a familiar native doctrine. The latter is what appears to have happened, for example, in certain recent interpretations of Russian socialism by American businessmen.

Assimilation through imitation, on the other hand, just reverses this process, adjustment here being achieved through the remolding of the native in the image of the foreign, as is illustrated in the case of expatriation.

Assimilation through fusion, finally, consists in so interacting with the alien element as to produce new patterns of group behavior, group thought, or even group appearance, totally unlike any which have existed previously, whether native or foreign. Under certain circumstances, this fusion will assume the form of hybridization, that is, be such as to submerge or blot out the separate identity of the elements being fused. Probably the clearest instance of this is to be found on the biological level and in the offspring produced by interracial marriages, but it is also often to be found at other levels, for example, in the subtle blending of foreign and native styles of painting, and in the merging of foreign and native ideologies. Assimilation through fusion may also, however, tend to assume the form of a federation, i.e., produce a pattern in which the original elements do not lose their separate identity but continue to exist side by side in harmonious relationship. This seems to be the kind of fusion aimed at in the present Soviet experiment in preserving the cultural autonomy of its many minority groups, and the kind also involved when a nation is able to tolerate and hold in perpetual suspension two quite different theories of government.

These three types of assimilation are not uniform either in the frequency with which they occur or as regards their social value. With respect to frequency, fusion seems to have occurred oftener in America than absorption, and absorption oftener than imitation. With the exception of the few Americans who have become expatriates, the tendency has been for the alien to become like us rather than for us to become like him, and for the foreign idea to be absorbed by the indigenous idea and not the reverse. Most characteristic of all, perhaps, has been the tendency toward fusion. Because of our general acceptance of the principle of "live-and-let-live," and the great flexibility of our cultural institutions, the alien born have usually been able to maintain a certain degree of independence and individuality, and foreign opinion to command a certain freedom of expression. As a result there has never developed a highly particularized American type to which all and everything must rigidly conform. The national character has remained fluid, and the succeeding waves of foreign influences, instead of being utterly suppressed, have been free to blend and fuse with the native culture.

On the whole, assimilation by fusion seems to be the most satisfactory of the three types mentioned. While assimilation by absorption and by imitation are probably just as effective in minimizing conflict through peaceful means, they cannot be as effective in preserving out of the conflict the best that each of the conflicting elements has to offer. In fact, they cannot be effective in this regard at all, since by their very nature they must remove and destroy all but one of the contending parties. Fusion, on the other hand, while not ensuring such preservation, does not, at least, rule it out entirely and, in fact, does much to promote it. As Robert E. Parks and others have shown, the individual or class which unites in itself the heritage of more than one culture is one of the most important vehicles of social evolution and progress.

We have now described some of the basic ways in which a group and its members may try to adjust to the presence of alien elements. We have pointed out, in addition, that these modes differ considerably in their general social value. We must now go on to inquire specifically into their effect upon group life in general.

3. Effect of Impact

The effect of alien impact upon any social group varies widely with attending circumstances and cannot, therefore, easily be described. Each instance of impact is different and produces a unique effect. It is possible, nevertheless, to indicate at least some of the features of this effect: viz., the points at which the impact may first be felt; the paths it may follow in pervading the group structure as a whole and some of the particular results incident to the several primary forms of adjustment listed above.

Every impact acts upon group life in two ways: first, directly, through the immediate action of the agent of impact, and second, indirectly, through the repercussions this first action may have. The first constitutes the impact's entry into the group structure, the second, its diffusion through the structure. Let us examine each of these phenomena in turn.

The Entry of Impact. The initial effect of an impact is to bring about an immediate alteration in one or more existing features of the group life. And since the importance of the impact is in part dependent upon the importance of the features affected, it is essential to understand what some of the principal features of group life are and in what basic ways they may be altered. I shall begin with a description of the features themselves.

The specific features, characteristics, and activities of a group may usually be defined in terms of (a) the level of group life at which they occur, (b) the class of facts on that level to which they belong, and (c) the way in which they are evaluated by the group majority.

(a) In regard to level, they may be said to occur either as elements in the terrain, as characteristics of physique, as particular practices, or as particular beliefs.

By "terrain" is meant the physical environment of the

group: the land it occupies or controls, together with whatever features or objects have been introduced into it by human
agency. The elements of terrain will include, therefore, not
only the soil, forests, waterways, etc., but also highways,
buildings, works of art, and everything else which the group
has physically created and preserved.

By "the characteristics of physique," on the other hand, is
meant the vital traits of the group: the physical appearance
and ancestry of its members; their number; their sex; their
birth-and-death-rates; their distribution as regards residence
and occupation; and the like. It describes the group, in other
words, in terms of its existence as a mere physical entity and
independently of its character as a society with definite ends,
purposes, and institutions.

The latter begin to emerge only at the levels of "practice"
and "belief." By "practice" is meant merely the characteristic
ways in which a group acts: the particular rules of procedure
which it or its members have evolved, and which have become
standardized. It thus includes all of the group's habitual
modes of behavior, whether they fall within or without an
institutional framework, whether they characterize the group
as a whole or only a part of it, and whether they are addressed
to important or unimportant ends, or indeed, to any end at
all. From this level the group may be viewed as a complex
and interlocking pattern of behavior which manifests a certain
degree of uniformity and stability, and which in part is pur-
posive and in part ritualistic or functionless.

The level of "belief," in contrast, represents the group at
the level of its motivations: what it or its members believe to
be true and hold valuable. Thus, to this level will belong all
of its opinions on all subjects and topics from its most ephem-
eral fancies to its most profound and sophisticated philosophical convictions. These will belong on this level, moreover,
whether they be vague or abstract, be conscious or unconscious, or represent the opinion of a single individual or of the
group as a whole. Similarly, there will also belong here all

the basic drives of the group and all its consciously accepted ideals whether the latter pertain to the most exalted conceptions of duty or to the price of mutton in a village butcher shop. It includes, in short, every conceivable attitude, individual or collective, on every conceivable subject.

(b) In addition to being either a belief, a practice, a characteristic of physique, or an element of the terrain, every specific element in the group life will be a certain kind of belief, a certain kind of practice, etc. Thus, beliefs and practices will be economic, literary, artistic, political, religious, philosophical, etc.; characteristics of physique will be physiological, ethnic, ecological, and the like; and features of the terrain will fall under the various categories of geography and geology. Many different methods of classifications are possible in each case, but classifications of the sort just suggested are the most common and therefore probably most pertinent to the study of impact.

(c) Finally, in addition to being a certain kind of belief, a certain kind of practice, etc., each element in the group life will be valued in a certain way by the group as a whole. In the first place, it will be either approved, disapproved, or tolerated. In the second place, it will be approved, disapproved, or tolerated in different degrees. Thus it will be assigned a certain definite place in the group's hierarchy of evaluations, and on the basis of this evaluation its continued existence will be specifically safeguarded, merely permitted, or definitely prohibited.

Every fact pertaining to the group life thus exists in a matrix or continuum having these three "dimensions" of level, kind, and evaluation; and in terms of these dimensions its relations to all other elements in the group structure may be specified. From this there will follow, moreover, certain conclusions regarding social change. In the first place, and most obviously, every change which occurs will occur at one of the four levels specified: it will be a change of belief, of practice, of physique, or of the features of the terrain. Moreover, it will always be a change of a certain *kind* of belief, a certain *kind* of practice, and so on. On this will be based, accordingly, the possibility of referring to it as a geographic, biological, institutional, or ideological change, or as a change in art, literature, politics, and so on. In the second place, the change will consist either in adding to, subtracting from, or in modifying in some form or another the existing beliefs, practices, etc., affected; or in altering the prevailing group estimation of their value.

As constituting one of the basic varieties of social change, the changes due to foreign impact will exhibit all the above characteristics. They will always occur at definite levels and will always consist of either changes in the group facts themselves or changes in the group's attitude toward these facts. In addition, however, they will manifest certain further characteristics:

First, the level and type of fact immediately affected by the impact will normally depend upon the character of the transmitting agent. Thus if the latter happens to be a newly current belief or practice, the group facts likely to be affected first are those native practices or beliefs which have something in common with it. On the other hand, if the agent of impact is a person, the group is apt to be affected on all levels simultaneously, with the type of change affected at each level being determined by who and what the agent is. Thus, for example, an immigrant professor is likely to have a different effect upon the group than an immigrant machinist because of the differences in their training and occupation.

Second, the initial and immediate effect of any impact is always in the first instance quantitative, and consists in changing the number of existing group facts. The immigrant, for example, in merely arriving in a new country automatically increases the size of the population, changes the proportion of the sexes, and adds to the store of existing practices and belief. And every agent of impact, ideal or human, has initially the same additive type of effect.

Third, if the agent does not merely increase the number of existing group facts but modifies them as well, this modification may assume different forms. In the first place, it may serve to reinforce or rejuvenate a native element already present. This is what happened, for example, when the influx of Irish and Italian Roman Catholics during the nineteenth century continually augmented the power of the American Catholic Church. In the second place, the modification may take the form of replacing or substituting for a native element, as when the influence of Herbert Spencer on American economic theory led to the formulation of a new defense of capitalism along evolutionary lines. Finally, the modification may consist of the alien elements fusing with certain native ones to produce a new type of element altogether. This has occurred, for example, in the American fusion of various ethnic stocks and in the frequently observed blending of native and foreign styles in the work of American artists.

The Diffusion of Impact. As noted above, the effects of impact are not limited to the direct effects of the impacting agent. These direct effects always have repercussions upon the group system as a whole and the latter are as much a part of the impact as the former. The character of these remoter changes, however, differs in no essential respect from that of the changes effected directly. They also always occur at certain definite levels, always affect certain definite types of group fact, and always change these facts or their evaluation by adding to them and by modifying them through reinforcement, replacement, or fusion. There is no need, therefore, to consider their character in detail. It is important, however, to note briefly the nature of the "paths" which an influence may follow in being diffused throughout the group life.

Causal interaction between different group levels, types, and evaluations is in no way restricted. The toleration of a particular political belief—say, the ideal of a collectivized democracy—may lead to the introduction and approval of a new literary practice, for example, the use of crowds rather than individuals as fictional heroes. The development of national parks, which are elements in the terrain, may affect not only the flow of tourist traffic (a matter of practice) but also the distribution of population (a matter of physique). Indifference toward a rapidly declining birth rate (again a matter of physique) will plainly influence economic practice, for example, the production and distribution of baby bassinets. In other words, any given type of event, occurring at any given level and group-valued in any given way, may, on occasion, affect the course of events at any other location in the group structure. Nevertheless, some of these paths of influence are more viable and more important than others.

In the first place, certain paths will be more frequently followed. For example, events of the same general type, whether on the same or on different levels, are apt to interact oftener than events of different types. A political belief is more likely to influence political practice or other political beliefs than it is to influence a religious or literary belief or practice. Again, so far as different types of events are interactive, any direct interaction between them is more likely to occur at the level of practice than of belief. This is because conflict of practice is usually more immediately interruptive of life than conflict of belief, and therefore more peremptory in character. In the second place, as between two types of interacting events, one will normally be more influential in the interaction than the other. Thus, in America today, it is probable that political, economic, and scientific events tend to affect, more than they tend to be affected by, artistic, religious, and philosophic events.

It is these more viable paths that an impact will tend to follow and it is by means of them, accordingly, that we are often able to trace its paths of diffusion in pervading a group structure. Two points, however, should be kept in mind: In the first place, an impact *need not* follow these paths and may actually cut across them. This may happen, for example, if the agent of impact is novel, striking, or odd in character and catches the attention of the group as a whole. Under such circumstances, all sorts of cross-influences between the different levels and types of group facts may result. In the second place, the more viable paths themselves do not remain constant. Paths which are the most viable in one period need not be the most viable in all. In general, viability will be a function of the manner in which the group itself conceives of the relationship between different kinds of fact and of the extent to which it organizes its life around this conception.

This means, accordingly, that in the study of foreign influence it should never be assumed that because two agents of impact are similar in character and have impinged upon the group structure at the same point, the course of their diffusion will always be the same. This is particularly relevant in the case of America where the societal structure has always been highly unstable and has frequently changed from one generation to another.

Effect of Different Forms of Adjustment. It remains only to describe some of the typical effects incident to the various forms of adjustment listed earlier.

(*a*) *The Policy of Exclusion.* If adjustment is sought by attempting to exclude the alien element through annihilation, exile, or segregation, the native group will be affected in three basic ways. First of all, any existing group tendencies in the direction of nativism and chauvinism will be encouraged to grow. Interest in, and loyalty to, existing (or even past) native institutions may be intensified and the prevailing group attitudes strengthened and consolidated. This follows from the psychological principle that in the mere act of defending something the sense of its value is usually heightened.

A second effect which also often results is the development of elaborate group rationalizations attempting to justify the policy of exclusion. These will frequently take the form of arguing that the foreign group or ideology excluded is "inherently inferior" or is "still not ready for assimilation." Thus, in America, to mention one instance, the policy of segregating the Negro has been consistently buttressed by arguments to the effect that the Negro is mentally inferior, that his vitality quotient is lower than that of the white, and that he is too childlike to be entrusted with full social responsibility, although careful and disinterested investigation has long since proved all such charges to be false.

Adjustment through exclusion tends, finally, to bring about certain changes at the levels of group practice and physique. A policy of exclusion cannot normally be put into effect without introducing new practices into the group life and without, therefore, producing certain malformations in the pattern of its existing institutions. By the same token such a policy cannot help but drain off group energies which could be more profitably expended in other ways. This purely negative effect of exclusion will often assume great significance, as when, through segregating an alien group, the various skills of the group or the sturdiness of its stock are not put to the most effective and productive use.

The effects of exclusion upon the invader are equally ramified, particularly when the invader is represented by a minority group, and where the exclusion consists of geographical, social, or industrial segregation. Constrained under these circumstances to move only in certain areas or circles, the minority's economic opportunities are correspondingly curtailed, and its members compelled to exist at substandard income levels. Accompanying this, in individual cases, will be a sense of bewilderment and instability resulting from having to accept a lower social status in the new country than that formerly occupied in the old.

In the second place, the excluded group will often tend to preserve and cherish as many of its original customs as the new environment and social status permit. Thus, it will retain not only its original language, dress, and social customs, but also, on occasion, its former commercial, agricultural, and manufacturing practices. If the isolation lasts long enough, the group may even undergo a cultural evolution all its own.

It may, for example, produce an indigenous art and literature of a relatively high degree of sophistication, as happened among the French in New Orleans and the Germans in Pennsylvania, or, still more fundamentally, it may even evolve new patterns of religious worship and political thought. In either case, however, it will represent a "cultural island" existing in the midst of another culture and having with this other culture no rapport or relationship of a significant sort.

In the third place, and again as a result of its isolation, the group may eventually be rent asunder by severe, internal conflicts. Its older members, still striving to preserve as much of their native culture as possible, will be challenged from time to time by younger members who no longer share this ideal. Some of the latter will desire to imitate the ostracizing group as closely as possible or, less radically, merely want to bring the older customs "up to date." Others, bitterly resenting their inferior status, will act collectively to improve it. Some of these will organize to procure a better recognition of the group's rights, while others will seek to reestablish new and direct relations with the fatherland. Such organizations as the National Association for the Advancement of Colored People and the German-American Bund have grown out of tendencies of this sort. But, whatever the issues, the old group unity is lost and the group as a whole tends to disintegrate into many separate factions.

Out of segregation, finally, may develop the individual phenomenon known to sociologists as "the marginal man," the individual who by birth or training belongs to two cultures instead of one but who, just by virtue of his divided origin, is denied full membership in either. The effect of such a situation is to produce a recognizable type noted for its unusual degree of intellectual and cultural emancipation, but one that is also noted for its sense of "rootlessness" and lack of adjustment. Perhaps the most striking example of the marginal man in America is the mulatto, as revealed in the studies of

Park, Reuter, and Stonequist, but the type is also often to be found among the offspring of white immigrants.

From all this it should be clear that a policy of exclusion is likely to prove, on the whole, unsatisfactory from the point of view of both the invader and the invaded. No matter how liberally we weight the fact that exclusion can, on occasion, be culturally fruitful, this will scarcely offset its effect as an economic depressant, its tendency to breed internal strife, and its rupture of normal intercourse between various segments of society. In the last analysis, cultural islands represent an abnormal type of human relationship which, if allowed to persist too long, is bound to result in the exhaustion and dissipation of group energies.

(b) The Policy of Assimilation. When adjustment is sought through assimilation, the effect is quite different than when recourse has been had to a policy of exclusion and, on the whole, more satisfactory, if it has been properly guided. As already indicated, a policy of assimilation allows for maximum flexibility in the removal of ethnic and cultural diversities harmful to either of the parties concerned and in the preservation of those which will ultimately enrich the group life as a whole. And it permits the accomplishment of these ends by a peaceful and orderly process. It is the one method of adjustment, in other words, by which the native group can absorb whatever of value the alien influence has to contribute and still preserve what is best in its own traditions.

For the same reason, the policy is one whose effects will always be profound and therefore difficult to trace or classify. This is particularly true in the case of assimilation by fusion, where the native and foreign may blend in altogether strange and unexpected ways, and where, accordingly, no one type of result can be considered characteristic. The very nature of the process is such as to keep the possibility of social development constantly open and to allow it to move freely in any number of different directions. In other words, where the process of exclusion is mechanical in character and produces more or less mechanically predictable results, the process of assimilation is in a literal sense creative and unpredictable.

4. *The Evaluation of Impact*

In evaluating any instance of foreign impact, two questions come to the fore: (a) How great an impact was it? and (b) To what extent were its effects desirable? The first question is concerned with the profundity of the influence—the degree to which it has affected the group life as a whole, the second with the extent to which its effect has been valuable. Both questions, however, involve an appeal to norms and it will be helpful before concluding to mention what some of these norms are.

Greatness or Profundity of Impact. In measuring the greatness or profundity of an impact, two distinct types of standard may be employed. One of these concentrates upon the *number* of changes the impact brings about, the other upon their *character*.

Norms based upon the number of changes introduced by an impact usually vary with the type of change emphasized. One such norm, for example, would emphasize the number of changes as such, irrespective of their magnitude or character. In using this norm, we should literally have to count every instance of change attributable to the impact—from the wear and tear of immigrant feet upon the dock at Ellis Island to the effects of electing a foreign-born alderman in St. Louis—and we should be forced to assume that the sum total thus arrived at was an accurate index of the profundity of the impact. Another such norm would consist in counting the number of group levels, types, or evaluations affected by the impact, considering it significant, for example, to discover that *both* belief and practice or that *both* literature and politics were affected instead of only one in each case. A third norm might consist in counting only the number of beliefs, practices, and other group features actually modified, a fourth in counting the number of agents, such as the immigrant, through whom the impact was transmitted, and so on.

These are the norms which naturally come to mind when our approach to the problem is quantitative. And it is important that the quantitative aspect be kept in view: unless we know something about the number of agencies through which an impact has been transmitted, the number of changes it has brought about in the group life, and similar statistical facts, we cannot properly appreciate its extent and therefore, also, its profundity or greatness. But although quantitative norms are thus necessary, they are not sufficient. Extent of change is not the same as profundity of change. To get at the latter, a consideration of the kind of change involved is just as relevant as a consideration of its extent. Quantitative norms, in other words, must be supplemented by qualitative ones.

The necessity for this may be made clear from a single hypothetical example. Suppose there were two separate instances of impact which have brought about exactly the same number of changes in the group life. Suppose, moreover, that all these changes were confined to the level of practice but that one of the impacts had altered the group's political practices and the other only its technique of barbering. Under such circumstances we should unquestionably maintain that the former represented the greater impact. And we should do this because we know that normally the political practices of a group are more fundamentally determinative of its life and character than is its style of hairdress. In other words, in gauging profundity we must always take into consideration what place the changes introduced occupy in the group's hierarchy of evaluation and the degree of change they represent, for to the extent that the alteration is one having to do with fundamental group policies or with basic values, to that extent also will the impact be great or profound.

But although both types of norm—the quantitative and qualitative—are thus necessary, there is no general rule governing their use in combination. Although neither one can be neglected entirely, sometimes one and sometimes the other must be given the greater weight. This will depend wholly upon the particular context and the attendant circumstances. For example, when the group values affected are exactly of the same order or rank, the mere number of changes involved assumes an unusual importance; on the other hand, where the number of changes is approximately the same, their character or rank becomes important. These are ideal cases, but they serve to illustrate the impossibility of proceeding here according to a fixed formula and the constant desirability of allowing each particular situation itself to determine the right method.

This lack of a definite rule of thumb is not, however, as great a handicap as it may appear at first sight. For in this case, as in other types of inquiry, the capacity for understanding and for judicious appraisal grows with the effort to exercise it. The more familiar we become with the data of a problem in all of its different manifestations, the more likely we are to develop insight and imagination in dealing with it, and the less likely we are to continue to feel a need for mechanical formulae.

Value of Impact. As indicated above we can estimate the importance of an impact not only in terms of its profundity but also in terms of its value, that is, in terms of the degree to which its effects have been generally good or bad. This second type of evaluation is not wholly independent of the first, since degree of value will depend in some measure upon degree of profundity. Thus the disvalue of an undesirable influence will be augmented or diminished in proportion as its effects are quantitatively extended or limited. But the two standards are not identical. In general, an impact may be described as desirable or undesirable only to the extent that it helps or hinders the group in realizing what is assumed to constitute an ideal goal. If it accomplishes the former, it is said to be good, if the latter, bad, and if it does neither it is held to be neutral.

Judgments on this score will differ depending on how the ideal goal is defined, and this may vary considerably. One possibility is to define the ideal in precisely the same way in which it has been hitherto defined by the invaded group. Another possibility is to accept without question the definition proposed by the invader. Still a third possibility is to define it without reference to the desires of either the invaded or the invader, but in a manner that is believed to be more objective. These are the general possibilities. A careful evaluation, however, will involve the application of all three: the first in order to see clearly the meaning of the impact from the point of view of the invaded; the second to make clear its value for the invader; and the third to adjudicate the difference between these two in terms of a more disinterested standpoint. It is only by this procedure that the evaluation can become genuinely comprehensive and be properly safeguarded against the dangers of bias.

Whether or not it is ever possible to regard any particular evaluation as final is another matter. Aside from the fact that any evaluation will always presuppose a certain interpretation of facts independently of their value and this interpretation itself will be subject to error, evaluation as such is a difficult and delicate feat. Even when its standards have been clarified and agreed upon by all concerned, the task of applying these standards in practice is rarely a mechanical process. It involves the discernment and weighing of many imponderables, the setting off of one fact qualitatively against another, and of being compelled to proceed without the assistance of formulizable rules. Evaluation, in short, is always a hazardous undertaking.

The same saving circumstance, however, that operates in the case of the estimation of profundity also operates here. Here, also, we grow by doing, and it is practice which makes us perfect. Although in the end we have no guide other than our own personal insight and understanding, the latter deepen with experience and ultimately provide us with at least some grounds for confidence in our own judgment.

III

This concludes our résumé of some of the problems that naturally emerge in the study of foreign impact, and it remains only to describe briefly what the broad objectives of such a study should be.

Obviously, the first task will be to understand what the principal ethnic and national impacts upon America have been during the period chosen for examination. This will involve: (a) a grasp of the history of American society previous to the dates at which the various impacts were first felt; (b) an understanding of the cultural and historical background of the foreign groups and ideas concerned in the impacts; and (c) a careful tracing of exactly what happened once men and ideas arising out of those backgrounds were brought into vital contact with the American pattern of their day. In the second place, and in line with the argument just concluded, we must also try to estimate the value of these impacts, to judge disinterestedly whether their effects upon American life have been good or bad, and in what sense.

As indicated earlier, however, the problem is too complex and too ramified to carry through either of these investigations, separately or together, in anything like adequate detail at the present time. What we should aim at here, accordingly, is not an exhaustive knowledge of the various impacts but one merely detailed enough to give a clear picture of their scope and sweep. If we can end by seeing in general what the German, the British, the Italian, and other such civilizations and cultures have meant in the development of America, what contributions for good or for ill they have made, this will be sufficient.

II · THE AMERICANIZATION
OF THE IMMIGRANT*

By STOW PERSONS

THE many students who have written about the history of immigration into the United States have shared in creating a vast composite panorama of one of the most important phases of our experience as a people. The causes prompting Europeans to leave their homelands have received much study; the narratives of their adventures before final settlement in the new world have often been told in colorful detail; and the contributions of each immigrant group to American life have been carefully noted. In contrast to the descriptions of historians concerning the unique events of immigration, sociologists have arranged the materials into classes and types of facts in order to deepen our understanding of the problems involved by relating the particular to the general. They have shown the difficulties of immigrant adjustment to a new community to be essentially those which any newcomer experiences in a strange group. Those who belong to the group are instinctively suspicious of outsiders, and admit them only with reluctance. They elaborate symbols of group identity and require the stranger to show an ability to manipulate these symbols as the password proving membership in the group. According to the sociologist, these are universal characteristics of social relationships. Immigration, wherever it occurs, will reveal the same patterns of dislocation and readjustment, of discrimination against the outsider by members of the in-group.

A consideration of the broader aspects of immigration into the United States suggests, however, that it is through a fusion of both the historical and sociological approaches that

* See also critical bibliography, "Immigration between 1800 and 1924," on page 175.

an understanding of the movement in terms of American civilization as a whole is to be gained. The universal characteristics of group behavior and attitudes as defined by the sociologist must be given the unique content of American experience. Many immigrants have testified to the peculiar and often annoying requirements exacted of them before they could consider themselves participating members of the new community, requirements which they had not anticipated and which in all probability no other land would establish. In fact, the assimilation of immigrants was a unique problem to the extent that America was unlike any other country. It is against the background of American history with its special problems that the story of migration as a universal phenomenon must be traced. The process by which a stranger is introduced into and becomes a member of an unfamiliar group is called assimilation. The immigrant who successfully adjusted himself in this country was Americanized, a special case of assimilation. It is our purpose to inquire into the nature of Americanization as it was elaborated through the years.

Only through an understanding of the major problems of American history can a satisfactory inquiry be conducted. Americanization was much more than merely a set of naturalization laws or formal requirements for admission to the country. It was a largely unconscious process by which Americans imposed their own standards and ideals upon newcomers. These standards applied at various levels of social utility. At a superficial level, the sense of newness and provinciality of American life might require defensive expressions of self-satisfaction and contempt for Europe and its institutions on the part of the native population. Many of the better educated immigrants noted and resented such a tendency. More fundamentally, the circumstances under which America grew, such as the availability of free land to be exploited by individual enterprise, might produce an independent type of personality, the components of which would also be inculcated in the immigrant through the Americanizing process. Such requirements could be laid down only as America became a distinct place, with its own characteristic frame of mind. In the early days, or for as long as America remained a geographical expression, these requirements were naturally less exacting. It was doubtless under such circumstances that the legend and the fact of America as a hospitable refuge for the oppressed grew. When in the course of time Americans came to establish their own identity as a national people they found that the ideal of America as a place of refuge seemed frequently to clash with its new function as a symbol of social unity. It might be said that when finally the cry of America for the Americans resulted in the closing of the gates to immigrants the process of Americanization for a majority of the people was completed.

The general outlines of the history of American immigration are familiar to everyone. The predominantly Anglo-Saxon population of the colonial period was supplemented by much smaller groups of Scotch-Irish, Germans, Celtic Irish, Dutch, and Negroes. From the close of the Napoleonic wars until the first World War—almost exactly one hundred years—the immigrant trickle increased to the proportions of a torrent, until freedom of access to the United States was virtually stopped by the restrictive legislation of the 1920's. The immigrant century was divided roughly at the year 1882, when the "old" northwestern European immigration gave way to the "new" southeastern European races and nationalities. Although legislation formally ended the era it is fairly clear now that the movement was terminating for natural reasons without the intervention of legislation. In America the frontier had disappeared by 1890; population was increasing faster than the demands for labor made upon it by the industrial plant except in peak years; and the frequency and severity of depressions attendant upon the "maturing" of the industrial economy all made the United States a much less attractive haven for the immigrant than formerly. At the same time the intensification of national rivalries with the ever present possibility of war caused European governments to look with less favor upon the loss of potential military man power. Nevertheless, it is a significant fact that Americans were not content to allow world events to achieve their destined effect, but that they insisted upon closing the gates by formal legislation.

Paralleling the facts of immigration we can trace the attitudes of Americans toward these events. At first, in the early nineteenth century, the land was a haven for the oppressed. The newcomer was welcomed on the assumption that he was honest and industrious and would in time adjust himself to the new world and become a worthy addition to the population. Such a complaisant welcome was naturally most easily extended to immigrants whose racial and cultural backgrounds were similar to the prevailing American type. In the later nineteenth century, when the character of immigration changed, the cordiality of the welcome cooled as many people began to doubt whether widely heterogeneous peoples could indeed be transformed into creditable Americans. It began to be said that the melting pot failed to melt, and ultimately restrictive legislation put an end to the whole movement. These changing attitudes revealed the fundamental point of view from which native Americans tended to view the problem. In every discussion it had been assumed that the immigrant must be "assimilated" in the sense of being absorbed into the population through the loss of his peculiarities; he must successfully undergo a process of "Americanization" whereby he was made to approximate an ideal American type. Finally, convinced of their failure to transform the immigrant successfully, the Americans nevertheless gave official sanction to the ideal when they passed the National Origins Acts of the 1920's. In this legislation the larger of the annual quotas were assigned to the northwestern Europeans who most closely conformed to the prevailing racial and cultural ideals of America.

It was almost inevitable that Americans of the early nineteenth century should consider the assimilation of the immigrant as essentially a problem of Americanization. The great task which they faced as a nation was the task of forging national, political and cultural unity. Evidences of preoccupation with this task everywhere intrude themselves upon the careful student. In political life one of the dominant issues was the need to transform federal union into truly national union. The arts reflected the effort to achieve emancipation from the "courtly muses of Europe" and establish an indigenous American idiom. Socially, a militant republicanism insisted upon the destruction of class barriers and privileges as the preliminary step in realizing the new ideals. These tendencies were evidences of the ethnocentric impulse—the primitive necessity for mankind to adhere together in groups. In our time and civilization the most significant of these ethnocentric groups is the nation-state. Fear, with a consequent desire for protection, has been found to be a universal element in the continuance of such groups. Group unity can best be secured through group likeness, which accounts for the preoccupation of Americans with Americanizing their immigrants. These nationalizing tendencies operated all the more strongly because of the will of a new and untried nation to establish and to prove itself.

Under the influence of these conditions a democratic social faith or set of popular beliefs emerged in the early nineteenth century in which the new national consciousness received expression.[1] This faith formed a common denominator among Americans, and filled the needs of the ethnocentric impulse. The first article of this faith was a belief in individualism. As used here the term designates the fundamental assumption of all American political and social theory and practice: that each individual possesses and should exercise the rights and responsibilities of democratic self government. The second article was a belief in the reality of a moral order underlying

[1] R. H. Gabriel, *The Course of American Democratic Thought* (New York, 1940), Chapter 2.

the universe, shaping its ultimate course and guaranteeing its value and meaning. Faith in the moral order was the product of the Christian outlook, but it was shared by many secularists and humanists who no longer called themselves Christian. The third article was a belief in progress, especially the progress of the American people. Americans had a mission to fulfill in lighting and carrying the torch of democracy to the world.

With the appearance of a democratic faith there also emerged the ideal American type figure in whom the faith would receive expression. The ideal American was imagined as being of British stock and English-speaking. He tended to be equalitarian in his social and political thinking and even more so in his immediate social relations. He was an individualist; ambitious in a material sense; optimistically devoted to *laissez faire* in economics and politics; fairly scrupulous in business but not possessed of a strong social conscience outside of his group. In private life he was puritanical, idolizing his women and imposing fairly close social restraints upon them. In religion he tended to combine liberalism with mysticism, producing what Horace Kallen later called a new combination of "smug devoutness and secular spirituality."[2] These were the qualities most prized by Americans. In professing allegiance to them they were forging another important social common denominator.

II

The America which was thus nationalizing itself was predominantly a rural society. The breaking up of the New England farming village and the pattern of dispersed settlement established in the Northwest land ordinances led to the scattering of the farm population over wide areas. The home rather than the community was the dominant social unit. Here the independent attitudes of the subsistence farm were in-

[2] Horace Kallen, "Democracy versus the Melting Pot," *The Nation*, Vol. C (1915), pp. 190-194, 217-220.

culcated. It was also the period in which the frontier exerted its greatest social influence. With its rapid advance through the Mississippi valley the frontier energized America with the optimism of creative effort and expansion. Isolation from Europe and almost complete military security inculcated an easy complaisance rarely enjoyed in the modern world. Personal intellectual security was also widely achieved through the mediation of vigorous Protestant churches of great power and prestige. The immigrants adjusted themselves to such a society with a minimum of difficulty. Forbidden by the Congressional Act of 1818 to purchase blocks of land in groups, they settled as individuals and families. The mobility of the farming population fostered the friendly acceptance of strangers noticed by so many travelers, and at the same time it discouraged the shy suspicion of newcomers frequently found among more isolated rural people. Living on the land, pursuing the same occupations as the native Americans, the immigrants commenced the process of Americanizing themselves under the most desirable circumstances.

Their reaction to these conditions has received classic expression in the *Letters* of the ex-Frenchman, Crèvecoeur. "We know, properly speaking, no strangers," he wrote. "This is every person's country." The prevailing social attitudes toward the newcomers in this rural paradise could only be described, curiously enough, as "urbane" and "cosmopolitan." Many languages might be overheard and diverse social customs observed. But the natives did not question the capacity of their society to assimilate and Americanize these strangers, largely by means of the transformation to be wrought in the second generation thought in the public schools. According to Crèvecoeur, this transformation took place even sooner. In response to the conditions of life in the new world a moral and spiritual awakening occurred in the soul of the immigrant. The prevailing social equality gave him a new sense of his own worth and dignity. He acquired new skills, made new friends, accumulated resources, planned new ventures, and ultimately was able to purchase land. By such experiences the immigrant was surely and imperceptibly Americanized. Crèvecoeur might have foretold the official welcome and encouragement extended to immigrants by many western states as long as good public lands remained unoccupied and a shortage of farm labor was felt.

In spite, however, of the many factors making for national unity there were equally strong centrifugal forces at work. They were largely the product of geographical diversity and rapid territorial expansion. The nation was growing with such rapidity that the nationalizing forces were scarcely strong enough to hold it together. From the Revolutionary War to 1850 the occupied area of the United States spread from the Appalachians to the Pacific, skirting the high plains and the Rockies. In this vast new settled territory distinct regionalisms developed to menace the national unity. Regional types and ideals matured and came into conflict with one another. Of these types, the northeastern progressive industrial individualism and the southern romantic paternal personalism were only the most pronounced among several local ideal patterns. A distinct frontier type in the old Northwest likewise bequeathed lasting characteristics to that region. None of these regional complexes were entirely incompatible. They were all variants of a more generalized democratic type and as such were generally able to sublimate their rivalries in mutually harmonious relationships. But this fact was not clearly recognized by the Americans of one hundred years ago, particularly as the deepening cleavage between North and South threatened to destroy national unity.

This is not the place to enter into an analysis of the American Civil War. It may merely be said that in the South for the only time in our history, and because of a unique combination of circumstances, sectional loyalty transcended national loyalty. That most Americans throughout the middle of the nineteenth century sensed the possibility of such a calamity seems indubitable. The political energies of the greatest

politicians were devoted almost exclusively to the preservation of the Federal Union. If we are asked why the unity of
so young and untried a nation should elicit such heroic defense we can only say that the ethnocentric impulse expressed
in its ideal form in the democratic faith commanded the burn-
ing loyalty of all Americans. Southerners as well as Northerners fought for what they conceived to be American ideals.

It is only against this background, in any case, that an understanding of American attitudes toward the immigrant is to
be gained. To a new nation struggling to unify itself the immigrant inevitably appeared as a potentially divisive force.
To sectional disunity was added the threat of social disunity,
and the result was the ideal of the stereotyped American
which we have sketched, and to which the immigrant was expected to conform. In some instances the alien challenge to
national unity was less immediate than in others. If the immigrant was so fortunate as to possess a knowledge of the English language and the Anglo-Saxon way of life he enjoyed an
enormous advantage over the non-English-speaking settler.
Even this recommendation, however, was not enough to guarantee a welcome reception to the large group of Irishmen who
entered the country in the thirties and forties. The reaction to
the Irish and German settlers of this period illustrated the
role of immigration in relation to the struggle to achieve unity
over sectionalism; it also foreshadowed the issues which were
to dominate discussion of the immigrant problem after the
Civil War.

The Know-Nothing movement, in which the anti-immigrant sentiment crystallized, was a national phenomenon. It
appeared in both North and South, and in each section it expressed the same fears. Everywhere a predominantly Protestant population revived its ancient hatred of Roman Catholicism. Southerners found especial cause for discontent in that
the immigrants would swell the ranks of free labor, increase
northern political representation, and possibly lend support
to the antislavery cause. Northerners resented the political

influence which the Irish soon exerted in the cities, while the lower income groups also suffered from their economic competition. But behind these immediate issues loomed the approaching struggle between the sections, and the nativist movement, both North and South, must be understood as in part a spontaneous reassertion of the democratic ideals in order to gain assurance and unity with which to meet the impending crisis.

The Know-Nothing Party was the first nativist organization to emphasize the potential threat of the alien to American institutions and ideals. Its fears failed to convince more people largely because the immigrants themselves were disproving them by their political activity, especially in the areas of German and Scandinavian settlement. Occasionally immigrant opinion might be construed as critical of American institutions, as when the German Democratic Association attacked representative assemblies and the privileges accorded organized religious bodies all in the interests of more direct democracy. German farmers in the Middle West were also active supporters of the movement for free distribution of the public lands, incurring the charges of "radicalism" and "agrarianism" by those who felt that the immigrants would thereby elude their share of the costs of government. But in general the immigrants submerged themselves in the dominant political issues of the day, and while politicians and observers reckoned with immigrant voters as forming distinct blocs of opinion, these blocs were nevertheless accepted as part of the regular stuff of political life, and were treated as any other economic or social pressure group.

The collapse of Know-Nothingism in the face of the slavery and sectional issues in the late fifties was indicative of the subordinate place of immigration among the major national questions of the time. In the beginning, nativism and sectional conflict had been closely related problems. In addition to the spontaneous nationwide insistence upon unity, whenever that unity was threatened by internal dissension, there were overt factors which had associated the two issues. Both nativist and proslavery groups had united to oppose early homestead bills which would have stimulated immigration. As long as immigrants tended to favor the Democratic Party both of these groups also supported the Know-Nothing Party, contributing to its rapid growth in the early fifties. But after the Kansas-Nebraska Act of 1854, the sectional struggle assumed its place as the major issue of the time, and all other problems oriented themselves in relation to it. The slavery question disrupted the national council meeting of the Know-Nothings at Philadelphia, in 1855, causing that party to lag behind the Republicans in the elections of the following year. At the same time, the immigrant voter became restive as he saw the Democracy emerging as the party of slavery. Eventually, with the addition of the homestead plank to the Republican platform, the rural immigrant vote overcame its fear of the latent nativism of the Republicans and went over to them in a body. Now the realignment of forces was complete; the immigrant vote, except in the large eastern cities, responded to the issues as they were outlined by the major parties; and the effort of the nativists to make a special issue of immigrant problems was temporarily submerged.

III

The transformation of American society brought about by industrialism after 1860 cannot be ignored in any effort to understand immigration in its larger aspects. The 1880's, dividing the "old" northwestern European immigrants from the "new" southeastern European migration, is usually indicated as a significant decade in immigrant history. The newcomers after that time are said to have been more difficult to assimilate and Americanize than their predecessors, and it is this change in the character of immigration which is held to be largely responsible for the agitation that the movement should cease. Without questioning the validity of the assumption it is nevertheless pertinent to point out that again other factors must be considered in gaining a comprehensive understanding of the situation. The industrial process wrought greater transformations in the American scene than any other single force, and it would be remarkable if immigrant as well as other social problems did not reflect its impact.

Before the Civil War the immigrant's chief task was to Americanize himself in a rural society. With his predominantly agricultural background the conflicts attendant upon his adjustment to a relatively mobile farming population were held to a minimum. Contact with the older Americans was less immediate in the physical sense but socially more personal than it would have been in the city. While rural spokesmen were still welcoming immigrants as industrious additions to the community, however, urban orators were beginning to emphasize the undesirable effect of immigrant labor in depressing wage standards for the native worker. It is significant that the strongest expressions of nativism before the Civil War appeared in the urban communities of the eastern seaboard. With the growth of industrialism in the later nineteenth century these urban conflicts were intensified, until in the twentieth century immigration had become largely an urban and a class problem.

Industrialism thus transformed the position of the immigrant as a subject for Americanization. The task of fusing national geographic unity was now completed in the fires of civil war. But the process only hastened the appearance of a new threat, that of class and race conflict. In this new challenge to American unity the immigrant occupied a central position. Always a potential recruit for the ranks of industrial labor, he now found this his major role. As a laboring man the immigrant's problems were easily confused with those issues which were generating conflict between capital and labor. Consequently, he suffered loss of prestige in the eyes of all those who were determined to maintain the traditional American patterns by then firmly established. In other words, in the early nineteenth century the immigrant had been compelled to Americanize himself as an incidental aspect of the struggle of the American people to establish their national identity and to defend their unity from sectional divisions. In the latter part of the century, because of his social and economic disadvantages, the immigrant became closely associated with the laboring class, and inherited its psychology and status in an industrial economy.

The "new" immigrants thus had to overcome handicaps never imposed upon predecessors. Although chiefly of peasant stocks, bred to the land, they found most ready opportunities as cheap labor in urban industrial and construction projects. With frontier settlement no longer possible, a few found their way to abandoned farming lands in the East. The majority, however, settled of necessity in the slum areas of the large cities, where "Little Italys" or "Little Polands" arose to disturb the exponents of Americanization. Social isolation more complete than had ever surrounded the frontiersman was now the lot of the newcomer. His children might experience the preliminary steps in assimilation in the public schools, but his own opportunities were severely limited by his position. Formerly, the normal process of settlement automatically promoted Americanization; now every circumstance impeded it. It was not surprising that few among these later immigrants broke through the bonds of their class.

For the immigrants were now frequently thought of as comprising a distinct class, in America but not of it. For various reasons many groups looked upon them with disfavor and suspicion. The middle classes, faithfully following industrial and financial leadership, became the great defenders of the American ideals. To them the difficulty of Americanizing the newcomers threatened the purity of national standards. Organized labor, with which the immigrants might have affiliated, found them difficult to organize, and resented their willingness to work for low wages, thus undermining labor's objectives. As evidence of illiteracy and poverty accumulated, the intellectuals and publicists began to question the wisdom of a national policy which permitted indiscriminate settlement of peoples who were not only difficult to Americanize, but who fell distinctly below the cultural standards already established in America. Plentiful statistical material presumably demonstrating this inferiority was amassed in the tests and records of the army during the first World War.

Perhaps the most striking aspect of the immigrant problem in industrial America has been the tendency on the part of the native Americans to transform the economic and social conflicts of industrialism into cultural conflict wherever the immigrant has been concerned. Cultural conflict in turn has almost always been expressed in terms of Americanization. The immigrant allegedly jeopardized native institutions because he resisted assimilation, or because his customs and ideals were so un-American as to give him an unequal advantage in the economic and social struggle. The spread of these views among thoughtful people constituted a major victory for nativism, since in the twentieth century the acceptable theories of Americanization have been largely nativistic in character. Instances of this new approach to immigrant problems began to appear immediately after the Civil War. In California a clash between Chinese and native shoe workers in 1867 initiated a long series of race conflicts. The Chinese had entered the country to work at the mines and railroads, and at first they were welcomed in a land where cheap labor was sorely needed. They were soon driven from the mining fields, however, and with the completion of the railroads they were released upon the community to fend for themselves. Economic conflict quickly ensued. In the shoe industry of San Francisco, where the Chinese became strongly entrenched, native shoe workers launched a campaign against them which ended only when the foreigner was completely ousted from the trade. In the course of the struggle a purely economic issue was transformed into a race problem. Chinese were said to be a peculiar and inferior people who lowered the standard of living. Their unsocial habits were believed to be the more dangerous because they resisted assimilation and thereby gave no promise of improvement through Americanization. By emphasizing the "un-American" characteristics of the Chinese these warnings made it clear that labor intended to participate in the traditional American patterns. It would insist upon a wage high enough to support a standard of living comparable to that of the middle classes. Such a wage would make possible a pattern of life according to the established ideals. It would also serve as a barrier to exclude from the laboring class those immigrants from lands where a comparable standard of living was not enjoyed. By such arguments as these the workingmen made it clear that their allegiance was committed to the older American traditions, now distinctly middle class in character.

The summary of attitudes expressed in the California race conflict fails to indicate the depth of hatred for Orientals and the determination of the native Americans to exclude them. Treaty, legislation, and court action were all employed to close the first chapter in immigration restriction. Demands for restrictions of other kinds were being made at the same time. Organized labor was again influential in securing the first really selective immigration statute, the law of 1885 forbidding the importation of contract labor. Anti-Catholicism reappeared in the American Protective Association of the nineties, part of whose program demanded immigration restrictions in view of the fact that most immigrants were then Catholics. The three major parties in 1892 included planks in their platforms advocating further restrictions. Most popular of the early methods of determining who should be admitted to the country was the literacy test. Congress three times incorporated it in immigration legislation before the World War, only to have the bills returned with presidential vetoes. Aside from the fact that a literacy test would have the practical effect of excluding much of the immigration at the end of the nineteenth century it would also serve admirably as an agent to promote Americanization. While literacy was a fundamental element of American social ideals it frequently had no place in the heritage of many peoples who sought admission to the country. The test of literacy would provide a convenient way to discriminate against those whose social backgrounds were least similar to the conditions which produced and fostered the American ideal type. The pressure to impose a literacy test became so strong that one was eventually secured over the veto of President Wilson during the World War.

In the meanwhile, Congress had created an immigration commission which was to study the problem in all its ramifications. The report of the commission, known as the Dillingham Report, represented an exhaustive study requiring four years and forty volumes. In separate monographs its agents examined many aspects of immigration, yet the recommendations of the commission bore little if any relation to their findings. It reported that no evidence substantiated the widespread conviction that the "saturation point" of American ability to absorb immigration had been reached. It could find no indication that immigrants willing to work for low wages deprived native workers of jobs, although they may well have served to keep wages down. Contrary to popular belief again, statistics did not show a preponderance of criminality among the immigrants, nor were they on the whole reluctant to be Americanized. On the other hand, the elements of economic struggle and class hostility resulting in discrimination against the immigrant were brought into clear focus. The low economic status of the unskilled immigrant worker was emphasized. The effect of immigrant communities in retarding the process of assimilation was shown, with the recommendation that rigid enforcement of school and child labor laws would greatly improve this condition. In spite of the generally favorable conclusions to be drawn from the report, however, the commission recommended that further restrictions be imposed in view of the fact that continued immigration at the volume reached in the first decade of the twentieth century would not benefit the country and would hurt native workers. It is hard to resist the conclusion that consciously or unconsciously the commission yielded to the growing fear of social disunity which expressed itself in a determination to ignore the industrial class struggle on the one hand, and to exclude the immigrant as a disruptive force on the other.

At the beginning of the twentieth century the immigrant reflected this hostility in his own theory of assimilation—the ideal of the melting pot. As made explicit by such spokesmen as the Englishman, Israel Zangwill, the melting pot preserved for the "new" immigrant at least shreds of self-respect by assuring him that the process of assimilation did not involve complete cultural extinction; that from the mixing of races and nationalities in the new land there would emerge a new and finer race, combining the most valuable traits of its component elements. Even the lowliest immigrant group might make some humble contribution to the character of the new American. The term "melting pot," had long been current in the American vocabulary. Without giving it precise definition, however, the popular usage had generally assumed that it implied the process of Americanization according to the pattern we have indicated. As the conviction grew that the later immigrants were not becoming Americanized with anything like the desired rapidity, widespread criticism of the melting pot was heard. At best the melting-pot theory anticipated the gradual fusing of peoples over a period of several generations, a pace far too slow for the exponents of Americanization. English and Scotch-Irish immigrants had frequently become completely Americanized in ten years, and any longer period seemed dangerous.

The first World War brought the whole issue to a head. The threat was now internal disunity in the face of foreign danger. The hated "hyphenates," to be sure, were German-Americans, a group which had always been considered most desirable and easily Americanized. This inconsistency did not deter the opponents of immigration, however, from basing their arguments on the assumption that only a completely

Americanized people could successfully weather a serious national crisis. Whatever the inconsistencies of the argument, it was now clear that in the face of international conflict and domestic class and economic tensions a large majority of the American people sought security in the common bonds of Americanism. The crisis of the war lasted beyond the armistice in so far as immigration was concerned. The German menace was superseded by the greater red menace, and the red constituted a threat to American economic as well as to political institutions. Organized opinion of many persuasions joined in demanding drastic legislation in order to preserve the "American type" from extinction. The principles governing restrictions in the regulatory legislation of the early 1920's were designed wholly for this purpose. Both the temporary method of allotting quotas according to the nationality groups in the country in 1890, and the permanent policy of allotment according to the national origins of the contemporary population, contemplated admitting in any appreciable numbers only immigrants of those nationalities among the "old" stocks who had easily and quickly undergone Americanization.

Throughout the immigrant century the usual problems of adjustment were in evidence and, in addition to them, the special requirement that the immigrant must Americanize himself. During the first part of that century, when, as Hanson and others acknowledge, American society was in a more fluid and adaptable mood, the greater tolerance of and patience with the vagaries of the newcomers should not blind us to the fact that the requirement was none the less in force. Later, with the profound social changes attendant upon the process of industrialization as well as in the character of the immigrants, the necessity for Americanization seemed far more urgent although it was by no means a new phenomenon in American life, as we have attempted to demonstrate. Ever since independence the process of forming an American nation and an American people has been the determining factor governing the prevailing attitudes toward the immigrant.

III · THE PROBLEM OF
ETHNIC AND NATIONAL IMPACT
FROM A
SOCIOLOGICAL POINT OF VIEW*

By JAMES G. LEYBURN

THE impact of millions of people upon other millions during the past century and a half in America interests the sociologist both in its effect upon the culture of the immigrants and upon the culture of the Americans.

It is easy enough to say that the influx of foreigners has inevitably had an effect upon American culture. But do we understand specifically what we mean by "culture"? We realize that the term means more than refinement and a broad education; what else does it mean? If this term is properly used, many of the problems of ethnic and national impact will be made clearer to us.

Note, first of all, that *culture is not biological*. It has nothing to do with physical heredity. One of the first lessons we learn in our biology courses is that all human beings, of whatever color or breed, belong to the single species Homo sapiens; any normal adult male can mate with any normal adult female; all normal human beings share the pangs of hunger, the drive of sex, the range of emotions from fear to exaltation, the ability to talk, and the power of reasoning. In these respects, black does not differ from white, nor Oriental from American Indian.

Our biology courses teach us next that heredity is a stable, relatively unchanging factor. Man's physical characteristics have not appreciably changed within the past ten thousand years. The physical traits of parents will be passed on to their children according to Mendelian laws. Tall black parents with

* See also critical bibliography, "The Pattern of Assimilation," on page 186.

JAMES G. LEYBURN

flat noses and kinky hair will have children who resemble them; parents of Mongoloid physical characteristics will produce children Mongoloid in appearance.

So much is patent. But is there a Negro *culture?* Does a baby born to Chinese parents have a predisposition to Chinese culture? The answer is No. Before we have been with a Frenchman and a German for ten minutes we recognize radical differences between them. But this difference may not be one of appearance. Indeed, many an expert anthropologist is unable to distinguish the nationality of a member of the white race (or of the black or any other) from his looks alone. What marks off the Frenchman from the German is his culture—not what he has biologically inherited, but what he has learned from infancy onward in his social environment: his language, his customs, his ideals, his preferences, his behavior.

Culture is not human nature, but second nature. If a French baby were adopted at birth by Eskimos, before he had begun to learn French habits of thought and action, he would grow up an Eskimo in everything but appearance; he would eat blubber, hunt seals, make kayaks, and he would lack all those characteristics which we commonly attribute to Frenchmen— logicality, thrift, excitability, and the rest—except in so far as they were also Eskimo characteristics. When we speak of such traits as French excitability, the Latin temperament, Dutch phlegm, English restraint, we tend to think that these are inherent in the people. They are not. They are culturally approved attitudes which are impressed upon a child almost at his mother's breast. To use our former illustration, an infant of typical Dutch parents growing up in Italy under normal circumstances, and with Italian foster parents, would have a Latin temperament.

Our culture, then, we get by imitation and inculcation from the people among whom we grow up. There are among us many hundred-per cent Americans who are children or grandchildren of tall blond Swedes or small swarthy Greeks. The hereditary physical traits have not changed unless there has been intermarriage, but the culture has.

The upshot of this matter is that we need never fear that alien *blood* can in any way affect our culture, nor need we fear intermarriage with any of our immigrants.

What precisely is culture? It consists of three parts: ideas, behavior, and material things. If you went on an ethnographical expedition whose purpose was to describe the culture of a primitive tribe, you would try to bring back a report of what the people thought, what they did, and what they had—as a group. And with your outsider's detachment, you would probably be able to give a pretty fair description of the essentials of their culture. It is not so easy to describe our own complicated American culture (not only because it is complicated, but also because, being parts of it, we cannot view it objectively), and I know of no one, historian, sociologist, anthropologist, or philosophical critic, who has been able to give us more than a partial picture.

These three components of culture (which we may call the mental, the behavioral, and the material) are all closely interrelated with each other, as we shall presently see. Bearing these three aspects in mind, wherein consists the problem of ethnic and national impact? What have the alarmists feared when they have warned that our American culture might be swamped by the millions of Italians, Slovenes, Poles, and others? Surely they were not concerned over the material things these immigrants might bring in with them. On the contrary, they have often even adopted some of their material objects, such as foods, furniture, and craft products. From your reading you will certainly have already seen that the divergent *behavior* first of all attracted unfavorable attention, and then the native Americans, their minds fixed upon this divergent behavior, assumed that the ideas and motives prompting it were likewise divergent, and if divergent, dangerous.

Being an American does not mean to us *primarily* the things we use—our automobiles, our houses, our machines, our roads, our chewing gum. It does not even mean *primarily* our behavior, although this touches us more deeply. What really stirs our hearts and minds is our set of ideals and values. Often we do not realize explicitly what these are until they are threatened. But in the present crisis we know with our innermost being how dear to us are our American ideals of democracy, decency, and individual freedom, our belief in free speech and in free elections and in the right to worship as we choose, our family mores, our religious faith, our respect for certain symbols which convey these ideals to our attention (the American flag, for example).

It is this *mental* aspect of culture which gives us what security we have in life. Conversely, it is a threat to this part of our culture which disturbs us most profoundly. By a perfectly understandable, if elliptical, bit of reasoning, we tend to conclude that when people look and act differently from ourselves, they must think and feel differently about basic matters. The more ignorant people are, the more suspicious they are likely to be of differences from the customary. Precisely because new immigrants are recognizable in looks, language, and acts, suspicion against them is aroused.

Our grandparents apprehended clearly that immigrants can bring this mental part of their Old World culture with them, unchanged, to the New World. When, therefore, they saw the German immigrants amusing themselves on Sunday in their beer gardens—"desecrating the Sabbath," as they called it—how could they be sure that this behavior did not betoken a lack of sympathy with all our American ideals and values, did not, in fact, constitute a threat to them? And when, in the last generation, the New Englanders, hardly yet accustomed to the presence of Irishmen, now saw southeastern Europeans with different folkways and standards of living actually outnumbering themselves, were they not justified in their alarm for American culture?

Increasingly through the nineteenth century, when the tide

of immigration was swelling, this perturbation grew. Distrustful of the apparent mental nonconformity of the immigrant, Americans took steps which made his assimilation all the more difficult. Feeling ourselves to be an in-group and the newcomers an out-group, we have segregated them in Little Italys and in sections across the railroad tracks. Certain native Americans have tried to keep them from voting. We have excluded them from various organizations and institutions. And by these very acts of self-defense on our part we have delayed their adoption of our own cherished values.

Yet despite such shortsighted, if understandable, policies of dealing with the immigrant, two factors have worked in our favor, helping us to preserve and enrich many parts of our culture. The first of these, which needs but little comment, has been the willingness, nay, the eagerness, of most of the immigrants to become Americans, not only in externals, but heart and soul. If the first generation often found this difficult —and they did, for the adult mind cannot easily take on new patterns of thought—the second generation found it much simpler; and the third generation has been no longer foreign, but truly American. In this same connection it might be pointed out that we were more numerous than any single group of immigrants; our American culture was one, while their cultures were many; ours was a single reservoir in which their diversities met and merged.

The other factor working in favor of the preservation of American culture is a subtler one; it has to do with a characteristic of culture itself. So closely related are the ideas, the behavior, and the material goods of a group, that each of them has an inner logic in terms of the others. *A change in one element of culture is almost sure to produce an adaptive change in other elements.* The obviousness of this simple, but significant, idea will be clear upon reflection. One illustration will suffice. When the automobile came into wide use in the United States, first our behavior patterns changed. We became more mobile as a people; cities grew, while rural population declined proportionately; new occupations were made necessary; styles in women's clothes were modified. The effects were even more far-reaching: our courtship customs changed, and church attendance was affected. And these are but half a dozen of the literally thousands of consequences attendant upon a change in our material culture.

Let us now apply this idea. The values and ideas of our immigrants *had been* logically related to the artifacts and to the behavior of the Old World regions from which the newcomers derived. Almost as soon as these people stepped upon our shores, however, they had perforce to use *our* machines and follow *our* economic methods. This adoption of our goods and our methods in order to gain an economic livelihood meant inevitably learning new patterns of behavior and new habits; and these in turn soon produced new ways of thinking —for, of course, our own symbols and mores had taken their logic from *our* material culture and behavior. It is, in fact, a generalization of almost universal application that adjustment and assimilation begin first in the material realm, since the immediate sense of the new *things* is obvious. The very absorption of these foreigners into our economic life meant the ultimate assimilation by them of our culture, or at least of a very large part of it.

Anyone who reads history, anyone who has heard his grandfather tell about how things used to be when he was a boy, knows that culture is dynamic. This is another of the aspects of the problem of impact which concerns us. Even within your own lifetime there have been changes in American culture; but such changes have been so slow, and you have felt so secure in the comfortable familiarity of American society, that you have been able to take these changes in your stride. Our culture is logical to us, and we are spiritually secure because of this. But put yourself for a moment into the place of the immigrant, particularly of the first generation. However much he might have told himself that he must expect to use new goods, new techniques, new habits instead of the old familiar ones of southern Italy or Yugoslavia, he can hardly have prepared himself to see dozens of his *moral* notions challenged. Much American behavior and many American ideas to which we do not give a second thought have struck first-generation immigrants as dangerous or even abhorrent. Girls in America went unchaperoned, children displayed little respect for parental authority, the hold of the church was relaxed, money was spent for pleasure of the moment instead of being put by with peasant thrift against a rainy day.

Whereas the cultural changes *we* have faced have come so gradually that we could make an easy and normal adjustment to them, the cultural changes the immigrant had to make were so sudden and radical as to be almost disruptive. As the writers on immigration point out, it is the usual course of events for the first generation to experience conflict and disorganization. Reorganization and assimilation come later. Had it not been for such immigrant institutions as foreign-language clubs and churches and newspapers, to renew the comfort of the familiar, undoubtedly many of the new arrivals would have become demoralized, or would have turned to criminal acts of violence.

Here again is a paradox. Many Americans have looked upon these immigrant institutions with suspicion, fearing them as centers of alien propaganda, citing them as proof that aliens could not be, or at least were not being, assimilated; yet actually they broke the shock of novelty and so made a new adjustment possible. All such institutions tend to die. The second generation has little need of them or desire for them, and the third generation practically never needs them. With the flow of immigration stopped, they will all disappear—or else they will radically change their character, as Tammany Hall has done.

The millions of immigrants who came to our shores before the 1880's have been so completely absorbed into the body of American life and culture that we no longer think of them as constituting problems. Despite the outcries of our alarmists, despite all the Native-American movements mentioned a moment ago, the average Americans have seen the need of assimilation and have fostered it—at times almost too fast. But if the process of absorption for the immigrants before 1880 has been fairly complete, the same is not true for the more recent ones. The reason is simply that there has not yet been time enough. We still have thousands of first-generation immigrants, and millions of second-generation ones. If it seems to you unlikely that they will ever be assimilated, because of their differences from us in background and culture, bear in mind that our ancestors felt the same way very often about the immigrants of their day. Scotch-Irish, Irish, Germans, Swedes—all those Northern Europeans whom our recent immigration laws have favored—were in times past looked upon as dangerous elements and harmful influences; yet we now know how much richer our national life is because of their presence. Given time, and a continuation of our present restrictive immigration laws, there is every reason to expect the absorption of the newer stocks.

This is hardly the place or the time to discuss specific problems caused by immigration. Courses are given in our various universities on "Immigration Problems." Any of the standard textbooks on the subject will treat these matters—labor problems, political chicanery, social discrimination, crime, urban concentration, and the like. To me the significant point is that these courses are every year becoming fewer, as the immigrants become Americans.

It is evident, then, that most of the problems of impact of ethnic and national groups upon American culture are temporary and soluble. Does immigration present any *insuperable* problems for America? It might do so, on two counts.

If we should open wide our door again, so that millions of foreigners poured in each year, most of them settling in one part of the country, the culture of that part of America would inevitably be radically and vitally affected by the culture of the immigrant group. It might even disappear. There are even now parts of Connecticut and Massachusetts in which one sees small trace of any characteristic Yankee culture, such as was familiar in the nineteenth century. The newcomers have outnumbered the Yankees, and the cultural ideas and values of the newcomers are preponderant. Yet even in those parts the tide of immigration has not been so great that *American* culture has disappeared. The second generation Poles and Italians of New England are hardly twentieth-century Yankees, but the great majority of them are nevertheless recognizably twentieth-century Americans. I say again that if immigration were completely unchecked, it might conceivably swamp a country, fundamentally altering its character and its culture. I consider it highly unlikely that our policy will change in this direction.

The other apparently insuperable problem is not in the realm of hypothesis. It is the problem of race. Negroes have been among us for three hundred years, and they still remain Negroes in appearance despite the American culture they all have. We have not yet absorbed our Orientals either. It would therefore be folly to admit large numbers of colored immigrants; under present circumstances, it would be folly to admit any at all. Amalgamation occurs along *cultural* lines easily enough in the case of both these racial groups. The rub comes in the fact that we can still tell a Negro by his looks, and that a Chinese still looks like an Oriental, while the grandchildren of the Swedes or Germans of two generations ago are indistinguishable from other Americans.

These physical marks are not overlooked by the average American; they are likely to set in motion a whole train of prejudices, not logical, but traditionally strong, and possibly all the more persistently held to because they rest on tradition and emotion. Whereas the Europeans have been able to amalgamate themselves both physically and culturally with the American whites, and so lose their separate national identity, the Negroes and Orientals have been able to achieve only half this amalgamation. The line of separation is sharply drawn at intermarriage. Racially these peoples are distinct; and because of this they have to suffer whatever prejudices we feel and display. Here is one of America's great unsolved problems. Personally, I see no solution for it until intermarriage has wiped out all distinguishing marks of race in this country. And this will hardly occur for centuries.

In conclusion, it might be suggested that the United States, in its experience with 38,000,000 immigrants, may have a contribution to make to our distraught world of today. We have, whether by sheer luck or by good common sense, effected a peaceful mingling of diverse cultures under freedom. Had we taken the contrary course of opposition, we should merely have perpetuated the diversities. Despite temporary discriminations and injustices, we have in the long run afforded our immigrants equal opportunity, full citizenship, and equality. And now, in this present crisis, we are being repaid with the loyalty of our so-called "enemy aliens" and of those of foreign stock. It is conceivable that our American experience might be taken as a model for post-war Europe.

IV · ETHNIC
AND NATIONAL FACTORS IN THE
AMERICAN ECONOMIC ETHIC*

By FRANK D. GRAHAM

ECONOMICS is a promiscuous discipline, its scope is very great, and, like the true sciences, large parts of it are ethically neutral. It is promiscuous in that it cuts across all volitional human activities. One cannot attempt to define its field, by vertically drawn lines only, as one may perhaps do with other disciplines such as chemistry, physics, botany, architecture, and so forth. On the contrary the most sweeping line of demarcation of economics is horizontal, that is to say, there is an economic aspect to all human activity and there is, in consequence, an economics of everything. Bridge whist, for instance, is an exercise in economics, as indeed are all games, since games consist merely of the effort, under various rules, to make the most, toward a defined end, of a given set of resources. There is an economics of art and of religion, of education and of science, of work and play. The whole of one's life is, in fact, an economic problem, viz., how to spend one's allotted time in the way which, with a given biological inheritance, will most effectually meet a given, or selected, end.

One branch of economics, therefore, is a purely technological, an engineering, science, ethically neutral and concerned solely with the method of handling the elements of the situation—as if they were inert, will-less, things—so as most fully to realize the end in view. There is, however, another, very different, branch of economics which is concerned with the selection of ends and with the fact that human factors of production are not inert, to be manipulated as some designer wills, but, on the contrary, resent manipulation, are recalci-

* See also critical bibliography, "The Economic Impact," on page 195.

trant about it, are themselves will-full and are interested both
in the ends selected and in the manner in which they are to
be furthered. The manner of furthering the ends to which
men will give their approval is, moreover, by no means necessarily that which would most effectually promote the end
selected were that end quite uncomplicated by the means
through which it is to be realized. If, for instance, one were
so naive as to suppose that the goal of economic endeavor is
simply to maximize the total output of material goods accruing to men who are otherwise to be regarded as mere instruments, or even to maximize the *per capita* receipt of material
goods on any given basis of distribution, the director of opera-
tions need take account of nothing more than his available
raw material and the strength and skills of his workers. Working conditions, and all living conditions apart from the ac-
quisition of the produced goods, would then be a matter of
complete irrelevance. The study of methods might, under
such assumptions, be called economic engineering, but it
would not be economics in any pregnant meaning of that
word.

So soon as we come to economics in the larger sense we are
involved in ethics, and ethical attitudes are always heavily
conditioned by ethnic or national backgrounds. Ethics, in fact,
is frequently held to be nothing but a body of customs which,
of course, vary from tribe to tribe and nation to nation. American economic thought has been greatly affected, and has
sometimes completely changed direction, as members of one
or another ethnic or national group attained a certain domi-
nance in the field of economic thought and shifted its ethic.
Their temporary eminence, of course, frequently arose from
the fact that the economic environment, largely as a result of
the impact of impersonal forces, was in constant process of
change. This made the way easy for one or another ethic and
therefore for the ideas of one or another ethnic or national
group.

Though ethics is, in my judgment, much more than mere

tribal custom, there is no doubt that men's notions of "good" and "bad," "right" and "wrong," are largely the product of their environment, of which their ethnic, or national, background is a very important part.

The settling of our North American continent was originally effected chiefly by British, Irish, French, and Spanish, but also by nationals of some other states which were, for the most part, of the Protestant faith. Protestantism was predominant in what became the United States. The faith is of some importance to the matter in hand since ideas on religion are, in part, a reflection of ethnic inheritance, and the Protestant or Catholic impact on economic thought is thus an ethnic, or national, impact. It is far from an accident that the Latins and South Irish have found Catholicism congenial to them while the predominantly Nordic peoples, such as the British, North Irish, Dutch, Danes, some of the Germans, the Swedes, and Norwegians have not.

Catholicism is authoritarian in essence,[1] Protestantism, individualistic.[2] Catholicism obviously retains its strength most readily among peoples predisposed to an authoritarian social organization. If such peoples ever renounce Catholicism, they are likely to embrace a new faith, such as *étatisme*, as a means of having their lives ordered by authoritarian edict. The distinguishing marks of any such authoritarian order are status and loyalty, a feudal regime, a system of homage, of personal dependence, submission, and service, with rather clearly defined rights and obligations on a basis of thoroughgoing inequality. Individualistic doctrine, on the other hand, repu-

---

[1] The early Christian church was, of course, democratic or even communistic, but, when it came to power, it quickly developed a hierarchy and supported a system of caste (status) in the secular world.

[2] The individualistic character of Protestantism is the reason for the general tendency of Protestant sects to disintegrate. It is very difficult, for any length of time, to maintain solidarity in a Protestant *church* and therefore to preserve its character as an effective organization. Wherever solidarity has been preserved, in an ostensibly Protestant system, this has been done only through a partial reversion toward Catholicism, as e.g., in the Anglo-Catholic and German-Lutheran churches.

diates status and puts its faith in contract. In its most advanced democratic form it spurns all personal loyalties, relies on the cash nexus rather than the bonds of homage, emphasizes equality (of some sort) rather than a "graded" society, proposes that every man shall be his own priest and his own master. Protestant societies tend to be of this character and any authoritarian organization must, by definition, suppress the Protestant spirit.

All this has its repercussions in economic thought and practice. The feudal system in Europe was merely the economic expression of the religion of the time. The Church claimed sway over the whole life of the individual; its *dicta* provided the great organon for the coordination, to a definite end established by the ecclesiastical "court," of *all* of man's activities. Under this system the end of economic endeavor was not riches or material comfort but rather the attainment only of the minimum, or perhaps optimum, of material goods necessary to a sober (that is, abstinent) and godly life. This was true, at least, for the public at large, whatever may have been the case for the princes of the Church and the State. All of such surplus, above this modest standard of living, as was not absorbed by the potentates, was devoted to the glory of God in outlays on expensive cathedrals, crusades, and similar worthy objects, and the economic goal of the society was luxury of this peculiar and pietistic character.

The feudal system was an almost inevitable result of the system of values established by the Church (unless, indeed, the chain of causation ran the other way). The feudal "man" was supposed to devote his penurious life not only willingly, but assiduously and joyously, to these purposes, since the chief end of man was to glorify God (in the manner prescribed by the Church). The (ideal) feudal "lord," in turn, was conceived to be a steward of that part of the heavenly Master's estate over which he had, by grace, been placed, and his duty (more honored in the breach than in the observance) was to manage it solely to the glory of God. As a check upon the old

Adam, which the ecclesiastical authorities all too well knew was like a Phoenix in the breasts of the secular lords, the Church asserted plenary powers over them, and this gave rise to persistent conflicts which culminated in the struggles between the kings and the popes.

The triumph of the kings was more or less coincident, if not identical, not only with the decline of the power of the popes but also of the feudal lords, and with the appearance of Protestantism. Protestantism was, in some places, merely a protest against the *power* of the popes while, in others, it was a protest against the *ideology* of the Roman Church. Where the protest was of the latter kind it was, in some cases, directed against what were conceived to be abuses of good ideas and, in others, against the ideas as such. The reformation in England, so far as it was effected by Henry VIII, was the result of a pure struggle for power. But complaints against the abuses of accepted doctrines of the Church had, for centuries, been current in England, and some of the Puritans were now challenging the doctrines themselves. In Germany it was mainly at abuses of doctrines that Luther thundered, and he later withdrew in horror from many of the applications of ideas which he had done so much to let loose in the world. Calvin, however, was a much more comprehensive reformer in that he set up a wholly new ideology, together with an organization for its application, and sought to make of himself a sort of Protestant pope, perhaps without the catholicity that the Roman pope asserted but with a much more thoroughgoing and detailed prescription of the conduct appropriate both to the elect and the (presumptively) damned.

It was with Calvin, and those that patterned themselves after him, that what we now call the economic virtues—enterprise, assiduous industry, thrift, foresight and sobriety—were given every encouragement, and God was felt to be most fully glorified in the life of the sober, rich, and righteous burgher. (It was the *rich*, the wise, and the good who were supposed to have an indefeasible title to rule the social life of New England, including the means and method of organization of the economic system.) Instead of the generous, good-humored, frequently artistic slovenliness which had characterized the economy of the Middle Ages (what the Germans call "Polnische Wirtschaft"), Calvin insisted upon a parsimonious efficiency in the conduct of business, and on efficiency, if not parsimony, in consumption. Under the Catholic regime it was the life of the spirit that was emphasized—it was much more important to live religiously (that is, according to the precepts of the Church) than to live what we have now come to call well—and the economic result was incidental. With Calvin, economics became religion. Calvin's theology was, in a very real sense, materialistic—the good life was that which would normally lead to the accumulation of wealth—and ethics was, in large part, determined by what was conceived to be economically desirable. Under the Catholic view, the economic life had been but a necessary and unhonored means in a wider scheme in which the things of this world were (officially) condemned. Calvinism, on the other hand, was the religion of the bourgeois, the creed of the capitalist, the cult of efficiency to economic (or perhaps merely pecuniary) ends, the faith, par excellence, of the business man. It provided a comfortable halfway house for those who had not fully shaken off the religion of the Middle Ages and, therefore, had not fully gone over to the evolving ideology of more modern times. It invested materialism with the de-jeweled robes of the Church.

Calvinism came to full flower in New England. It suited the English temperament and was highly favored by the natural environment it found on this side of the water. The inherent conflict between the self-regarding virtues, which it so greatly stressed, and the regime of ecclesiastical authority, on which it still more vigorously insisted, was temporarily assuaged in the comparative uniformity of religious notions and the kinetic character of the economy. Calvinism, in distorted form, still exerts a powerful influence on the American economy. The individualism it fostered, however, soon broke the bounds set upon it in the Massachusetts Bay Colony and was reflected much more fully on the later frontiers than it ever had been on the stern and rock-bound coast.

A century and a half was to pass, however, between the founding of New England and the expansion into the first "West." In this period a profound change was occurring in the intellectual climate of Europe and its influence quickly made itself felt in this country. Mercantilism which, on its political side, exalted the Prince or the State, and, on its economic side, the interest of the merchant as the main support of the Prince or State, was on the whole irreligious and derived its philosophy from Machiavelli and the Renaissance. So far as Mercantilist writers were not agnostic they regarded the Prince as the vicegerent of God, but they showed a progressive forgetfulness of God in their enthusiasm for the Prince. Hence the doctrine of the divine right of kings and an acceptance of the view that the *Vox principis est vox Dei*. The Mercantilists more and more insistently asserted that the religious and the economic life were separate, on quite different planes, and they felt increasing irritation at the interference of the Church in economic and business affairs such as in the prohibition of interest, the emphasis on the "just price," and the like. Economic evolution was bringing the merchants to power. The more frankly agnostic or atheistic Mercantilists repudiated medieval concepts root and branch and assumed a pagan, or even a more or less refined, jungle attitude toward life. Neither the semireligious nor the wholly irreligious Mercantilists regarded the bulk of the population as anything other than raw material for the advancement of *their* interests (which they identified with those of the Prince or State) in a religion of nationalism. The common people remained the mere pawns they had always been (though possibly to a lesser extent) under the princes of the Church, but now their lives were doomed to the (alleged) glory of the State rather than to the (alleged) glory of God. The Mercantilists believed in individualism for themselves but for no one else.

The first chapters of Benjamin Franklin's *Autobiography* show clearly enough the degree to which mercantilistic concepts had invaded the thought, and conditioned the practice, of the colonists of the middle colonies. These concepts were also steadily breaking down the theocracy in New England. The South, in turn, was just on the verge of the development of the new feudalism associated with cotton culture. It seems certain that that culture could never have taken the form that it eventually assumed had the planters been forced to rely on Anglo-Saxons for their labor. As it was, however, an economic ethic, entirely alien to what we like to think is "American," was promulgated by the "philosophers" of the slave states, and quickly won acceptance in that region. Those ethical concepts on which a free economy is based were readily repudiated when the ethnic background of the laboring men permitted a fastening on them of the shackles which Englishmen had struggled to strike from their own limbs. The plantation system was not necessary, it was merely profitable, and it is in an emphasis on pecuniary profits that Mercantilism was blended with the feudal regime to produce an economic "ethic" completely devoid of any type of moral restraint. The sole purpose of the system was to produce planters' profits. The attitude is still present among those who imagine that economic systems are mechanisms for producing entrepreneurial profits rather than that profits are as yet a very imperfect mechanism for driving the economic system in a regime of freedom.

As the notion of an anthropomorphic God came to be regarded as naive, and the divine right of kings was more and more questioned, the "state of nature" became a substitute for a more personal deity in the philosophical salons of Europe. The "state of nature"—an Arcadian, not a jungle, concept—had no historical, or prehistorical, basis. It was pure fiction but it rapidly came into fashion, nevertheless, among the philosophically inclined. In the world of economic thought it was the inspiration of the Physiocrats who, in reaction against mercantilistic ideas, exalted the agriculturist as against the merchant, declared that the only source of wealth lay in the soil and natural resources, and that neither manufacture nor trade added anything, net, to product. The early Physiocrats were also aristocrats and can, in some respects, be regarded as reactionary in the sense that they wished to restore, in part at least, that type of status which had characterized feudalism, as against the different type which the Mercantilists had promulgated and more or less established. The landed gentry were to regain the place from which they had been pushed by parvenu bourgeoisie.

Later Physiocrats were more liberal but they were only in process of putting the first bloom on their ideas when the French Revolution broke. With it, ideas of status, for the time being, went out of the window. The liberty, equality, and fraternity of all citizens was ardently preached, and all systems of caste were, temporarily at any rate, shaken to their foundations. The French Revolution was the real birth agony of democracy. Democratic ideas had been expounded by the Levellers in England a century and a half earlier, and had even been put into partial practice on a small scale in Rhode Island, but, on the whole, had until 1789 received short shrift. The American Revolution was not really democratic and was, in any case, followed by reaction, since the Constitution was in no small degree an aristocratic document. As already noted it was not until the West was opened up that democracy on this side of the water began to make real strides and caste was widely impugned.

The period of the American Revolution had been marked by that struggle of liberalized physiocratic ideas with the tenets of Mercantilism which was dramatized in the conflict between Jefferson and Hamilton. Fundamentally the issue here was whether the economic ethic was to be that of a classless society or that of a society based on status. Ethnic and national factors played a minor, if any, part in this conflict, though the comparative triumph of Hamilton's notions in the evolution of our economy was facilitated by the immigration, in the late nineteenth century, of large numbers of workers from eastern Europe who fitted rather easily into a regime of status.

The shift to a Hamiltonian economy was, of course, not without its vicissitudes. It had already been noted that the opening of the West furthered the acceptance of Jeffersonian ideas and, so long as the frontier played a prominent part in our history, our economic ethic was never fully converted to the uses of Hamilton.

The facts of the environment supported, and their influence was supported by, the evolution of general philosophical concepts. Coincident with the development of liberal ideas (of which the first real, if still partial, expression in economic thought was Adam Smith's *Wealth of Nations*) was the replacement of the notion of God as Father by that of God as the Great Artificer, or Clockmaker, who made the world at the Creation, wound it up, and set it running as a machine under immutable laws, the "laws of nature." In Smith's terminology, the Great Artificer, who had been progressively depersonalized, had become an invisible hand, or merely the simulacrum thereof, which did not of course intervene to change the inherent course of things but only to correct the results of the action of fallible human beings with a disposition to meddle. All of these notions were a product of the enthusiasm which Newton's great work had aroused, and it was perhaps not strange that ethical ideas should be derived from the principles of celestial mechanics.

With Smith, and more particularly with his followers, the less there was of human government (whether ecclesiastical or secular) the better it would be for all concerned, and it was thought that, with some slight reservations, men needed only to be left to their own devices if the plan of the Great Artificer was to be realized with a minimum of friction. The frontiersman was very sympathetic to this point of view. The English philosophers, moreover, such as Smith and his friend

Hume, were comparatively matter-of-fact, even earthy. Englishmen have never been greatly inclined to indulge in the metaphysical flights of the Germans. Their thought was well adapted to the matter-of-fact technique which, as a result of the growth in the use of machines, was steadily becoming indispensable, and it fitted nicely into the one-man or one-family units by which Northern agriculture, and, to a certain extent, industry, was then conducted.

It should be noted, however, that Smith's belief in *laissez faire* rested on the assumption of natural laws of a very different character from those in which thinkers of the nineteenth century came to believe. The "state of nature," which had existed in a somewhat nebulous past, was conceived to have been a state of practical perfection, from which the world had lapsed largely because men would not leave it alone. All that was necessary to recover this lost Eden was to take, and keep, hands off the laws on which it rested. The writings of Malthus and Ricardo partly, and of Darwin preeminently, shattered this dream of a pristine Arcadia but, strangely enough, did not shake the hold of *laissez faire*, which it was supposed would promote the survival of the "fittest" and thus, in an evolutionary way, lead to a progressively better world. The doctrine was seized upon by apostles of things as they are, and any condition of misery was cheerfully accepted, by those who were not affected, on the ground that this was an inevitable accompaniment, and even the mechanism, of constant upward progress. The result was to establish a more or less complete reversion to something like the law of the jungle, slightly modified by the humanity which still issued, in a not very swelling stream, from sources in the ancient religious faiths.

Economic thought long continued to be dominated by the concept of the state of nature. Though it made some room for Darwinism, it began to move more and more fully into abstractions and became a dismal science not only in that, under the influence of Malthus, it was giving countenance to pessimistic views on the possibility of improving standards of living but also because it was moving so rapidly away from reality as to deprive the discipline of all human interest. The views of the English philosophers, in twisted form, nevertheless proved useful to those who were coming to dominate our economic life, and the ethic of an economics based on freedom, to which lip service was steadily given, was gradually brought into a support of status.

Karl Marx, in attempting a well-nigh miraculous synthesis of classical English thought with Hegelianism, put human interest back into economics and, whether because or in spite of his mysticism, has cut an enormous swath in modern economic life. Marx laid emphasis on institutional processes, materialistically determined, and must be set down as one of the world's great optimists inasmuch as, after a predicted period of steadily accumulating friction and misery, he assumed that his Utopia would suddenly emerge from a final cataclysmic upheaval. The plain fact is that Marxism, instead of establishing a classless society, leads to the dictatorship of the proletariat, that is, to a society of classes turned upside down. Marx was a typical German of the have-not school.

While we are on the Germans we should notice the influence of German economists on the young Americans who left this country, in the 1880's, for post-graduate work in Germany and became alien to the English classical school. The principal result was the advocacy of state enterprise in various fields and, in general, a diminished enthusiasm for *laissez faire* and, perhaps, for freedom. The state, in Germany, had, of course, never been subject to the dis-esteem with which it had been regarded in English thought, and the steady tendency to expand the role of the state in economic life has, in this country, been following a path which, in the country of origin, has led to the extravagances that are now so evident.

The most original, and perhaps the most significant, of American economists, Thorstein Veblen, was, in some respects, a Marxist, but Veblen had comparatively little of Marx's optimism. Veblen asserted that economics had never been a science since, until *his* entry into the field at any rate, it had never partaken of the *method* of science which is a study of process, without preconceptions, and without any emotion beyond what he calls "idle curiosity." Economics in the past has been dominated by ideas of the design of a personal, and wrathful God for humankind, or of the scheme of a less personalized deity, or of the alleged operation of natural laws, or what not, all of them teleological in character. But, says Veblen, we ought to study economic phenomena purely as a process moving to no known or posited end, kinetic, always in a stage of becoming (but never becoming anything in particular).

Veblen's views have had great influence on American economic thought, even on the thought of those who repudiate him, and this has been marked by apathy toward conscious social reform. The American dream has been fading and, instead of the widespread enthusiasm for its progressive realization, once so intense, we have been moving toward an amoral struggle between classes in a climate singularly devoid of confident hope. Anglo-Saxon ideals of freedom have not been realized in the economic sphere but the Anglo-Saxon tradition in America is much too strong to permit ready acceptance of the notions of status under which a more or less authoritarian state might function without intolerable friction.

We need, therefore, a new economic ethic. My own view, which I hope is making headway, is that we should neither accept an hypothetical ethic imposed from on high, or from below, nor yet abandon all ethical notions and sit down, in perfect objectivity, to find out what is going on as if there were nothing that we could do about it. On the contrary, we should establish our own ethic in the belief that, within wide limits, we can shape our destiny, that man is free to make of himself what he can, that his fate is not foreordained by God, or natural laws, or "history," that it need not be a mere haphazard "process," and that the "American dream" can be realized.

Let us now review, a little more closely, the reflection on American economic thought and life, so far, of the ideas that have here been sketched. The impact of ethnic and national factors will perhaps be exaggerated, in the effort to bring them more clearly to view. If our melting pot is to prove effective, their influence must, of course, be merged in a synthesis distinctively American.

In the French and Spanish settlements on this continent, the Catholic and feudal way of life was introduced. The conquest of the French by the British (including American British) gave the *coup de grace* to the French feudal *seigneurs*, but the Church retained its hold, and a semifeudalistic regime developed which persists to this day. In the Spanish settlements both the Church and the feudal lords secured their power, and most of the unrest in Central and South America issues out of the struggle to supplant a system of ancient status by one more consonant with modern ideas.

The English settlers in Massachusetts established a Protestant hierarchy with a secular arm under the control of the Church. The latter was run on Calvinistic lines and was, therefore, undemocratic, with a strong feudalistic tinge. The *organization* was much like that of the Catholic Church. It was merely a question of ins and outs. Against this Roger Williams revolted, was thrust out, and set up a somewhat more democratic society in Rhode Island. The other colonies along the Atlantic seaboard were more secular in character than New England and the current economic thought was mercantilistic of an areligious type. This was more or less true of the settlements from continental European states as well as of those from the British Isles. But the quasi-religious deification of the State had here, of course, little chance to flower since the State that controlled their territory was not that to which they had been born and toward which they still felt close ties. Democracy was thereby prospered. As the English colonies began to feel "American," moreover, the political aspects of Mercantilism were weakened, so far at least as the mother state was concerned, though in its economic aspects it retained full vigor.

When Negroes were brought into the South, as slaves, a feudal or prefeudal economy grew up there and the South went clean through Protestant, and indeed all Christian, thought, all the way back to pagan Greece for a philosophical justification of the dominant institution.

The American Revolution was the child of the philosophy of John Locke but Locke's philosophy had little immediate influence in the field of economics. The year 1776 is, of course, also the date of *The Wealth of Nations*. Alexander Hamilton, and his group, however, were thoroughgoing Mercantilists and the economic freedom that Smith preached had no attractions for them. On the other hand, Jefferson and his followers were deeply influenced by physiocratic ideas. The French influence, in general, was strong at this time.

The English liberal school of economics found perhaps its strongest advocate in the United States in Albert Gallatin (a Swiss) but Ricardo's ideas were ardently attacked by Matthew Carey and his son, Henry C. Carey, who, being Irish, were no doubt convinced that nothing good could come out of England. It should be noted, however, that the ideas of the two Careys were in part indigenous and sprang from the natural environment in which they found themselves, rather than from any inherited ethnic, or national, habit of thought. The degree of interaction between the ideas of the Careys and those of Friedrich List, who later founded the German Zollverein and wrote the *System of National Economy*—on the basis of ideas developed in America—is close if not quite clear. But the so-called American system of Henry Clay and the economic system of the later Imperial Germany have much in common, and both are a reaction against English economic liberalism. The "American system," in fact, did not differ

very greatly from Mercantilism, and the contest between mercantilistic ideas and those of the classical English political
economists, represented in the field of foreign commercial
policy by the North and South respectively, continued until
the triumph of the North in the Civil War.

Henry George's thought, and the Single Tax movement,
a reaction against the perversion of frontier ideals, was directly
inspired by the Ricardian, that is the English classical, theory
of rent, even though most neoclassical American economists
repudiated what they conceived to be George's misinterpreta-
tion of it. The growth of monopolies, which was the result of
an undue reliance on the validity of the doctrine of natural
law with the consequent failure to realize that free competition had to be established and maintained—that it was not
automatic and self-perpetuating—was responsible, in the latter
decades of the nineteenth century, for the reintervention of
the State in economic life. But, instead of the employment of
the power of the State to establish the essential conditions of
freedom, there has been a tendency toward an allegedly be-
nevolent autocracy. The influence of the American economists
who had studied in Germany is here in evidence. Trade union
action was, on the other hand, mainly inspired by English
nonclassical precedents, social insurance partly by English
and partly by German, and there has, in recent decades, been
a much stronger undercurrent of Marxism than might, at first
blush, be supposed.

The growth of the institutional school of economics traces
to Veblen who was always harping on the ethnic basis of much
of our thought but was, on the whole, a believer in materialistic determination. Veblen's chief contribution lay in pointing
out the continuing conflict between pecuniary (that is, business), and productive (that is, economic) motivations, and
between the predatory psychology and institutions associated
with a regime of status and the workmanlike psychology and
institutions associated with the development of the machine.
He was by no means certain of the outcome of this struggle.

The status formerly built on an aristocracy of blood has been replaced in Britain, and particularly in America, by a status of plutocratic character, but the ideals (peculiarly German or Prussian) associated with the aristocracy of blood have been widely adopted by the plutocracy. The hold of the matter-of-fact philosophy, which is peculiarly Anglo-Saxon and highly appropriate to the early machine age as well as to frontier conditions, is under steady, subtle, and often triumphant, invasion by the ancient philosophy of status.

The present upshot is that we are not very sure of our democracy, for a long time hardly seemed to know whether or not we were prepared to defend it, and, even if we are successful in the military phase of the defense, are not very confident of the kind of society we want to establish when we are free to do what we will.

This result would seem to show that we have not yet been very successful in melting the elements in our melting pot. They have been impinging on one another, have been setting up frictions of which we were scarcely conscious but which were nevertheless gravely disturbing to our solidarity, and have left us confused. The building of an American civilization is yet in a stage of chaos and immaturity.

V · THE IMMIGRANT AND AMERICAN POLITICS*

By OSCAR HANDLIN

IN THE century and a half of its existence, this republic welcomed to its shores some thirty-five million representatives of almost every nation on earth. For better or for worse, immigration was one of the main currents in the history of the United States and, in politics as elsewhere, was a dominant factor in the evolution of American life.

It is true that the relation of the immigrant to politics—to the struggle for possession and control of the instruments of power as organized in the state—presents only one phase of a complex problem. For politics in the life of the immigrant, as in the life of the entire community, occupied only one limited and restricted sphere. Other foci of interest, beyond the scope of this paper, were often more important. But in government the instruments of social control received their most formal organization and in that sphere they are most readily subject to analysis.

In the bewildering array of climates, backgrounds, cultures, and traditions that produced America's immigrants there was little that was common beyond the fact that there were emigrants. The crossing supplied a universal element which justifies generalizations that comprehend Irishmen and Japanese, Germans and Chinese, Scandinavians and Slavs. For all these left an old world to come to a new, all made the perilous transition from one society to another. The diverse groups here considered felt the results of migration with varying degrees of sharpness and of permanence, but all were influenced so long as they retained their immigrant character.

Those factors which are not the products of migration can only be confusing and must be eliminated even if they are,

* See also critical bibliography, "The Political Impact," on page 207.

somehow, otherwise connected with the immigrants. The second generation, for instance, is subject to so many unique influences that it presents a problem in itself. Similarly certain individual variations must be excluded. Not all newcomers have acted like immigrants. The role of such men as James Wilson, William Cobbett, and Joseph Pulitzer would have been the same had they been born in America rather than in Scotland, England, and Germany. Nor could it be reasonably asserted that the ideas of Francis Lieber who came to the United States had more influence here than those of Adam Smith who did not. In the realm of individual ideas and personal development, place of birth was of only slight consequence; the universal currency of thought enabled the exceptional man to make his mark wherever he was. Only in respect to movements by masses of people was migration significant, for only in the mass was common foreign nativity strong enough to outweigh the other factors which entered into the formation of political attitudes.

Immigrant influence impinged upon American politics in two ways. Immigrants became citizens and, as participants, as voters and officeholders, made American government feel the effects of migration directly. At certain moments they also became an issue, a subject for debate, and consequently significantly affected political developments.

As voters, newcomers stood apart from the rest of the community in the character and direction of their reactions. These differences were not due, as contemporaries thought, to the fact that foreigners were "ignorant, credulous . . . brutalized by oppression,"[1] for native voters of the same class were rarely more enlightened. The divergence arose from a difference in background and experience which invariably colored responses to new and complex problems.

With few exceptions, immigrants were complete strangers to the democratic process. In no country where emigration

---

[1] E. L. Godkin (1866) quoted in Edith Abbott, *Historical Aspects of the Immigration Problem* . . . (Chicago, 1926), p. 649.

was a considerable phenomenon did the suffrage extend to those sections of the population which departed for America. Even in England, property qualification kept farm and city laborers from voting until the Reform Bill of 1867. Where the right to the ballot did exist, it had little meaning. The Irish peasants, for instance, had that privilege before Catholic emancipation in 1829; but they were the tools of their landlords. Carted off to the polls in groups, cheered by the abundant flow of liquor, they voted in public as the Tory bosses told them to. Even further from self-government were the depressed subjects of the feudal monarchies of eastern Europe. To all, the very techniques of democracy were foreign. In no case was politics anything real or close to the people. Government was simply a taskmaster, a tax collector, a crime punisher, over which they had no control and from which they wanted most the favor of being left alone.

With no experience to guide them, immigrants were hardly prepared to act intelligently about the problems of American politics. A few, but very few, had read and thought about America, and had an inkling of what its democracy meant, but the overwhelming mass rarely knew what to make of the new circumstances they faced. Indeed, on arrival, the more pressing problems of finding a job and making the countless physical adjustments to the new life, completely overshadowed the question of participating in the government of their new country. Out of the welter of strangers about them there often emerged a compatriot here long enough to know the ways of the new world, who could furnish assistance. This aid paid heavy dividends. For when the voting privilege came—a privilege which had no meaning because it had no counterpart in their previous existence—it was inevitable that the newcomers should turn to the same source for advice and guidance.

Here originated the immigrant boss.[2] He did not always

[2] A description of this process may be found in Joseph F. Dinneen, *Ward Eight* (New York, 1936).

have to be an immigrant; the new citizens were preyed upon by ambitious politicians whom Godkin described as "keen, shrewd, cunning, unscrupulous Americans, determined to live on the public and ready to do anything that may be necessary for that purpose." Trained to cajole the newcomers, they had learned all their foibles and prejudices, and "knew how to pander to them with unequalled dexterity."[3] Through immigrant middlemen, or directly, they could buy and sell, ruthlessly manipulate large blocks of voters, grasp control of governments, and use them as they liked in their own interests. These practices were undoubtedly often corrupt. But, in the immigrant's scale, a vote weighed against five dollars, an unmeaningful "X" on an unintelligible paper against a week's wages or a month's rent, rendered the very notion of corruption irrelevant.

In any case, the outright buying of votes was often unnecessary; more powerful ties held the immigrant to the boss and to his machine. Countless social clubs, lodges, and associations were affiliated to the party, sometimes directly, sometimes through key individuals. Wherever the immigrants' gregarious instincts took them among their compatriots—in saloons, on picnics, at balls, even in churches—there was a link with the ubiquitous machine. Most of all, the machine understood the immediate practical needs of the foreign born far better than did the idealists and reformers who may have had their ultimate interests closer at heart. Hughie Donnelly knew that a public bath in the North End was more important to slum dwellers than a balanced budget, or Proportional Representation, or Civil Service reform. He also knew that the frigid uplift of the settlement house could never replace the rowdy good-natured camaraderie of the political club or of his henchmen's corner saloons. Mingling with his own kind, in these hospitable gathering places, the immigrant acquired a sense of his own dignity, a feeling of importance and value, that

[3] Quoted in Abbott, *op. cit.*, p. 650.

held him to the boss more closely than did the city job or the free beer.

The influence of the machine was strengthened—sometimes consciously, often unconsciously—by the immigrant press. These newspapers were the most important interpreters of America to the new citizens. For many foreign born the only key to what went on about them was the daily or weekly paper whose interpretations of current issues and political advice carried tremendous weight. Some journals were outright party organs. But whether they were or not, they invariably fortified immigrant separatism, and thus indirectly strengthened the machine. The desire to support and applaud a successful compatriot, combined with the realization that circulation depended upon the perpetuation of group consciousness, resulted in a continuous emphasis upon favoring members of the group. Almost always that meant maintaining party regularity.

The significance of this factor must not be underestimated. The consistent adherence of the Irish-born to the Democratic Party in the nineteenth century, for instance, was largely due to the influence of a relatively small group in New York City. T. A. Emmett and his followers had given their allegiance to Jefferson's party shortly after 1800 and, in the next decade or so, had developed close ties to its organization in that city. There the earliest and most powerful Irish newspapers were set up and these fostered an attachment to the party which ultimately spread to many parts of the country. Newly arrived Irishmen, even in Boston, Philadelphia, and the West, found their first information on American politics in the pages of the *Truth Teller* and its successors, and from their columns imbibed a lasting prejudice and habit of voting for the Democratic Party.

There were native machines, too. But the factors already mentioned gave the immigrant organizations peculiar strength and, at the same time, exceptional pliability in the hands of native interests. The boss whose control rested on foreign-born voters rarely faced the danger of revolt because his power was independent of the issues he faced. The great questions which plagued Americans in the nineteenth and early twentieth centuries meant little to the newcomers. Manifest destiny, tariff, soft money, progressivism, even slavery, were subjects which they neither understood nor pretended to understand. Unprepared to deal with these questions, they followed the party line unquestioningly.

The issues which did concern them were completely different, hardly touched the affairs of the native born at all, and generally tended to bring the immigrants even closer to the machine. Almost all came from countries in which nationalism was already a potent force; and the process of emigration stimulated further what was already latent. Contact with other groups generally heightened pride in the homeland. Outside local politics, therefore, the chief interest of foreign-born citizens lay in developments in their native countries and that interest invariably affected their attitudes toward American politics. There is little doubt, for instance, that the anti-British feeling of the Democratic-Republican Party first attracted Emmett and the Irish émigrés, and that frequent twistings of the lion's tail by Democratic presidents from Madison to Cleveland were required to hold the Irish vote.

The intrusion of these attitudes into American politics gave rise to the charge that the immigrant became "a naturalized *foreigner*, not a naturalized citizen; a man who from Ireland, or France, or Germany, or other foreign lands, renounces his native country and adopts America, professes to become an American, and still . . . talks (for example) of Ireland as 'his home,' . . . resents anything said against the Irish as said against him, . . . forms and cherishes an Irish interest, brings hither Irish local feuds, and forgets, in short, all his new obligations as an American."[4] But more important, the persistent nationalist sentiments, to which the machine could

_____
[4] S. F. B. Morse, quoted in Abbott, *op. cit.*, p. 449.

cater without hesitation, at once obscured more immediate issues and ensured party loyalty.

Sometimes the party which profited from the firm grip of the machine on the immigrant vote was Republican, sometimes Democratic, sometimes both. For there was never a foreign vote, always foreign votes. One could not expect the Scandinavians and Slavs, the Irish and Orangemen, the Greeks and Turks, Protestants and Catholics, Jews and Gentiles, to work together. Old world rivalries frequently made these more hostile to each other than to the natives. In addition, the conditions of settlement often turned one group against another. The Italians of Boston turned the Irish out of the North End by working at lower wages and living in cheaper quarters, so that an inveterate enmity arose between them. And because the Irish were Democrats the Italians became Republicans. But though there was no general "foreign vote," perhaps not even a Greek or German vote for the whole United States, there were in each community specific immigrant votes, marshaled and controlled by organizations. The concern with foreign problems, the absence of interest in the important American issues, and the lack of familiarity with the techniques of American political life, drove the immigrants into the control of the machine. Group loyalty was equated with party loyalty, and one sentiment strengthened another.

A second set of conditions shaped the reactions of foreign-born citizens as voters. Immigrant ideas—the fundamental assumptions and attitudes basic to their thinking—differed widely. There were few similarities between Germans and Italians for instance. In some ways the ideas of one group were closer to those of the natives than to those of another group; the Irish were more like Americans than like Chinese. But in one respect, a product of the transition, there existed a fundamental cleavage between the ideas of immigrants and those of native Americans.

The process of migrating perpetuated a conservatism alien

to the dominant trends in American political life. Perhaps the most prevalent myth about immigrants links them with radicalism, but nothing could be farther from the truth. The overwhelming majority were exceedingly conservative in politics, as in other forms of social expression. The peasant origins of many, and the comparative backwardness of the societies from which they emigrated, bred a submissiveness which was not shed in the crossing. In fact the very process of emigration fostered it. Forms, ways of doing things, which in the old country needed no justification, in the new had to be bolstered continually by a rigid traditionalism. Thus, the Polish or Italian peasant, transplanted to Warsaw or Naples, might become a socialist or anarchist; but, in Chicago or Cleveland, he was so preoccupied with defending what was familiar that disruptive influences made no impression upon him. Migration froze development.[5]

One important aspect of this conservatism was a respect for, and willingness to accept, authority; another was the weighty influence of clericalism. Both diverged radically from the American pattern. The insistent individualism of the nineteenth century left little place for authority as such. In the political life of the period, the influence of the native churches was waning; religious factors played only a minor role in the great decisions of the era. But among immigrants, both were powerful. Feudal backgrounds, rigid class lines, and oppressive governments at home left no room for doubts in their minds as to the part of authority in man's life. And religious influences, already strong to begin with, were immeasurably strengthened by the transition to the new world. The Church was one of the few institutions that crossed the ocean with them, and its influence mounted steadily under the pressure of new circumstances. The activity of the Catholic Church is most familiar but the same part was played, at the begin-

[5] Cf. M. L. Hansen, *Immigrant in American History* (Cambridge, 1940), p. 77 ff.; Oscar Handlin, *Boston's Immigrants* . . . (Cambridge, 1941), p. 128 ff.

ning at least, by others—Lutheran, Jewish, and Greek Orthodox, for example.

The pressure of this conservatism was reflected in the failure of immigrants to participate in the widespread radical
movements that swept the country up to 1914. The pre-Civil
War humanitarian reforms drew their numbers almost entirely from native elements. The Granges and the Populist
Party found no support in the German and Scandinavian
areas of the Middle West; in fact, these groups actively opposed them. The socialists drew few recruits from the Jews,
Italians, and Irish of the cities, and, in the labor movement,
the unions in which immigrants were strongest, the cigar
makers, for instance, were among the most conservative. Like
the factors which made them members of political machines,
those which encouraged their conservative ideas kept the foreign born apart from the native citizens and encouraged the
immigrant groups to lead political lives of their own.

Both sets of influences waned as immigrants adjusted to
their new milieu. In some groups they disappeared within
the first generation; in others they persisted for three or more.
The general complex of social factors which determined the
rate of immigrant adjustment is beyond the scope of this
paper, which can only point to the inverse correlation of immigrant adjustment with political separatism. Those groups
like the English and Scotch, which came from societies most
similar to that of the United States and which adjusted most
readily to the new life, rarely acted as a unit politically; those
which had difficulties in the process of settlement retained
their distinctiveness longest.

While these forces operated to separate the immigrant
from his native fellow citizen, pressures equally powerful at
times cut apart the native from the immigrant. Expressed in
movements that were sporadic, violent, and largely irrational,
these operated sometimes on a local, sometimes on a national,
scale. The circumstances which encouraged these forces will
emerge from the three examples which follow.

Immigration and the political influence of the foreign born became a serious issue in the 1850's. Nativist lodges of various kinds had existed throughout the East for many years, particularly in New York and Pennsylvania, and occasionally had played a transient role in local politics. Sometime around 1850 a number of these had banded together as the Order of the Star Spangled Banner, a secret, oath-bound society, and in 1853 emerged suddenly as a national party. In the next year they gained rapidly in strength, carried a number of state governments, and developed a widespread organization. By now known as the Know-Nothing or American Party, they called for the complete exclusion of the immigrants from American political life, and gathered adherents with amazing rapidity everywhere from New Hampshire to Texas. By 1856 they held the balance of power in Congress and ran a former president as their candidate for the highest national office. But within two years their strength ebbed and the party disappeared from the American political scene even more quickly than it had appeared.[6]

Shortly after the discovery of gold in California, the immigration of Chinese began. By 1850 they were there in considerable numbers. Their presence became a political issue once in 1852-1853 but evoked little real hostility for more than two decades. But in September, 1877, a new party appeared in San Francisco dedicated to the purpose of driving out the Mongolians. Led by Kearney and Day, both immigrants, the Workingman's Party grew rapidly in strength, captured the Democratic Party, and by 1878, controlled the state. In the constitutional convention of that year they sponsored a set of provisions which, if enacted and enforced, would have compelled the emigration of the Chinese. Forbidden to hold

[6] On this movement, cf. Ray A. Billington, *Protestant Crusade 1800-1860* ... (New York, 1938), p. 380 ff.; Handlin, *op. cit.*, p. 184 ff.; William G. Bean, "Puritan Versus Celt 1850-1860," *New England Quarterly*, VII, p. 70 ff.; H. J. Carman and R. H. Luthin, "Some Aspects of the Know-Nothing Movement Reconsidered," *South Atlantic Quarterly*, XXXIX, p. 221 ff.

property, to fish, or to engage in any trade, orientals were to be taxed $250 each year and, in addition, were to be subjected to many civil disabilities. The debate over Asiatic immigration continued for many years, but the party which had so dramatically raised the issue disappeared within two years.[7]

In 1915, an obscure Georgian founded a fraternal society which differed from countless others only in that it revived the name of the defunct reconstruction organization, the Ku Klux Klan. In the next five years, the new group grew slowly, if at all; by the beginning of 1920 it had perhaps 5,000 members, almost all in the state of Georgia. In the next three years it expanded tremendously until almost 4,000,000 were enrolled in it. By then it was no longer the old Klan. Its geographical center had shifted to the old Northwest and its strongest support was drawn from Ohio, Indiana, and Illinois. Its program became primarily anti-Catholic, then anti-Jewish and anti-immigrant; the Negro issue was not very important. By 1924 it was a local power everywhere, had gained control of some states like Oregon, and was strong enough to swing the Democratic nomination away from Al Smith. Yet the very next year it began to disintegrate and soon was again a fraternal society of no political importance.

These three movements differed in time, in locale, and in objectives. Yet they had some element in common that produced their animus to the foreign born.

The simplest explanation is that nativism, or anti-Catholicism, or anti-Semitism, or racism, the various elements from which the anti-immigrant movements are compounded, are natural and inherent in the character of American society and emerge more or less frequently and continuously. If that were true, one could expect to find Americans always hostile to foreigners, Catholics, or Jews. Yet the signs of general anti-immigrant feeling were rare in the nineteenth century, there

[7] Cf. R. W. Paul, "Origin of the Chinese Issue in California," *Mississippi Valley Historical Review*, XXV, p. 181 ff.; Mary R. Coolidge, *Chinese Immigration* (New York, 1909).

was no sentiment against the Catholics before 1830, or against the Jews before 1880. Even the Chinese in California were not always unwelcome; as late as 1852, the leading newspaper of San Francisco predicted, "The China boys will yet vote at the same polls, study at the same schools and bow at the same altar as our own countrymen."[8] The elements of the anti-immigrant movement were not always present; they were produced after the newcomers arrived.

Nor did immigration alone create the anti-immigrant movements. For there was no correlation at all between the arrival of foreigners and the intensity of the hostility to them. The period of greatest immigration in terms of numbers was the decade after 1905. That was also the period when the "new" immigration from southern and eastern Europe was heaviest. Nevertheless, there were no important traces of enmity then.

The ultimate causes for these movements must be sought in the character of the adjustment of the immigrants within the community after they reached it. First, two distinct reactions must be differentiated. On the one hand, there is the vague dislike of strangers, the prejudice against that which is different—a reaction probably found in every society. To the extent that immigrants retained the characteristics that segregated them from the natives, there were always some who felt them alien and resented them. But that is quite different from the organized attempt to turn the machinery of the state against the foreign born, to place them under legal disabilities, and to consign them to an inferior political status. Even if they were considered different, there was an added factor which made the immigrants the subjects of political attack.

Certain similarities are at once visible in the three illustrations above. Each movement arose at a time of crisis when other, more important, problems faced the community. In the 1850's, Know-Nothingism intruded at a moment when sec-

[8] Coolidge, *op. cit.*, p. 15.

tional divisions threatened the union and when the impetus
of the humanitarian reforms had upset the internal equilib-
rium of American society. The Workingman's Party arose in
a period when the effects of the panic of 1873 and of the exhaustion of the mining frontier necessitated a radical change
in the economy of California. The Klan gathered strength in
the wake of a postwar reconstruction and serious economic
depression.

In each case the origins of the movement lay in a source
not directly connected with immigration. The American Party
gained its support from the antislavery agitation; the Workingman's Party from the effort to improve labor conditions;
and the Klan from the reaction to the internationalism of the
war years. In each case the ultimate objectives of the party
had little connection with the immigrants. The New England
Know-Nothings were abolitionists and reformers; those in the
middle states were anxious to evade the slavery issue and were
most concerned with stressing national unity; while the Southerners were primarily interested in perpetuating slavery and
in repressing the abolitionists. The Workingman's Party was
actually a workingman's party; as such it cooperated with
the Granges in enacting the radical constitution of 1878. The
Klan was most interested in restoring the American way of
life as of 1913 and in spreading its gospel of 100 per cent
Americanism. In all three, anti-immigrant policy was conceived as a means toward an end—abolition, higher wages,
and conservative, middle-class Americanism.

To some extent there was a basis for linking the immigrants
with these issues. The Irish in the North were proslavery, the
Germans in Texas were antislavery, Chinese labor was cheap,
and there were undoubtedly radicals and internationalists
among the foreign born of 1920. But in each case the immigrants were not the essential element in the situation. The
Irish were not the most important proslavery element in the
North, nor were the Germans the greatest threat to slavery.
The Chinese did not cause the depression of 1873 or exhaust

the Comstock lode; usually their labor did not even compete with that of the whites. And the influence of aliens in the radical movements of the early twenties was slight. That hardly mattered though, because in each case the means soon became far more important than the ends. The American Party's Philadelphia Convention of 1856 saw the strange spectacle of delegates from Massachusetts who were antiforeign because they were antislavery, and delegates from Virginia who were antiforeign because they were proslavery join in the same party because they were both antiforeign.

The first reaction of the community entering a crisis was to find a basis of unity. Characteristic of all three movements was the "insistent, imperative, and even intolerant demand for likemindedness."[9] Thus T. R. Whitney, a Know-Nothing apologist, insisted in 1856, with the Civil War already in sight: "The American people, those born and reared on American soil have but one opinion as to the general principles which embody our institutions, or, in other words, our system of government. They differ only in measures of immediate or local policy."[10] Such unity was, however, artificial, and could be supported only when it centered in something to oppose. At this moment, any group which, for one reason or another, stood apart could become a scapegoat. The outsiders furnished a *Gegenidee*, a "counter-conception" to which all the qualities the community feared and disliked could be ascribed and around opposition to which it could unite.[11]

Therein lay the significance of the immigrant in American politics. The practice of politics was not often rational. The elements that went into the struggle for, and the exercise of, power rarely permitted neat delineations in terms of class, interest, or ideas. The presence of immigrant groups at criti-

[9] John M. Mecklin, *Ku Klux Klan* . . . (New York, 1924), p. 18.
[10] Quoted in Abbott, *op. cit.*, p. 819.
[11] For a development of this concept in other contexts, cf. Erich Voegelin, *Rasse und Staat* (Tubingen, 1933); L. C. Copeland, "Negro as a Contrast Conception," E. T. Thompson, ed., *Race Relations and the Race Problem* . . . (Durham, 1939), p. 152 ff.

cal moments presented a unique obstacle to the clear-cut apprehension of issues. The immigrants themselves reacted in terms of adherence to a party machine and of stubborn traditionalism, while, from time to time, others discovered in the persistent strangeness of the newcomers a continual temptation to evade instead of to face problems. Sometimes, as in 1854-1856, that merely delayed the ultimate solution. But it was also a substantial factor in preventing political parties from acquiring a rigid class or ideological affiliation, and thus contributed to set one of the conditions of American democracy.

VI · FOREIGN INFLUENCES
IN AMERICAN ART*

By DONALD DREW EGBERT

A s EVERYONE knows, works of art, like other products of
man's handiwork and imagination, are historical documents, and consequently are bound to reflect the time,
place, and society in which they were produced. For that reason, American art necessarily registers various important racial
and foreign influences which have had a significant impact
on life and thought in the United States. In this essay, works
of art will be used as documents, quite regardless of their
artistic merit, to illustrate these influences. However, it must
always be remembered that in making use of works of art in
this way we are dealing with them from what is really a limited and secondary point of view, for obviously an artist is not
primarily interested in producing an historical document. Instead he is intent on expressing something which he feels can
best be said through the medium of his art; and on the originality of what he has to say depends, of course, much of the
significance of his work. This dual aspect of a work of art—its
importance as an historical document on the one hand, and its
primary artistic significance on the other—serves to remind
us that the artist, like any human being, is largely determined
by history, yet at the same time may help to determine the
course of history by means of what he expresses in his art. In
short, works of art are both an effect and a cause of history.

Before turning to the effect on American art of one aspect
of history—foreign and racial impact since the Revolution—
it will be necessary to indicate the chief "native" qualities
which have tended to characterize American art throughout
its history, and which have been affected by this impact. Only

* See also critical bibliography, "The Artistic and Literary Impact," on
page 220.

thereafter can we indicate and endeavor to account, briefly and superficially, for the most important non-native influences which have affected the art of the United States.

It has often been pointed out that the Puritan, middle-class, and frontier aspects of the American background have all in various ways given rise to suspicion of the fine arts. Indeed, with much truth it can be said that the average American has tended to be suspicious of all the arts except those in which the general Anglo-Saxon artistic tradition could be modified to express some specifically American quality. As a result, artists and works of art have usually achieved wide renown in the United States only if they expressed some aspect of American democratic nationalism, of American individualism, or of the American regard for such things as literal representation in painting and sculpture, for the immediately "practical" in architecture, or for technical ingenuity and virtuosity in all the arts. And if such qualities have been achieved in a completely novel way and on an imposing scale, so much the better. It is perhaps unnecessary to add that at times some of these characteristics have been in conflict with others.

But generalizations such as the above can be made clearer as well as more concrete by reference to a few specific examples. Thus, by way of illustrating the American propensity for stressing in a nationalistic way the democratic spirit of the American republic, let us consider a portrait of *Sam Houston as Marius* (Fig. 1). The crude original from which this was copied is said to have been painted at Nashville by an anonymous itinerant artist in 1831. At that time Houston was attempting a political come-back shortly after he had resigned as governor of Tennessee following his disastrous marriage, and some years before he became the hero of Texas. Here, in his character of Marius, Houston is clad in "classic" garb and stands upon the ruins of Carthage where Marius had once meditated. Now Marius (d. 86 B.C.) was a national hero in the Roman republic who was, at the same time, the leader of the Roman democrats in a bitter struggle against the aristocrats under Sulla. Similarly, Houston, the protégé of Andrew Jackson, was in his own right a leader of the American democrats on the frontier, and as such was something of a national hero to many admirers. The portrait, in its direct reference to a classic statesman and soldier, is characteristic of the neoclassic kind of art that was internationally popular during the late eighteenth and early nineteenth centuries. But though neoclassicism was an international style, as will be indicated in more detail later, it has here been given a specifically American, democratic, and nationalistic cast.

Another of the American characteristics cited above is the tendency to emphasize the individual in art, a tendency that might well be expected to accompany a democratic point of view. As is well known, such things as the Protestant emphasis on the direct relation of the individual with God, the freedom of the individual on the frontier, and the nineteenth-century spirit of economic *laissez faire*, all served to accentuate this tendency. One result of this individualistic spirit in American art has been to give a preponderant place to portraiture, and especially to portraiture of a specific and literal kind. Thus John Neagle's portrait of *Pat Lyon at the Forge* (Fig. 2), painted in 1826, shows a well-to-do blacksmith who insisted on being represented in an individual and characteristic pose surrounded by the tools of his trade, all quite literally depicted. Furthermore, the portrait reflects a democratic approach to portraiture which at that time could scarcely have occurred outside the United States. For Pat Lyon instructed the artist to "paint me as a blacksmith. I don't want to be represented as what I am not—a gentleman."

In addition to giving portraiture an especially prominent place in American art, the peculiarly American insistence on individual personality further served to encourage the eclecticism in art which was so characteristic of the nineteenth and early twentieth centuries in general and of this country in particular. For eclecticism, which involves the simultaneous existence of many different styles in art, implies that the individual artist considers himself free to express himself as he wishes. Consequently, it has been particularly strong in the United States where American individualism served to reinforce the internationally widespread insistence on artistic self-expression which resulted from the romantic movement.

Another characteristic of the American approach to art has been its liking for those kinds of art which, in some way or other, permit a "practical" emphasis, and especially if some technical or scientific problem is also involved. As is well known, the Puritan arts were mainly the more utilitarian ones, partly because in his opposition to Catholicism the Puritan feared that fine art might be, as John Adams once said, prostituted to the service of superstition. Hence the simple and utilitarian meeting houses of the seventeenth and early eighteenth centuries—such as the one at Cumberland, Rhode Island (Fig. 3)—partly, at least, reflect the Calvinistic fear of art as something "popish" that might interfere with the direct reception by the individual of the Word of God. On the frontier, too, aside from a few simple folk arts, the exigencies of mere existence necessarily allowed little opportunity for the cultivation of arts other than the most practical ones. And the middle-class business civilization of the United States in the Machine Age directed both art and science mainly toward practical ends achieved by means of large-scale production. It is certainly significant that the last major fine art to develop in the United States was sculpture, the least practical of them all, while, on the contrary, practical and technical arts such as prefabricated housing and "industrial design" for mass production have been carried further in the United States than elsewhere.

It is significant, also, that in the arts as in other things, Americans have tended to worship sheer technical novelty, ingenuity, and virtuosity as ends in themselves. Thus when Clark Mills ingeniously succeeded in the novel technical feat of casting his bronze equestrian statue of Andrew Jackson (Fig. 4) so as to balance on the horse's hind legs without additional support, a grateful Congress voted him $20,000 in addition to the contract price of $15,000. This despite the fact that the work was artistically negligible! Everyone knows, too, that for reasons of technique the musical virtuoso is likely to be particularly glorified in this country, and that one explanation for the great vogue here of even the poorer portraits of John Singer Sargent (Fig. 5) was his extraordinary technical ability with the brush.

The same American middle-class sense of fact which has made for an emphasis on practical and technical problems in American art has often demanded literal and "realistic" representation in painting and sculpture to a degree even more pronounced than in English art. Thus the literal likeness in wax of the elder Pitt in Westminster Abbey (Fig. 6), executed about 1775 by Patience Wright, the first American "sculptor" to achieve international fame, reflects a tendency in art that again is peculiarly American. The same tendency can also be seen in the carefully detailed landscapes of Albert Bierstadt (Fig. 7), which were so popular after the Civil War. These had the additional attraction of being tremendously large, and thereby both satisfied the American love of size and convinced the parvenu patron that he was getting his money's worth.

This literal approach to art has at times, however, often been forced to compromise with certain romantic tendencies in American art. Notable among the latter is that specifically American brand of romantic idealism which so often has resulted in the romanticization and glorification of young womanhood. In part, at least, this originally arose from the relative scarcity of women on the frontier, but was reinforced by the general romantic idealization of the "dream-woman." As a consequence, the literal romanticized is still a fairly accurate description of the pretty-girl, magazine-cover art that remains a popular American ideal, and one that has helped contribute to the immense popularity of such diverse figures as Florenz Ziegfeld and Charles Dana Gibson, and that was in part responsible for the reputation of Sargent as a portraitist (Fig. 5).

So much, then, by way of summation of the chief characteristics—the democratic individualism, the literalism, the romantic idealism, the regard for the practical and for technical virtuosity—which have tended to dominate American art except when it has been strongly modified by influences from abroad. We can now turn to the impact of the most important foreign influences that have affected these native tendencies—the topic which is, after all, the real subject of this essay. In discussing such foreign influences, it will first be advisable to indicate the chief *ways* in which they have entered this country. After that, the major *types* of foreign influence will be distinguished according to the degree and nature of their impact on the already existing arts of the United States.

In general it can be said that the foreign influences have usually entered this country in one of three ways. At times, as in the case of the Pennsylvania "Dutch," they have been introduced by closely knit bodies of immigrants who bring in their native tradition and continue it even after connection with the homeland has been broken, or at least has become very weak. At other times, the foreign influences have come in through ethnic or national groups who continue to keep up-to-date with developments in what they still consider to be the homeland. To a considerable degree this has been true of the arts of the French in New Orleans. Thirdly, and most important, the foreign influences have come in through Americans who, much more than the Pennsylvania "Dutch" or the Louisiana French, consciously regard themselves as American nationals, but who, for one reason or another, have kept open to influences from abroad. Such native Americans are usually affected by foreign arts for reasons that may be primarily intellectual and artistic, or snobbish, or religious in character. Examples of each variety of reason will be given below when the chief types of artistic influence which have entered the United States in these various ways are investigated. For the foreign artistic influences which have thus modified the arts of the United States can be grouped into four chief types distinguished by the degree and nature of their effect on the art already existing here.

One type consists of those foreign influences which have not only been imported but long kept alive by immigrant or ethnic groups existing in a kind of cultural island, and which hence have had little or no effect on the more characteristically American art of the surrounding regions. In such cases, the art of the cultural island is usually limited to provincial versions of the minor arts of the homeland, as in the case of the household arts and crafts of the Pennsylvania "Dutch" (Fig. 8). Ordinarily, too, the continued survival of such folk art is the result of a more or less blind adherence to tradition, with the result that—as in so much folk art—there is likely to be a lack of sufficient originality to make either for artistic greatness or for any significant progress. However, the relative simplicity and directness of this kind of art, its loving craftsmanship and its feeling for the qualities of materials, appeal strongly to our own sophisticated age in which primitive art is glorified both for its direct and immediate expressiveness, and for its unsophisticated expression of "natural" man.

A second type of foreign influence includes those foreign artistic currents which by their very nature could strongly reinforce some already existing American tendency or tendencies. A good example of this is the German painting of Düsseldorf which was so highly regarded in America during the mid-nineteenth century. Indeed, from 1840 to 1870 or so, after the decline of the English portrait tradition which had dominated American painting from Colonial times, the academy at Düsseldorf was the favorite place of study for those American painters fortunate enough to be able to secure training abroad. The Düsseldorf style, based as it was on a revival of the literal, highly finished, middle-class genre of seventeenth-century Holland, appealed both to the American middle-class love for literal storytelling in art, and the American regard for technical polish. It is therefore not surprising that so mediocre a painting as Emanuel Leutze's *Washington Crossing the Delaware* (1851) has enjoyed such great popularity in America. For in it Leutze—who worked both in Germany and the United States—shows most of those characteristics of Düsseldorfian painting which also had a great appeal to the average American, even though, in this particular example of it, the scale and subject matter of the painting are more monumental than was usual. In this respect, Eastman Johnson's *The Old Kentucky Home* (Fig. 9), painted in 1859—a much smaller work dealing with an everyday scene—is more typical of the paintings produced by Americans trained at Düsseldorf. Here again, however, is the detailed storytelling and characteristic careful finish in a picture in which the more directly visual qualities of the art of painting are largely ignored. For the artist has painted each detail in the scene with equal care so that there is no real visual focus to the composition. He has, in short, put in everything he *knew* was there rather than just what an observer could see if he were far enough away to take in the whole scene at a glance.

A third variety of the outside artistic influences that have affected our art consists of those which, while foreign to characteristic American tendencies, appeal to a relatively small number of Americans for some special intellectual, artistic, snobbish, or religious reason. For instance, Americans who received their education—artistic or otherwise—abroad, have often been attracted by European movements in art which have had no wide appeal for the average American. Similarly, sheer snobbery has at times produced small cliques who have adopted certain European vogues merely from a desire to keep ahead of the Joneses. Such a desire has determined the character of many American art collections, and of course can also be clearly seen in such things as the influence of Paris on the styles of women's dress. Finally, as a good example of a foreign religious influence with a strong appeal for a limited group of Americans, we can cite the Victorian Anglo-Catholicism which was so largely responsible for introducing the Gothic Revival into church architecture in this country. It was directly responsible for the Gothic style of Trinity Church in New York (Fig. 10), built between 1839 and 1846 by Richard Upjohn, one of the first "high-church" architects in this country. Upjohn was influenced by the Oxford and Camden movements in England, and by that famous English architect of the Gothic Revival, A. W. N. Pugin, who was so very high-church that his interest in the Christian Middle Ages eventually led him to become a Roman Catholic. And for Trinity Church, Upjohn not only chose Gothic, to him the most Christian style, but insisted on a deep chancel and a cross on the spire against the opposition of a low-church vestry. It is amusing to note that the only way in which he finally won his point about the cross was to place it atop the steeple just before the scaffolding was hastily taken down, so that, in order to remove it, the vestry would have been forced to rebuild the scaffolding at considerable expense. As a result, the cross remained in place.

The three types of influence from abroad which have already been considered—the foreign influences restricted to a small cultural island, the foreign influences reinforcing already existing American tendencies, and the foreign influences appealing for some special reason to a small group of native Americans—are not, however, so important as the fourth variety which combines the second and third types already discussed. That is to say, it consists of foreign tendencies that appeal *both* to widespread tendencies already existing in this country, and also, for particular reasons, to certain small groups of artists, intellectuals, snobs, sectarians, or to some other kind of sharply delimited body.

For example, the Gothic Revival which has affected our architecture so strongly from the end of the eighteenth century to the present day, had an appeal not only to the religious needs of a limited group of high-church Episcopalians as indicated above, but also to certain widespread American tendencies, which in turn were reinforced by romantic and scientific currents characteristic of the nineteenth century in general. For one thing, the complicated structural problems implicit in Gothic vaulting and buttressing appealed to that romanticization of the technical and scientific which was both peculiarly American and particularly characteristic of the nineteenth century. Thus Ralph Adams Cram, the architect in charge of the Episcopal Cathedral of St. John the Divine in New York from 1911 until his death in 1942, was not only an extreme Anglo-Catholic, but in addition was very proud of the structural thinness of the intermediate piers in the Gothic nave (Fig. 11) which he added to the cathedral. Indeed, he boasted that before the vaults were placed on these stone piers, they could be made to sway by the mere push of a man's hand. It was this sort of delight in the skeleton construction made possible by Gothic methods of building that helped lead many architects to an interest in other materials which would make even thinner structure possible, so that the introduction of iron and steel as structural materials was frequently fostered by Gothic Revivalists. Furthermore, many steel-framed skyscrapers, such as Cass Gilbert's Woolworth Building in New York (1912), or the Chicago Tribune Building (Fig. 12) by Raymond Hood (1922), were covered with Gothic detail as particularly suited to expressing tall buildings of light construction.

Like the Gothic Revival, the corresponding international style known as the Classic Revival, which greatly influenced American art from the Revolution to 1850 or so, appealed both to certain restricted groups for very special reasons as well as to certain general American tendencies. In addition, unlike the Gothic Revival which was limited mostly to architecture, neoclassicism strongly affected sculpture and painting as well. One restricted group with whom it was especially popular for political reasons consisted of the slave-holding planters of the southern states simply because the Greek republics and the Roman republic of classic antiquity had all

accepted slavery without question. It is therefore not surprising that the Classic Revival in architecture was so all-
prevailing on the great plantations of the South, or that the
Richmond residence of Jefferson Davis, Confederate President, originally built in 1813 but later known as the White
House of the Confederacy (Fig. 13), was in the style of the
Classic Revival.

However, besides the special appeal which neoclassicism
had for the slave holders of the South, it also had a powerful
nationwide vogue because of its connotations of liberty and of
republican government. From the time of Milton and through
the eighteenth century and the romantic movement, the classical idea that freedom and the arts rise and fall together—an
idea derived mainly from Cicero and Ovid—had been very
strong in the English literary tradition. As a result, it had
gradually come to be felt that the spirit of freedom could best
be expressed by classical forms, a belief which naturally had a
profound effect on the arts of the young Republic when independence from England had been achieved. Furthermore, our
early statesmen tended to model themselves on the republican
heroes of Plutarch, so that classic art in this country came to
connote not only liberty, but particularly the individual liberty
made possible by a republican form of government. And, in
addition to its republican connotations, the neoclassic style in
architecture possessed certain connotations of civic and official
grandeur, largely as a result of association with the buildings
of ancient Rome as the greatest capital of antiquity. It was
doubtless partly for this reason that Thornton's original design (1792-1794) for the Capitol at Washington (Fig. 14),
the building which established a precedent for so much of our
official architecture, had a dome directly modeled on that of
the Roman Pantheon.

To occupy the center of the rotunda beneath the dome of
the Capitol, Horatio Greenough carved in Italy between 1833
and 1843 his well-known statue of Washington (Fig. 15).
However, because the only light on the figure came directly

from above, the effect was so bad that Greenough secured permission to have the statue moved outside. It stood before the western façade of the Capitol until 1908 when, because of weathering, it was given shelter at the Smithsonian Institution where it is today.

Greenough had represented Washington as seminude in the classic garb of a Plutarchian statesman in order to suggest the great leader of the American republic by association with Plutarch's heroes, so many of whom were leaders of the republics of antiquity. There was, of course, European precedent for such neoclassic sculpture, although in Europe its republican connotations were usually less pronounced. For example, in 1807-1810 the same general style had previously been used by the famous Italian neoclassic sculptor, Canova, in his nude statue of Napoleon (Fig. 16), but obviously with the intent of suggesting a semideified emperor on the Roman imperial model, rather than the leader of a republic.

As might have been expected, in spite of its more-or-less symbolic association with liberty and with a republican form of government, Greenough's statue aroused considerable opposition in this country, both because of the nudity of the figure which was so foreign to the Protestant heritage and because its idealization of Washington as a hero of classic antiquity was so far removed from the American sense of the literal in art. In this case, then, various characteristic American tendencies were in sharp conflict with one another.

This particular kind of conflict was, however, limited to the representational arts and hence did not occur in the non-representational art of architecture. For this reason it was in architecture that neoclassicism became most widely popular, especially as an expression of the republican spirit. So completely, indeed, did neoclassicism become associated with the idea of liberty and of the American republic that when various South American republics achieved independence from Spanish rule, they erected a number of neoclassic public buildings —such as the Senate House in Lima, Peru—based on examples in the United States. However, the Monroe Doctrine (1823) and the Mexican War (1846-1848) caused the South Americans to look with increasing suspicion and hatred upon Yankee imperialism, and their architectural attention was soon focused elsewhere.

By the middle of the nineteenth century the neoclassic style had begun to wane even in this country, and other artistic influences, native and foreign, had developed. In the representational arts, as the spirit of Jacksonian democracy gradually replaced the more aristocratic points of view of the Federal period and as the opinion of the man-in-the-street became more influential, the demand for literal representation, particularly in painting, became ever stronger. The one variety of European painting which could then reinforce this demand for literalism was that of the academy at Düsseldorf. Consequently, as previously noted, the influence of Düsseldorf on American painting was very great from the 1830's until after the Civil War.

Following the war, however, as wealth and sophistication increased, certain foreign influences less bourgeois and more sophisticated than those of Düsseldorf became influential in this country. The greater sophistication of the new influences naturally made them appeal first to those small groups of Americans who considered themselves to be either cultural aristocrats in the forefront of fashion, or rebels against the crudities of American life. However, each of these foreign currents had certain qualities which also appealed to one or more native American tendencies. As a result their popularity in the United States often eventually became widespread.

The first of the new influences to take effect came from centers of more aristocratic kinds of European academicism than that of Düsseldorf, particularly from Munich and Paris. The influence of Munich was mostly limited to painting but, from the close of the Civil War until about 1900, large numbers of American painters, especially those of German-American stock, went to the academy at Munich for training. Like the art of Düsseldorf, that of Munich was inspired by seven-teenth-century Dutch painting. However, the Munich style derived, not from ultrabourgeois and literal Dutch genre painting, but from the somewhat more aristocratic style of Frans Hals. In his portraits, Hals' technique was character-ized by very free brushwork, with little or no preliminary drawing. This technique, which was revived at Munich in the second half of the nineteenth century, implied a more visual approach to the art of painting than had prevailed at Düssel-dorf, for the free Munich style required the spectator to stand at a distance from the picture in order to see it as the artist intended. While this technique did not, of course, permit the tight finish and literal representation beloved by the average American, it did require a mastery of the brush and a flashy directness that appealed to both the German and the American love of technical virtuosity. Perhaps the ablest American prac-titioner in this style was Frank Duveneck, who himself came of German-American stock. Duveneck was called by Sargent the greatest talent of the brush in his generation, and his *Whistling Boy* (Fig. 17), painted at Munich in 1872, clearly shows the free brushwork, brownish tones, and studio lighting characteristic both of Hals and of the Munich school.

Much more important than the academicism of Munich was that of Paris because—beginning about the same time—it affected American architecture and sculpture as well as painting, and prevailed in this country for a longer period. Indeed, in American architecture and sculpture its influence was dominant until well after the first World War. Thus, for approximately sixty years, the national French art school, the Ecole des Beaux-Arts, and the private Parisian academies modeled on it, made Paris the great Mecca of the American art student. The principles taught in the Ecole des Beaux-Arts were in most respects very different from those of the academy at Munich, even though both went back to seventeenth-century precedent. At the Ecole there had been preserved an almost continuous tradition stemming from the French academies of art established in the seventeenth century under Louis XIV. This tradition, reinforced in the nineteenth century by Napoleon III, was mainly based on rather rigid codifications of the canons of design which the artists and critics of the Italian Renaissance had previously derived from careful study of the arts of ancient Rome. Consequently, the style taught at the Ecole des Beaux-Arts was a relatively narrow version of the classic tradition somewhat modified by the baroque art of the seventeenth century. As such it emphasized formal and monumental design as well as more-or-less classic subject matter and treatment. Unlike the neoclassic art discussed earlier, however, French academicism did not usually result in the copying of specific examples from the classic past but instead followed what it considered to be the general classic principles of design. Despite rigid interpretation of those principles and a hard dry style very different from the flashy technique of Munich, the Ecole des Beaux-Arts did place heavy emphasis on technical proficiency and particularly on proficiency in drawing as the basis for the arts. As a result, the Ecole played an important, if limited, part in raising the technical standards of art in this country.

The French academic style, as it had been formulated under Louis XIV and revivified under Napoleon III, was primarily a monumental style with imperial and civic connotations. Consequently, it was attractive to Americans of the post-Civil War period, not only because of its snob appeal as an imported style but also because it offered an expression in art for the newly developing American imperialistic spirit; furthermore, at this time American cities were expanding in size and wealth, and were calling for a more impressively monumental kind of civic architecture with painting and sculpture to match. But there was still another reason for the strength of Beaux-Arts influence in the United States. During the nineteenth century the Ecole des Beaux-Arts added to the French academic tradition a new emphasis on fitness to specific purpose and to the direct expression of that fitness, particulạrly in architecture. Within the limits of the rigid academic formulas, buildings were now more conveniently organized for their use and given a character more directly expressive of that use. This new importance of specific character and convenience doubtless reflected the emphasis given by romanticism to the characteristic in art, as well as the general utilitarian spirit of the nineteenth century. And it made this very French style of architecture appeal to the American love of direct and literal expression, and to the American respect for the practical.

At first the influence of the imported Beaux-Arts style was mostly restricted to a relatively limited group of Easterners who prided themselves on being cosmopolitan and up-to-date. However, because the style also appealed to certain native American tendencies, it soon spread widely and, with the Columbian Exposition at Chicago in 1893, began to sweep the whole country. For most of the architecture, painting, and sculpture at the Exposition was executed by Easterners trained at the Ecole des Beaux-Arts and working under the leadership of Richard Morris Hunt (Fig. 18), the first American architect to study there.

As a result of the strength of this new French influence various well-known French buildings became the inspiration for their American counterparts, because the expression of suitable character in Beạux-Arts design was customarily achieved by association with some previous solution of a similar problem, though usually without literal imitation of the earlier solution. For example, the Bibliothèque Ste.-Geneviève in Paris (Fig. 19), built in 1843-1850, in some respects directly inspired several American designs for large public libraries. The façade of the Boston Public Library (Fig. 20), begun in 1893, and the rear of the New York Public Library (Fig. 21), completed in 1911, both show its influence; and they were designed respectively by Charles McKim and Thomas Hastings, both of whom had studied at the Ecole des Beaux-Arts. All three examples show the same direct expression of the vast reading room by means of a series of great arched windows to suggest a large well-lighted room. In each of the three there are screen walls placed in the lower part of the arches to indicate wall space for books within, and also to express the fact that a reader does not want direct sunlight falling on his book. To make clear that these walls are nothing but screens, they are recessed between the piers, and tiny openings are placed either in the screens themselves or in the piers between, thereby showing that the floor level within is at the base of the screen wall and not at its top.

On the rear of the New York Public Library the suggestion of use was carried still further by the direct expression of the stack floors beneath the reading room. It is amusing to note that most critics of the building have preferred the back of this Library, with its frankly functional character, to the more "monumental" but inexpressive Fifth Avenue façade, much to the horror and disgust of the architect. While both the New York and the Boston Public Libraries can certainly be criticized as sacrificing convenience in plan to monumentality —a frequent Beaux-Arts failing when conflict arises between these two considerations—nevertheless, the two American libraries are better organized for use than were most of the public buildings in this country before the influence of the Ecole des Beaux-Arts became strong.

The painting and sculpture used to decorate monumental buildings such as these were based on the same general principles of classic design. For example, Kenyon Cox's *Tradition* (Fig. 22), executed in 1916, is characteristic of the sort of monumental painting executed by Americans who had studied at the Ecole. In technical proficiency, in recollections of Renaissance classicism, and in pseudomythological subject matter —all reduced to a dry-as-dust formula—it is typical of the Beaux-Arts approach to monumental painting. To that approach, however, has been added here, as in so many works by American painters and sculptors trained at the Ecole des Beaux-Arts, a characteristically American idealization of womanhood. As this kind of nonfactual and moribund classicism occurred again and again in our public art, it is not surprising that reactions against it set in, following the lead of similar reactions in France itself. Nor is it surprising that some of these reactions turned to the representation of everyday people and everyday scenes.

One of the most important of the French reactions against the academic tradition of the Ecole des Beaux-Arts was that of Millet and the Barbizon school, and this began to affect many American students in France including even some of those who were studying at the Ecole des Beaux-Arts itself. Nevertheless, most of these men retained enough of the Beaux-Arts doctrine to follow the pseudoclassical tradition in monumental work, although in small easel pictures they now often turned to representing ordinary people, like the peasants in Millet's paintings, or to everyday landscapes like those painted by Théodore Rousseau and other members of the Barbizon school. Thus William Morris Hunt, one of the first American painters to study at the Ecole des Beaux-Arts, used the monumental style of the Ecole for his great murals —later walled up—in the New York State Capitol at Albany. But he was also the first to popularize the works of Millet in this country, and his smaller pictures clearly betray the influence of Millet and of the Barbizon school (Fig. 23). Because so many of the Barbizon artists made careful studies from nature, and because they represented ordinary people, their work naturally appealed both to the American liking for literal representation and to the American democratic spirit. Even Winslow Homer, perhaps the most completely American painter and the one least influenced by foreign art, copied lithographs of the Barbizon school.

However, though the influence of the Barbizon group was pronounced in this country during the eighties and nineties, it was gradually supplanted by that of another French style, which sought to be more realistic and scientific in its technique and consequently made a strong appeal to the American love for technical problems. This new style—which affected American art and particularly American painting from the late nineteenth century until well after the first World War—was known as Impressionism. Under the leadership of the French painter, Monet, the Impressionists reacted against the studio formulas of the academic tradition and against detailed literalism in painting, because both are visually unrealistic. For really the first time in the history of painting in oil, the Impressionists insisted on executing their landscapes out of doors and hence direct from nature. Their chief interest lay in representing the visual effects of sunlight as it falls on the surfaces of things. In their attempt to depict the brilliance of light more-or-less scientifically according to laws of physics, the Impressionists placed on their canvases separate contrasting dabs of the pure colors of the spectrum which constitute light. These are fused together by the eye of the observer at a little distance from the canvas and give more of the effect of real light than when the colors are mixed in advance on the artist's palette, as had previously been customary. An example such as *The Little June Idylle* (Fig. 24) by the American Impressionist, Childe Hassam, shows the characteristic Impressionist technique, but the reproduction in black and white cannot give the sense of light which pervades Impressionist paintings in color. However, the reproduction does manifest certain characteristic limitations of Impressionistic painting. It shows, for instance, that the effect of three-dimensionality in solids and voids has been sacrificed to effects of light. Furthermore, it shows that the more truly "scientific" the technique of an Impressionist painter, the more will his work resemble that of other scientific Impressionists; and the less can he express his own individuality and thereby contribute to the significant originality necessary for a great work of art. For this reason, the greater artists among the Impressionists have been much less objective and scientific in practice than in theory.

In reaction against the loss of three-dimensionality and

self-expression which occurred in Impressionism, in reaction also against the stale academic formulas, and against over-literalism in art, the movement known as Post-Impressionism developed on the Continent during the early years of the twentieth century. Unlike Impressionism, the new movement was not restricted mainly to painting for it has had a profound effect on all the fine arts. As might be expected from its re-action against Impressionism, Post-Impressionism made a conscious effort to reemphasize three-dimensionality and self-expression in art, and in a very nonliteral way.

That variety of Post-Impressionism which particularly stressed three-dimensionality and simplified "abstract" form, became known in painting and sculpture as Cubism. Cubism was "invented" about 1907 by the French artists, Picasso and Braque, and while, like all Post-Impressionistic art, Cubism gave great importance to self-expression, its cubistic qualities were what mainly impressed most beholders. A typical ex-ample of Cubist painting is Picasso's *Woman of Arles* (Fig. 25), executed in 1911-1912. The geometric, abstract shapes so far removed from the literal reproduction of nature were in part derived by Picasso from certain statements of the early Post-Impressionist painter, Cézanne—statements such as: "Deal with Nature by means of the cylinder, the sphere, the cone, all put into perspective"; or "I have not tried to reproduce Nature, I have represented it." In part, also, the Cubists were inspired by the simplified forms of primitive African Negro sculpture. In theory, at least, the Cubist artist sought to express simultaneously all aspects of a subject even including the interior, so that various features are repeated in different positions somewhat as they might have been seen from different viewpoints in walking about the subject over a period of time. Thus the Cubists sought to represent a new relation-ship of space and time in painting. Furthermore, they sought to do so by nonnaturalistic means, for they deliberately dis-located the world of appearances, recombining the disjoined elements according to a new order of their own arrived at

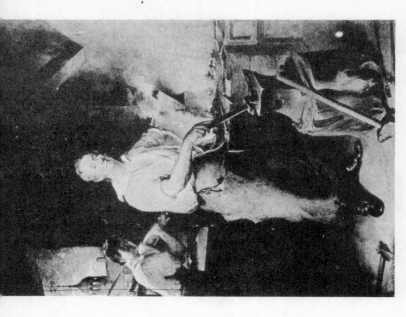

Fig. 2. *Pat Lyon at the Forge*, by John Neagle (1826; loaned to the Boston Museum of Fine Arts).

Fig. 1. *Sam Houston as Marius*, copy by Rouland, from an anonymous original of 1831 (State Capitol, Austin, Texas).

Fig. 3. Meeting House, Cumberland, R.I. (1740).

Fig. 4. *Andrew Jackson*, by Clark Mills (-1853; Lafayette Square, Washington, D.C.).

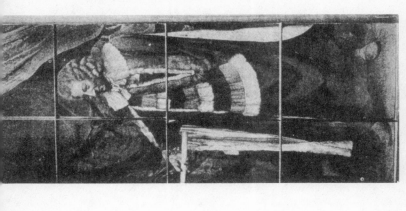

Fig. 6. *William Pitt, Earl of Chatham*, by Patience Wright (c. 1775; Westminster Abbey, London).

Fig. 5. *The Ladies Acheson*, by John Singer Sargent (1900; Duke of Devonshire Collection, Chatsworth, England).

Fig. 7. *Mount Corcoran*, by Albert Bierstadt (c. 1871; The Corcoran Gallery, Washington, D.C.).

Fig. 8. Dining-room furniture, Pennsylvania "Dutch" Gallery, The Metropolitan Museum of Art, New York.

Fig. 10. Trinity Church, New York, by Richard Upjohn (1839-1846).

Fig. 9. *The Old Kentucky Home*, by Eastman Johnson (1859; The New York Public Library).

Fig. 12. Chicago Tribune Building, Chicago, by Howells and Hood (1922-).

Fig. 11. Cathedral of St. John the Divine, New York, nave by Ralph Adams Cram

Fig. 13. "White House of the Confederacy," Richmond, Va., by Robert Mills (1813).

Fig. 14. Dr. William Thornton's Design for the Capitol, Washington, D.C. (1792-1794; now in the Library of Congress).

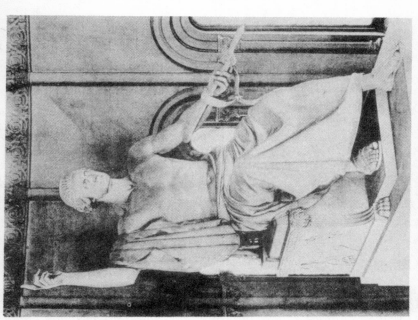

Fig. 15. *Washington*, by Horatio Greenough (1833-1843; Smithsonian Institution, Washington, D.C.).

Fig. 16. *Napoleon*, by Antonio Canova (1807-1810; Brera, Milan).

Fig. 18. Chicago, Columbian Exposition of 1893, Administration Building, by Richard Morris Hunt.

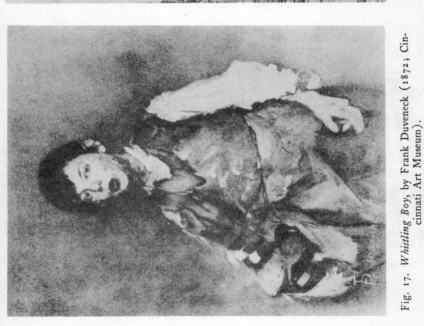

Fig. 17. *Whistling Boy*, by Frank Duveneck (1872; Cincinnati Art Museum).

Fig. 19. Bibliothèque Ste.-Geneviève, Paris, by Henri Labrouste (1843-1850).

Fig. 20. The Boston Public Library, by McKim, Mead, and White (1893-).

Fig. 21. The New York Public Library, rear, by Carrère and Hastings (-1911).

Fig. 22. *Tradition*, by Kenyon Cox (1916; The Cleveland Museum of Art).

Fig. 23. *The Belated Kid*, by William Morris Hunt (Boston Museum of Fine Arts).

Fig. 24. *The Little June Idylle*, by Childe Hassam (Miss R. B. Moore Collection, New York).

Fig. 26. *New York at Night*, by Max Weber (1915; Max Weber Collection, Great Neck, New York).

Fig. 25. *The Woman of Arles*, by Pablo Picasso (1911-1912; Walter P. Chrysler, Jr., Collection, New York).

Fig. 27. Bauhaus, Dessau, Germany, by Walter
Gropius (1925-1926).

Fig. 28. *Jealousy*, by Edvard Munch (1895; National Gallery, Oslo, Norway).

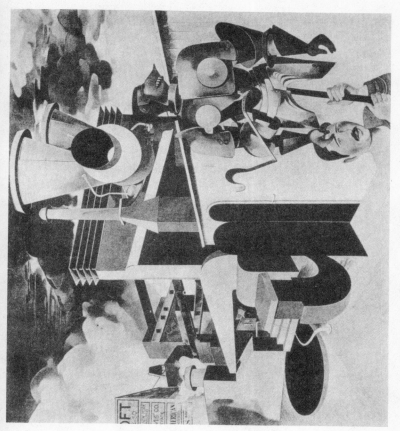

Fig. 30. *Parade*, by Peter Blume (1930; Museum of Modern Art, New York).

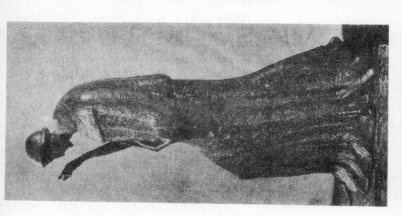

Fig. 29. *St. Francis*, by Alfeo Faggi
(c. 1933; Museum of New Mexico,
Santa Fe, N.M.).

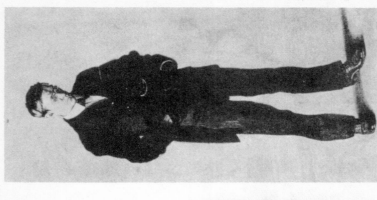

Fig. 32. *The Thinker*, by Thomas Eakins (1900; The Metropolitan Museum of Art, New York).

Fig. 31. *Baptism in Kansas*, by John Steuart Curry (1928; Whitney Museum, New York).

solely by intuition. This they did in an effort to reveal, by nonnaturalistic symbols, essences beyond the everyday world. Hence in its theory Cubism had a direct connection with the Symbolist movement in literature.

Cubism per se has had relatively little vogue in American painting and sculpture because it is so extremely unliteral and non-matter-of-fact. It first became known to the American public in 1913 with the famous exhibition held in what was then the Armory of the 69th Regiment in New York, an exhibition which aroused tremendous interest and controversy. The relatively few American artists who wholeheartedly adopted Cubism about this time were avowedly under very strong European influence, and most of them, too, were expressing their American individualism by revolting against what they considered to be limitations in American art and American life. However, American Cubists have very frequently chosen subjects which, by their very nature, are somewhat cubistic, and hence could be treated in a somewhat more literal manner than was customary in European Cubism. Such an example as Max Weber's *New York at Night* (Fig. 26), painted in 1915, deals primarily with architectural forms which, from the nature of architecture, are necessarily abstract and cubistic.

Because of the inherently cubistic quality of architectural shapes, the influence of Cubism on architecture has remained strong long after the decline of Cubism as an independent movement in painting and sculpture. Indeed, about that time in the 1920's when the Cubist movement was already dwindling in the representational arts, its influence on architecture became particularly powerful. In this country Cubism could have much more effect on architecture than on the other arts because the absence of literal representation which made Cubism in painting and sculpture so foreign to the American man-in-the-street, had little bearing on the nonrepresentational art of architecture.

In American architecture today the direct influence of

Cubism can still be felt in what is known as the International Style, which has combined an interest in modern materials such as reinforced concrete, steel, and glass, with Cubistic methods of composition. The influence of the International Style began to affect American architecture only about 1925. It became much stronger a few years later when various German practitioners, many of whom were either Jewish or had socialistic leanings, were driven out by the Nazis, who wanted a national, rather than an international, style of architecture. One of the leading German architects of the International Style who left Germany and eventually came to this country was Walter Gropius, now Chairman of the Department of Architecture at Harvard University. In Germany Gropius had founded, and for nearly a decade directed, the famous modern school of architecture and of industrial design known as the Bauhaus. Gropius had built at Dessau in 1925-1926 a building for the Bauhaus (Fig. 27) which was one of the most influential monuments of the International Style; and this building not only reflected Cubistic methods of composition but also showed an interest in new materials and methods of construction typical of the International Style. Modern materials made it possible to replace whole walls with glass and thereby express—simultaneously and from a single viewpoint—numerous aspects of the building, including the interior. In short, the simultaneity of expression called for in Cubist theory was now achieved in architecture more completely than had been possible in painting or sculpture. In this country, however, the International Style gradually won popularity almost in spite of its Cubistic connotations which appealed only to relatively limited groups of American cosmopolites or rebels. Its wider popularity was based on the new materials and techniques which made an appeal to the American admiration for sheer novelty and to the peculiarly American interest in technological problems.

In painting and sculpture most of the abler Cubists, both European and American, gradually passed from Cubism as an end in itself toward those other varieties of Post-Impressionism which are grouped together under the name of Expressionism. Actually, Cubism and Expressionism cannot be completely separated one from the other, for just as Cubism involved much self-expression on the part of the artist, so Expressionistic art has generally been marked by some Cubistic simplification of form. In other words, all varieties of Post-Impressionism tend greatly to distort and simplify the forms of the world of appearances for purposes of conscious self-expression. In contrast to Cubism, however, Expressionistic art may or may not be cubistic, and, though distorted, the forms of the natural world are generally more recognizable in it.

Like Cubism, Expressionism derived from many different sources, but its chief place of origin was not France but Germany. One of the main sources of German Expressionism was the Norwegian painter, Edvard Munch; and his painting, *Jealousy* (Fig. 28), executed as early as 1896, directly foreshadows the Expressionistic movement as it developed in Germany shortly before and after the first World War. At this early date a very subjective interpretation is already achieved through great distortion of human figures and other aspects of the natural world, even though the various elements are still quite recognizable.

Not until well after the first World War did Expressionism begin to have much effect on American art. Then, however, the emphasis which Expressionism placed on artistic self-expression appealed to American individualism in general, and particularly to those American rebels in revolt against the sheer literalism of so much American art. In so far as Expressionism, unlike Cubism, has tended to retain some semblance of the forms of the natural world, it has had more influence on American art than Cubism itself. In the works of American Expressionists, however, the distortions are likely to be relatively restrained, and are often used primarily to emphasize certain fairly obvious qualities of the subject. Thus in Faggi's statue of St. Francis (Fig. 29), the artist has elongated the figure to stress the asceticism of the saint in a relatively "literal" American way.

One variety of Expressionism that has had comparatively little influence on American artists is Surrealism. Mostly limited to painting, it has not been widely popular here. For in its attempts to express the subconscious—attempts which, of course, parallel Freudianism and similar developments in modern psychology—Surrealism has dislocated and distorted the world of appearances too completely for the average, matter-of-fact American. It is significant that the foreign Surrealist who has had the greatest vogue in America is Salvador Dali, whose popularity in this country has probably resulted more from the extraordinary technical finish of his paintings than from their content. The best known of the few American practitioners of Surrealism is Peter Blume, whose *Parade* (Fig. 30) is typically Surrealistic in combining the incongruous in such a way as to produce something of the sharp intensity of a dream. Yet the individual objects depicted by Blume are more literally rendered than are the details of much European Surrealistic painting, and consequently clash less sharply with the American regard for the everyday appearances of things.

However, because all forms of Post-Impressionism tend to be very nonliteral in some respect or other, it is not surprising that there have arisen in this country sharp national and regional reactions against them, reactions which today are very popular particularly in the Middle West. For example, John Steuart Curry's widely known *Baptism in Kansas* (Fig. 31), though painted in 1928, represents a present-day nativistic and Middle Western tendency to return to literal representation, and this despite the fact that Curry had studied abroad. So literally does the painting tell its story that it is often criticized for being little more than a sheer illustration of the scene, and as such it runs the risk of failing to make any aspect of the subject as painted seem more significant to the beholder than would the actual event itself. In so far as it may fail to give intensified expression to some aspect of reality and truth, the painting lacks the significant reality of really great art. Nevertheless, the importance of Curry's work in making Americans aware of the possibilities of American subjects for art cannot be denied.

Today, then, there still prevail in the United States the same interplay and conflict between native tendencies and foreign influences noted throughout this essay. American artists are aware of Europe, just as they have always been, even while reacting against its influence. Today, some American artists insist that everything European is bad, and that we must consciously cultivate our native tendencies while shunning Europe. The danger of this self-consciously regionalistic point of view is that only sheer provincialism may result, and Curry's *Baptism in Kansas* is on the edge of such provincialism. Other American artists, at least until the outbreak of war in 1939, have tended to follow European developments slavishly. The danger of so doing is that only second-rate imitations of European developments may be produced, giving rise to another kind of provincialism. Thus Weber's *New York at Night* (Fig. 26), despite its American subject matter, runs the risk of being merely a provincial version of French Cubism. It is only fair to add, however, that most of Weber's paintings are more distinctively original in spirit, and that in any case he has played an important part in familiarizing Americans with artistic developments abroad.

It can be said with considerable truth that at least a majority of the American artists generally considered to be the greater ones have neither self-consciously avoided nor self-consciously imitated Europe, but have taken inspiration wherever they could find it for developing their own individual modes of expression. If they have worked in the United States and have not consciously sought to escape from or rebel against their native land, their work has almost inevitably been American in some respect or other. Thus, while the portrait by Thomas

Eakins known as *The Thinker* (Fig. 32) betrays some evidence of Eakins' French academic training, the effects of that training have been entirely assimilated to Eakins' own purposes. The final result is entirely un-French and completely American: democratic, individualistic, and relatively literal yet much more than just a transcription or illustration from nature. If we could compare the portrait with the typical American who served as Eakins' model—actually his wife's brother-in-law— it would undoubtedly be found that the portrait is more immediate, more real to us than the man himself. For the portrait presents the essence of the man as seen through the extraordinary eye of a great artist. As a result, this portrait, like any great work of art, can heighten the beholder's awareness of reality and of life and thereby make him more understanding and more truly alive.

In conclusion it can be said that—largely as a result of American individualism reinforced by the general individualistic spirit of the nineteenth century—American art has developed no single dominant tradition of its own. For this reason the individual American artist has usually been forced to work out for himself his own particular mode of expression to a much greater degree than many foreign artists who have been able to work within a developed tradition. Nevertheless, art in the United States has been characterized by certain pronounced native tendencies, although somewhat modified by influences from abroad. As might be expected, the foreign influences which have had the widest effect have been those that buttressed certain of our native tendencies. In general, the greater the number of native tendencies thus reinforced by a given foreign influence, the more that influence has been likely to affect American art. But even those imported styles which have had relatively little in common with the general American trends of the day have often been accepted by a limited group of Americans who in this way have sought to express their characteristically American individualism.

THE author wishes to thank the publishers, institutions, and individuals who gave permission to reproduce the illustrations used in this chapter. The sources of these illustrations are as follows:

Sam Houston as Marius from Marquis James, *The Raven*, Bobbs-Merrill, 1929, and courtesy of Orlando Rouland; *Pat Lyon at the Forge* by Neagle, courtesy of the Boston Museum of Fine Arts to which the painting has been loaned by the Boston Athenaeum; Meeting House, Cumberland, R.I., from *Old-Time New England*, Vol. 13; *Andrew Jackson* by Mills, from *The Pageant of America*, Vol. 12, "The American Spirit in Art," Yale University Press; *The Ladies Acheson* by Sargent, from Mrs. Meynell, *Work of John Singer Sargent*, Scribner's, 1903; *William Pitt, Earl of Chatham* by Wright, from *The Connoisseur*, Vol. 19; *Mount Corcoran* by Bierstadt, courtesy of The Corcoran Gallery of Art; Pennsylvania "Dutch" dining-room furniture, and *The Thinker* by Eakins, courtesy of The Metropolitan Museum of Art; *The Old Kentucky Home* by Johnson, courtesy of The New York Public Library; Cathedral of St. John the Divine, from the pamphlet, *The Cathedral of St. John the Divine*, 1928; Chicago Tribune Building, from the *American Architect*, Vol. 128, courtesy of the *Architectural Record*; "White House of the Confederacy," from H. M. P. Gallagher, *Robert Mills*, Columbia University Press, 1935; Thornton's design for the Capitol, Washington, D.C., from I. T. Frary, *They Built the Capitol*, Garrett and Massie, 1940, courtesy of the Library of Congress.

Also, *Washington* by Greenough, courtesy of the National Collection of Fine Arts, Smithsonian Institution; *Napoleon* by Canova, from a Brogi photograph; *Whistling Boy* by Duveneck, courtesy of the Cincinnati Art Museum, Cincinnati, Ohio; Administration Building, Columbian Exposition of 1893, from *Blätter für Architektur*, Vol. VII; Bibliothèque Ste.-Geneviève, from Kimball and Edgell, *A History of Architecture*, Harpers, 1918; The Boston Public Library and The New York Public Library, from G. H. Edgell, *The American Architecture of Today*, Scribner's, 1928; *Tradition* by Cox, courtesy of The Cleveland Museum of Art; *The Belated Kid* by Hunt, courtesy of the Boston Museum of Fine Arts; *The Little June Idylle* by Hassam, photograph copyrighted by N. E. Montross, reproduced from N. Pousette-Dart, *Childe Hassam*, Stokes, 1922; *The Woman of Arles* by Picasso, courtesy of the Walter P. Chrysler, Jr. Collection and The Museum of Modern Art, New York; *New York at Night* by Weber, courtesy of the artist and The Museum of Modern Art; Bauhaus, Dessau, from W. Gropius, *The New Architecture and the Bauhaus*, Museum of Modern Art, n.d.; *Parade* by Blume, courtesy of The Museum of Modern Art; *Jealousy* by Munch, from R. Goldwater, *Primitivism in Modern Painting*, Harpers, 1938; *St. Francis* by Faggi, courtesy of the Museum of New Mexico; *Baptism in Kansas* by Curry, courtesy of the Whitney Museum of American Art.

VII · THE AMERICAN
LITERARY EXPATRIATE*

By R. P. BLACKMUR

O F ALL the terms used to argue the peculiar relation of the American to his Europe there is none that argues on more confused premises than the term "expatriate." There is none, either, that has been so used to judge by default or in ignorance of the issues. It is only today—in 1944—that we can understand our ignorance and can distinguish some of the forces we had felt as confused. We know now that the expatriate is not a monster overseas, for he is with us, here at home, in the only sense that he was ever actually elsewhere, whether in Paris or London or Rome. The expatriate is the man or woman who chooses to live in a country not his own because he cannot do his serious work as well in his own country as he can in another. His reasons may be good—as were the reasons of the scholars who settled at the medieval universities; or they may be dubious—as were the reasons of some of the Americans who went to Paris to die but who lived to languish on the Riviera; or they may be bad—as were the reasons of the young Russians who went for culture to the German Spas in the seventies. But in few cases was the expatriate a monster, or more than usually depraved, either for what he sought, for what he took with him, or for what he found in his exile. The expatriate is orthodox as a human type, classic in the nature of his struggle, romantic only in the ordinary sense of being strange in appearance or nostalgic in some of his attitudes.

We see all that now. We have in the cities and university towns of America large numbers of distinguished men and women from the countries overrun by the war or by the manias of the years preceding the war, and a few Englishmen besides.

* See also critical bibliography "The Literary and Artistic Impact," on page 220.

We call these men and women refugees, exiles, men in flight
and condemned. Their own countries may in later years call
some of them expatriates, precisely to the extent that they
will seem to have *chosen* America as their place of exile—
chosen America rather than Australia or South Africa or the
Argentine, in any of which they could equally well have made
a mere living, and where, perhaps, they would have been
more warmly welcomed as examples of economic man. They
came to America—these distinguished scientists, artists, scholars, professional men—because America exerted attractive
forces upon them which were not merely economic or even
merely political, but which were cultural. Thus many of them
plan never to return, for they see that it is in America they
can best use—or sell—their special talents.

For us the situation is unusual. We know the half-truth
that money breeds money, and we know that America has been
the economic capital of the world since at least 1917. There is
another half-truth, in the expression of which we are not so
skilled, that culture breeds culture, and it has taken the re-
newal and intensification of war since 1939 to show—whether
in actuality or in hope—that the only immediately possible
capital of the world's mind is also in America. It is our refugees, our new host of exiles, who declare the possibility. We
should be grateful to them less because they will enrich our culture than because of the reasons implicit in their coming itself.
A century and a half ago America showed the first plasticity
of youth, which was political; today we show a second plasticity, which has to do with the arts in all their versions. But
we show it less in ourselves than in the European expatriates
among us who hasten to block themselves off from subsequent
return to Europe by the process of naturalization. We had
better see if they are not right, and if they are, act accordingly,
responding fully and consciously to the stimuli which our
visitors feel, not so much in ourselves as in our situation. The
chance may not be single but certainly it is not frequent.

It is a chance to reverse our historic role, to cooperate with history in playing fully the role she seems to have cast for us. But we shall reverse nothing but the perspective of our snobbery unless we understand better the cultural roles we have played in the past. For seventy or eighty years before the war—back to 1860 or 1870—it was customary for America to expatriate annually good numbers of its blessed or its damned to one or another European capital. Men went away more or less permanently because they couldn't stand themselves in America—though some of them thought it was America that was intolerable. They starved, they shriveled, they yearned; they cultivated a positive avarice of exile; also they fled where no man pursued, out of inner guilt, themselves pursuing the chimera of a European salvation. Others thought they heard the sirens sing in their own ears. Others— the rarest of the lot—heard the sirens sing in Europe, and of these a few actually not only heard, but wooed and won the muses in London or Paris or Rome. What is striking is that all of these men behaved reasonably enough in the circumstances as they saw them.

Their fathers or grandfathers behaved reasonably, too, but differently. During the first seventy years of American national life—that is, roughly up to the Civil War—men had gone abroad with the clear purpose of returning with one or another thing that America needed, or, in some cases, with the even clearer purpose of playing America's part abroad— for safety, for growth, for doctrine, or for money. In the thirty years divided at 1800, America was far more integrally—and consciously—a part of the European political and commercial system than she was in the thirty years that divided at 1900, when the system had become in fact, if not in consciousness, an intercontinental system. Where in 1800 the capitals of economic, political, and cultural power were the same, sometime between 1900 and 1920 they had become different. London, New York, and Paris made a division of human roles—of human powers or subjection to powers—that has seemed in its present consequence very near fatal to human intelligence.

The peculiar chimera of the American cultural expatriate developed by metamorphosis during the interim till he became portentous. Looking at the chimera solemnly, made us think that there was either to be no culture in America or that the new American culture would differ in essential quality from the European culture which had preceded it, and in any case it seemed to many that the cultured man or woman who was cultured in the European sense could not find himself at home in America. Often, besides, it seemed that the man who aimed at culture in purely American terms—Mark Twain or Hawthorne—found himself even more homeless than the other fellow, who aimed, however wildly, at the old European bull's-eye. It seemed to those who did this thinking that as America aimed at democratic content, so it ought to produce contented great men.

There would seem to be two main lines of argument by which the chimera can be successfully exorcised. One is the argument attached to the fact that the cultural centers of the western world were not to be found in America at any time between 1870 and 1930. The second has to do with the peculiar relations between the artist and the social institutions of the modern world. The second argument is more significant than the first, but it gains its full significance only if the first argument is understood to begin with.

By 1870 a good deal of money had concentrated in America in such a way as to release the energies of those who possessed it. Of these many had social ambitions which could not be gratified at home, and of these some also had artistic ambitions. Henry James has given us the records of this group in his novels and tales of the International Scene, and in his life of Story; and in a famous paragraph of his life of Hawthorne, he summarized the snobbish form of the forces that drew them abroad. The snobbery comes from the terms in which the values of these forces were felt and has nothing to do with either the values or the forces. The whole passage is worth examining, not only for its application to the American gen-

eration of 1840-1875, but because it throws light on the bias
of the chief American expatriate artist, James himself. He was
making apologia, as he never ceased doing, for his own action.

James has been describing the early entries in Hawthorne's
journals, and has begun by quoting a sentence from Hawthorne's preface to his novel *The Marble Faun*: "No author,
without a trial, can conceive the difficulty of writing a ro-
mance about a country where there is no shadow, no antiquity,
no mystery, no picturesque and gloomy wrong, nor anything
but a commonplace prosperity, in broad and simple daylight,
as is happily the case with my dear native land." James then
proceeds in commentary upon Hawthorne's text: "For my-
self, as I turn the pages of his journals, I seem to see the image
of the crude and simple society in which he lived. I used these
epithets, of course, not invidiously, but descriptively; if one
desires to enter as closely as possible into Hawthorne's situation, one must endeavour to reproduce his circumstances. We
are struck with the large number of elements which were
absent from them, and the coldness, the thinness, the blank-
ness, to repeat my epithet, present themselves so vividly that
our foremost feeling is that of compassion for a romancer
looking for subjects in such a field. It takes so many things, as
Hawthorne must have felt later in life, when he made the
acquaintance of the denser, richer, warmer European spectacle—it takes such an accumulation of history and custom,
such a complexity of manners and types, to form a fund of
suggestion for a novelist. If Hawthorne had been a young
Englishman, or a young Frenchman of the same degree of
genius, the same cast of mind, the same habits, his consciousness of the world around him would have been a very different
affair; however obscure, however reserved, his own personal
life, his sense of the life of his fellow-mortals would have
been almost infinitely more various. The negative side of the
spectacle on which Hawthorne looked out, in his contempla-
tive saunterings and reveries, might, indeed, with a little
ingenuity, be made almost ludicrous; one might enumerate

the items of high civilisation, as it exists in other countries, which are absent from the texture of American life, until it should become a wonder to know what was left. No State, in the European sense of the word, and indeed barely a specific national name. No sovereign, no court, no personal loyalty, no aristocracy, no church, no clergy, no army, no diplomatic service, no country gentlemen, no palaces, no castles, nor manors, nor old country-houses, nor parsonages, nor thatched cottages, nor ivied ruins; no cathedrals, nor abbeys, nor little Norman churches; no great Universities nor public schools— no Oxford, nor Eton, nor Harrow; no literature, no novels, no museums, no pictures, no political society, no sporting class —no Epsom nor Ascot! Some such list as that might be drawn up of the absent things in American life—especially in the American life of forty years ago, the effect of which, upon an English or a French imagination, would probably, as a general thing, be appalling. The natural remark, in the almost lurid light of such an indictment, would be that if these things are left out, everything is left out. The American knows that a good deal remains; what it is that remains—that is his secret, his joke, as one may say. It would be cruel, in this terrible denudation, to deny him the consolation of his natural gift, that 'American humor' of which of late years we have heard so much."

The catalogue, and the bitterness of its iteration, are exhaustive. James has simply expanded for his own generation what Hawthorne saw for his; but he sees what Hawthorne saw with a greater intensity and a more passionate sense of lack. He goes on to argue that what the American kept in reserve—his "joke"—does not appear anywhere in Hawthorne's journals, but he does not argue that the joke did not exist; he was to spend the greater part of his artistic life in the effort to dramatize images which should express his ineradicable, but intellectually ineluctable, conviction that he knew what that secret joke was. What it was, it may be said in passing, shows clearest in the sacred rage for goodness and charity, fine feeling and candor in human relationships, that inhabits all his works like the atmosphere of a house; and it shows most precisely as he discovered that the English also had their joke—their reserved being—quite aside from their symbolized and catalogued possessions.

But at the time James wrote, perhaps even more than at Hawthorne's time, what a certain number of cultivated Americans wanted could only be expressed in the values symbolized by the social and institutional features which England and the Continent had and which America did not have: an available formula in which a man's mind could be taken up, standards by which corruption could be understood as well as virtues judged. For men weak in will and ability the symbol was equivalent to the substance, and the formula—because easier to handle—was better than the form. Symbol and formula represented the overwhelming desire of the weakness of free men to be absorbed into an institution. For men of great will, desperate to capture ability, the symbols could be personally enacted and the forms could be made to enclose whatever the men could compass of the substance of experience. Thus the desire of strong men was, if anything, greater than that of the weak for the release of imaginative energy, otherwise merely personal, through objective institutions. Through institutions a career seemed possible.

If, in the pursuit of a career, the American discovered that the English or the French or the Italians turned out frauds or fools, brutes or pirates, it was because they had failed of possibilities which London and Paris and Rome still presented to those able to take them up and which America did not present at all. London, Paris, and Rome—and in their special way the university towns of Germany—remained the magnetic capitals of civilization. London was politics and society, Paris was art and light, Rome was the corrupt face upon the purest or at any rate the most ancient vein of the European tradition. It was not only Americans who felt the magnetic attraction; the rest of Europe was drawn to the same centers, more to Paris than to Rome, more to Rome than to London. Only the American was drawn culturally to London because of his special ancestral craving for the Old Home. The British themselves were drawn like the Russians and the Spanish and the Scandinavians to Paris and Rome and the international resorts.

This account is of course a simplification; it is accurate only of tendencies along which social patterns shifted, and these tendencies may be thought of as directed by the double rise of economic and "scientific" power without a corresponding rise in political and cultural powers. At any rate the cultural and political intelligence of man seemed unequal to controlling or understanding the actual changes which great access of economic and physical power had brought about in society. But society reacts to the forces which shape it whether consciously or not, and it makes symbolic gestures to affirm its reaction. We may risk saying then that society began to make the experiment of setting up cultural capitals separate from political and economic capitals. America was rich enough and energetic enough to help the experiment along with certain of its chosen or prodigal sons whom in giving it tended to cast off. In doing so, America only ratified the general heresy of the late nineteenth and twentieth century that the arts and learning can be divorced from the power and the resources of society without danger to both.

The danger involved is social impotence. When the divorce reaches its greatest extent—it is never complete—the economic power distrusts first the cultural power and second the political power; the political power tends to submit to the economic because it has no cultural assurance to confirm its policy; and the cultural power either refuses contact with both politics and economics or whores after both in the dark. The relation between what was meant by the symbols of New York, London, and Paris during the 1920's and 1930's makes a paradigm of the disintegrations which followed the divorce. More important, the relation during the fifty years from 1870 to 1920 within the American experience, taken separately, between the business man, the statesman or politician, and the artist or scholar, suggests that, *at least on the conscious level*, the same disintegrative disease was prevalent within the unit of society. What was happening unconsciously, what was really happening, is another matter; the unity of culture is not killed by attitudes and relations, but it is made impotent, and it is the impotence with which we are concerned. The expatriate as a class was the extreme or hysterical symptom of the general disorder; he was held in contempt by the business man, ignored by the statesman or politician, and regarded with either hatred or envy by the artistic or scholarly man who had to stay at home.

In each case the attitude toward the expatriate was justified. He *was* contemptible, ignominious, and treasonable from every nationalistic point of view; he was in fact an anti-nationalistic phenomenon in the supreme age of economic nationalism. That he was also a product of the same economic nationalism made only the more excuse to mistreat and misunderstand him—especially if he came or stayed at home and practiced ingrown expatriation like Melville or Ryder or Dickinson or Adams, who by silence, remoteness, moral isolation, or enriched irony reacted to the scene from which the others fled. The only form of artist or scholar the economic nationalist could tolerate was the dilettante or the freak who had the sanction of conspicuous waste. There were exceptions: Whitman had the advantage of scandal and Mark Twain had the prestige of the clown, but each was treated, not as an artist or a great man (let alone with tolerance or indifference), but with the fickle alternation of privilege and obloquy usually afforded to commercial entertainers, to the dilettanti of low life. America was, as Van Wyck Brooks observed, not mature enough for poetry.

But the expatriate was justified also. One of the reasons that he went abroad was because of his delusion that the American view that culture *belonged* abroad and could be *brought from* abroad was right; and another reason was in his corresponding illusion that the symbols of full social unity —and those listed by James will do—were actually sustained by an existing and developing tradition. Sometimes the two reasons impelled the same individual—perhaps William Wetmore Story was an example, with his sculpture and living poetry in Rome; but generally speaking there were, in the period between the Civil War and the first World War, distinct classes of expatriates who based their flight either on one reason or the other. In the one class were the refined "men of the world" who sought neither to discover living culture nor (James' phrase) "to reascend the stream of time," but who sought to be exiled, to be strangers in a far land, and sweetly to do nothing; that is to say, they wanted to be men of the world divorced from the world. Since they needed a situation where privileged waste could be exchanged for money with no loss but a gain in the sense of occupation, they were drawn to Europe and became the living representatives of all that is dead in the general idea of culture. The later version of this class may be seen in the coveys of zombies who hustled back to the United States from France and Italy in 1939 and 1940 and settled in the neighborhood of the Ritz, the Modern Museum, and the proper, sheltered shores of Long Island.

The other class, which banked on the existence of "Europe," if not less numerous was less conspicuous: they went abroad for ideas, for growth, for work, and went as men have always done where the chance of those riches was propitious, where the conditions were tolerable, and where acceptance at potential value seemed possible. If most of them did not succeed abroad, neither would most of them have escaped failure had they stayed at home. The best of them knew that success in the great affairs of the mind was providential, but they knew also that they had to help themselves as far as possible into the general situation where on the evidence providence was most likely to strike. They made a gamble where if they won they had an exile in honor and if they lost an exile in defeat, but in any case an exile in the end. Your serious expatriates are like the Swiss a kind of nation of exiles who cannot exist without Paris or Rome, or like the Jews who have a culture in many lands but no nation of their own so that they swarm by second choice to the cultural capitals of the world as if, always, it might be the everlasting home they seek—as indeed someday, if the human race is to succeed, it must be.

In short, the American expatriate through the first World War was either a waste product thrown off like a rash on the face of the economic system or he was a serious and significant phenomenon—and the more so when he failed—of the disintegration consequent upon the division of function in the social system of the western world. If he idled, he idled with less need of apology in Europe; if he worked, like as not he worked in Europe because he felt that elsewhere he could not work at all. In point of fact, both most of the idlers and most of the workers returned to their native country and served to transmit and circulate ideas—either the "European" idea or the idea gained through revulsive reaction to "Europe," or some combination of the two. Perhaps we may say that in the American experience of this period the expatriate as a type—whether he returned or not—almost uniquely served a major social function; almost alone as a class he made it possible for America to see the disorder and the confusion and the rich possibilities of the world of which America was a continuing and emergent part. And he had, too, the subtler function of reestablishing that pattern of thought which had been lost since the time of Jackson and buried since the death of Emerson, that recognizes that culture, that politics, that economics even, cannot exist and grow in one place alone.

But in a later manifestation the American expatriate had still another function, rising from still another difficulty. During the twelve years between the first World War and the world depression, the increasing numbers of young Americans who sold dollars at high prices in francs, liras, pesos, and marks—and at a smaller profit in pounds—had, it seems to me, as their clearest function to show that nowhere in the world was there a society that believed either in the enterprise of culture or in the adequacy of human intelligence to cope with human life. That is, he pointed the consequence of the division of political and economic and artistic powers in western society by living a life and producing an art as far as possible without meaning to a wide audience and as far as possible without resort to the intelligence. I do not refer to the great exceptions nor to the great masses, but to the run of the mill *valuta* expatriates of the arts and the bars who joined movements and lived lives which were deliberately forced to a maximum unavailability to the society which produced them. They were an accidental result of the disfunction of society known as *valuta*: speculation on an unstable, unrelated, and inflationary exchange depending on a European political situation which alternated between violence and the apathy of dissolution. It was not the men so much as the arts themselves that had become expatriated. Extreme examples may be found in the American group which attached itself to The Black Sun Press of Harry Crosby, whose relation to society was expressed in black magic and the Black Mass, or in the group which inhabited the later pages of the magazine *transition*, for in that journal was found the Revolution of the Word, which deprived words as far as possible of their history and their idiom and aimed at a free polymorphism of spontaneous expression. *Valuta* was counterfeit.

With the New York crash of 1929 the supply of bad currency dried up and a great many of the expatriates had to return, I will not say to sound money, but to a kind of severely reactionary Marxist currency at first, and later, with the war, either to a blinkered nationalism or to a distrustful, self-persecuted moral isolation. But through these shifts there persisted, whether in the same men and women or in others who followed them, all that the expatriates of the twenties had so sharply symbolized: the inability to believe either in the dignity of the cultural enterprise or the power of human intelligence. In fact, the depression and the war have only made clearer the significance of the true inward expatriation of the larger figures—the men who make the study and clarification of coteries and their snobberies and agonies either possible or desirable. The cult of expatriation, and a cult is what it had become, may be said to represent the worst difficulty the modern artist has in his relation to society.

This brings us to our second argument. The first argument, to repeat, is that what we call expatriation is a natural consequence of living in a country which does not have a great cultural capital and in a world where the cultural, political, and economic capitals are not the same. The second argument represents the inevitable difficulties of the artist in making and maintaining his attachments to the institutions of such a world. It is along the lines of this argument, with the presence of the first argument for external aids and props, that the inward expatriation of such figures as Hawthorne, James, Whistler, and Eliot can be made plain.

But to begin with, let us get rid of the demon of external expatriation. Hawthorne, of course, never remained abroad, and his attempt to live in the Old Home was a failure, as, in a sense, his effort to live anywhere was a failure. He makes thus a good archetype of the kind of man who becomes an expatriate in the external sense without showing any of the accidental or secondary features. His society did not feed him either because of an unwillingness, an inability or a disability within himself; and he had therefore to create a society in his imagination, which instead of enriching the values he found, asserted the values he could not find; but his creative powers being limited—except in *The Scarlet Letter* and a handful of tales—he was left in both his life and letters short-rationed. It was not that he repudiated anything American that he would not have repudiated in Europe, but that he could not find in America the values that he needed for his art. Neither, in the main, could Byron and Shelley find the values they needed in their England, nor Turgenev, for most of his life, in his Russia. All of these figures felt the absence of a cultural capital, the absence of the institutions of a cultural capital in absolute operation; but all succeeded, soon or late, in overcoming that absence to one degree or another. They had the quality, lacking in Hawthorne, which enabled them to create a capital within themselves corresponding somehow to the society outside themselves, or at any rate responding to it. So did Flaubert, with his hatred of the bourgeois whom he made his subjects; so did Dostoevsky, with his inability on the practical level to accept any society at all; so did Baudelaire, even, with his positive sense of sin. Poor Hawthorne's luck was perhaps not bad enough to compel in him a positive reaction as it was not good enough to permit a positive assent. His unwillingness or disability remained all his life. Let us say then that his failure was the failure of human weakness in the individual rather than a failure of the artist in relation to his society.

It is a very different matter when we come to Whistler and James and Eliot. Reaction in them was positive, and for each of them reaction meant a cumulative act of personal expatriation against which each of them struggled. In Whistler the struggle was not long and he came to an obvious conclusion: Art, he said, was international, and since he was all artist, where he was not all butterfly, he was himself, like one of his paintings, a kind of international arrangement, a *modus vivendi*, a persuasive pastiche good through the accident of its lasting. That true internationalism was something deeper than that, and depended on the fundamental unity rather than the superficial sameness of the arts, depended on the source rather than the execution, Whistler never suspected. He was safe in the aesthetics of the eighties, where men much smaller than he have been safe ever since, in the unconscious exile of art for art's sake. Of his essential attitude, Ezra Pound is a modern example, and, in the doctrine of his life rather than of his art, the James Joyce who wrote *Ulysses*, is another only less complete example. Pound in Rapallo has lost himself in one adventitious international "movement" after another, primarily because he did not have the ability to play the single role of Whistler, and was thus far more completely divorced from his audience as a poet and his society as a man. If Whistler was the expatriate as butterfly, Pound was the will-o'-the-wisp: the illusion is desperate only to those who follow, intelligible only to those who do not.

The positive reaction of Whistler and Pound, then, can be put as envelopment in illusion and the transformation of the illusion into a cult, almost a religion. James and Eliot made their positive reactions in different directions. Each attempted to seize, to understand, and to use the institutions of English society, the parallels to which they found tragically wanting in American society. Instead of adopting illusions wholesale, they struggled without end—Eliot is still struggling—to achieve them piecemeal. That they found, in Hopkins' phrase, piecemeal peace but poor peace, in short that the struggle can never end between society and the class of artist of which each is an illustrious example, is what made James, and seems likely to make Eliot, the permanent symbol of genuine expatriation. This is, to repeat once more, the expatriation which an artist—or any man—experiences to the degree that he feels the fundamental failure of coherence between the cultural, political, and economic energies of contemporary society, whether in his homeland or in the whole western world.

This is to contend that the symbolic value of James and Eliot would most likely have been the same if they had stayed at home, and that their going abroad—their physical expatriation—only furnishes external drama, for themselves and for us, to bring out the value of their experience. The psychological reality of expatriation is not, then, American: Americans have no mortgage on the insights concerned; and we could as well have made our points in terms of the careers of Thomas Mann, Marcel Proust, André Gide, and James Joyce as James and Eliot. For the values of psychological expatriation have two main features, which are perhaps fundamental to all the arts at certain stages of their over-all relations to whole cultures, and it is these values—found alike but variously—in all the writers named, with which we are concerned.

There is the value connected with the relationship between the outsider and the insider, the unique and the representative, as groups and individuals feel it, which may be expressed, when it is an imbalance, in the outward act of expatriation. This is the case with both James and Eliot.

There is also the parallel value connected with the balance or imbalance between anarchy and order, the rebellion against or the reliance upon imposed external forms, whether cultural, political, or economic, in terms of which groups and individuals frame their response to society, and which again, when the imbalance is severe, may be expressed dramatically in expatriation. Both James and Eliot seem in the terms of their respective expatriations to symbolize such imbalances.

Throughout the work of both men the protagonists have tended to be cast as artists or saints or seers or men of an intelligence so high as to be generally unavailable; and in each case these figures have been presented both as outsiders to the world in which they lived and as desperately engaged in the effort to capture the sense of that world. Similarly, both men went abroad in a combination of rebellion against the institutions at home and in predisposed submission to the institutions they expected to find in Europe and particularly in England. And in the careers of both men a part of the drama is the gradual revelation of the corruptness and inadequacy of the institutions in which they hoped to find strength. James came to see through "society" and was compelled to retreat for an imaginative moral order upon a concept of the candor of the American soul which apparently rejected social institutions altogether so far as the individual was concerned; yet when the first World War came, he found himself plunged to the full back into the authoritative mystery of British institutions. With Eliot, the case seems to me little different. He too went abroad for British institutions, but judging by his journalism, he has had to a considerable degree to make them over for himself in order to make them tolerable, and has found himself arguing for Scottish nationalism and the disestablishment of the Church of England, for which, it once seemed, he had quite settled.

This is to say that the imbalance between the insider and the outsider, between anarchy and order, which both men felt in their lives, was never settled, but was left, rather, always teetering on the little fulcrum of the soul's balance, always precariously perched on the branch of consciousness just beyond reach but fascinating full attention. The struggle for balance, not balance but the struggle for it, preoccupied both, and became the major theme in the work of each as they dramatized it, hopefully or desperately, in expiation or in pride. The expatriation was almost exile. Perhaps we should think of Dante exiled from Florence, Villon with his murderous luck, and the deep-riven swindling chasm between perfection of life and perfection of work and the stresses between these in a society which, for whatever reason, leaves the soul exiled in its only home.

There is luckily a tale of Henry James and a play of T. S. Eliot which combine to produce a single image upon which our sense of the maximum drama possible to the struggle with expatriation, with exile, may be left to rest. In James' "The Jolly Corner" we have dramatized the homecoming of Spencer Brydon, an exile from New York—from economic America—who has been spending a rich life in the great world of Europe. It was his business affairs that brought him back, and once back he becomes obsessed by the possibility of what he might have become had he never gone away. The house in which he was born and in which he grew up—which the family called the Jolly Corner—is empty and about to be torn down to make room for the growth of the New York monster. With the image of the Jolly Corner always in mind, Brydon works up his obsession of what he might have been and begins to prowl from room to room of the house after midnight, stalking the big and dangerous game of his unrealized self. After a few nights he begins to feel that it is his unrealized self that is haunting, hunting, ambushing him. Finally he finds himself actually ambushed and forces himself to meet, at dawn, in the vestibule, his beast of prey. Its hands are raised over its face, and from one of the hands two fingers have been shot away. When the hands drop there is revealed the face of a stranger: evil, odious, blatant, vulgar, and mutilated; the figure overwhelms him and he collapses. Though he recovers, later, and his other self has been exorcised, we have to remember, for the significance and the drama of it, that the other self has been in him, unrealized, all his life long, and that he could never assent to it except as intolerable, which is no assent at all. Yet it was part of the whole man, made monstrous only, it is possible to think, by the imbalance of the society which he represented. The monster had lived, so to speak, in the Jolly Corner of Brydon's happy childhood all his life long.

Eliot's play, *The Family Reunion*, deals, as its title indicates, with the return of a man to his family after a long absence. Unlike James' tale, however, it is not an American who returns to his home and makes an exorcism by the power of imagination; it is an English nobleman who returns to his mother's country house—the deserted temple of dead institutions—to find himself driven out and on by the Furies— the Eumenides—whom he had brought with him. The play could have as well been called The Family Destroyed, for when the protagonist, Harry, Lord Monchesney, departs to renew his inexplicable mission of expiation in exile, it is the family, the whole institution of British society, that has collapsed, though it has not, as in James' tale, been exorcised: it is perhaps one of the Furies pursuing Harry.

But there is in the first part of the play one speech in which James' and Eliot's versions of the theme of spiritual expatriation become united. It is Harry's Aunt Agatha who speaks out of her special knowledge. Wishwood, with its Dantesque overtone, is the name of the country house in which the family reunites and collapses. Agatha and Harry's mother have been arguing as to whether Harry will find anything changed, and for Agatha it is everything that will be changed even though and because everything will be the same.

"Yes. I mean that at Wishwood he will find another
      Harry.
The man who returns will have to meet
The boy who left. Round by the stables,
In the coach-house, in the orchard,
In the plantation, down the corridor
That led to the nursery, round the corner
Of the new wing, he will have to face him—
And it will not be a very *jolly* corner.
When the loop in time comes—and it does not come
      for everybody—
The hidden is revealed, and the spectres show
      themselves."

F. O. Matthiessen, in his *American Renaissance*[1] supplies two lines from Eliot's manuscript which should be read just after the phrase "*jolly* corner."

"I am sorry, Gerald, for making an allusion
To an author whom you never heard of."

In the context, Matthiessen has been demonstrating the connections between Hawthorne and James. "Certainly there is no question of any specific debts to Hawthorne at this point, but of a fundamental reassertion of kinship in moral values, which defied for both writers any merely realistic presentation."[2] The reader is referred to the whole chapter on Hawthorne and James for material which, from another point of view, illustrates the strength and continuity of the themes which rise from spiritual expatriation or exile through the work of the two novelists into the poetry of Eliot.

[1] Page 295 n.   [2] *Ibid.*, p. 294.

The search, the struggle, which James and Eliot pursued in England for the strength and solace and the comfortable words of old and living institutions, came, if this account is correct, to no more than the outward and personal dramatization of their inward and inevitable experience which they made objective and permanently symbolic in their art. If we exclude from consideration what seems the physical accident of alien citizenship, I think we can see clearly that their lives and their works were neither eccentric nor escapist, but orthodox and direct in their seizure of a theme which has been both fundamental and inevitable, as well as tragic, in the European and American world since 1860 or 1870. It was merely the newness of the country, the doubtfulness of its experiment, and the relative absence in it of formalized institutions, that made the American experience of cultural, political, and economic imbalance more consciously anguished. That this same western world is now pressing upon us the opportunity to make a society where these forces reach a balance and to which artists cannot help giving assent as a whole, will never prevent individual artists returning to the theme of inward dissent and dismay, for that theme will always represent one aspect, if he can be but persuaded to see it, of every individual's actual experience.

VIII · HEGEL, DARWIN, AND THE AMERICAN TRADITION *

By DAVID F. BOWERS

PHILOSOPHY and religion, like other intellectual disciplines, must disclaim national and geographic boundaries. Since their avowed purpose is the disinterested search for truth, they must welcome and study new hypotheses wherever they are to be found. This spirit, at any rate, has characterized philosophy and religion in America where the cultural ties with Europe have always been close. Early or late, all major European systems have eventually reached our shore and in some manner or another have left their imprint upon our intellectual development. For this very reason, however, it is impossible to trace the full tide of the European influence within the limits of a single essay. At most it can be illustrated with reference to particular examples, and it is the latter course I propose to follow here.

I have chosen, for this purpose, to trace the influence of Hegel and Darwin, whose systems of thought became well known in America at about the same time in the latter part of the nineteenth century. I have selected these two philosophers specifically for a number of reasons. In the first place, each belonged to a different and contrasting philosophic tradition—Hegel to the tradition of German romanticism, Darwin to the British empirical tradition—and each reflected in his own way the main currents of the national culture from which he sprang. In the second place, in spite of their differences in background, method, and conclusions, each was in closer agreement with the other than either was with American ideology as it had been constituted up to that time. Finally, in the third place, by means of this common opposition, each

* See also critical bibliography, "The Religious and Philosophic Impact," on page 235.

succeeded in modifying the American philosophic and religious tradition in a revolutionary manner. The influence of the two thinkers illustrates, in other words, how two radically different ideologies were able to reinforce each other at given points in their impact upon American thought and through common action effectively alter its course and direction.

For convenience, I shall begin by sketching in briefly what seems to me to have been the basic tenets of American thought prior to the time this influence was first felt.

I

Until 1860 American thought was prevailingly religious in tone. The religious tradition, which had been planted originally by the Puritans and Quakers and which had been still further enhanced by the early influx of Ulster Presbyterians and other religious groups, had taken firm hold and had eventually permeated American culture as a whole. Although the Enlightenment had later shaken this hold by creating minor flurries in the direction of deism, naturalism, and anticlericalism, that hold was by no means loosened entirely. By 1815 the most radical of these tendencies had largely disappeared and the church was free once more to assert unopposed its right of control over all matters of faith and conduct, including public morals and public instruction. Thus, even as late as 1879, G. Stanley Hall, reporting on the state of philosophical instruction in the United States still found that "there are less than half a dozen colleges or universities . . . where metaphysical thought is entirely freed from theological formulae," that "many teachers of philosophy have no training in their department save such as has been obtained in theological seminaries," and that "their pupils are made far more familiar with the points of difference in the theology of Parks, Fairchild, Hodge and the like than with Plato, Leibnitz or Kant."

Yet it would be a mistake to suppose either that within this religious framework wide differences of opinion did not exist or that the framework itself was purely Christian in origin. At one extreme, to be sure, there still flourished an active group of "high" Calvinists—for the most part professional theologians such as the Alexanders and Hodges of Princeton —whose opinions as expressed in *The Princeton Review* derived from the teachings of the great Edwards himself, and whose continued control over the Princeton and Andover seminaries still gave them great power in the councils of the church. But this group by no means had the field to itself, even within the church proper. At other extremes were to be found the liberalizing forces of Universalism, Unitarianism, and transcendentalism, and, at still another, the trend toward Christian primitivism as embodied in Methodism and Mormonism. The period was thus one of intense sectarianism, of great and violent dogmatic controversy.

In spite of this, however, there also existed a certain residue of belief common to all partisan groups and acceptable not only to the loyal Christian but to almost all literate Americans of the time. This common faith, which was founded in part upon the Christian tradition but also in part upon the great secular movements of the seventeenth and eighteenth centuries, constituted the fundamental philosophy of the period, the ideological matrix within which all thought and discussion were normally carried on, and one so naturally taken for granted that its validity was rarely questioned or doubted. In essence, this view involved the acceptance of three articles or postulates; the postulate of dualism, the postulate of fixity, and the postulate of atomism. And since it is precisely these three postulates which Hegelianism and Darwinism were later to challenge, it is important to examine them more closely.

The postulate of dualism, the most distinctively religious of the three, consists in the belief that there are two orders of being or existence, the natural and the supernatural, and that man as a miraculous union of soul and body is a denizen of both worlds. First clearly expressed in the philosophy of

Plato, the view in its purest form holds that the world of space and time is but the shadow or projection of a more fundamental realm, one with which it is perpetually at odds and in comparison with which its value is as nothing. Where the mundane sphere has little to offer which is not material, fleeting, and brutal, and serves at most as a preparation or discipline for entry into the other, the second realm on this view is held to be changeless and eternal, to be the source and locus of all order, all worth, and all creative energy. To put it in the metaphor of Plato himself, the two worlds stand forever in the relationship of light and shadow, reality and dream.

It was in a Christian, rather than Platonic, form, however, that the postulate had passed into the American tradition. In the fusion of classical and Hebraic culture which marked the rise of the early Christian church, the postulate had survived in a modified form to become one of the cornerstones of Christian theology. To the doctrine of the two orders of existence there had been added, among other new elements, a faith in a trinitarian god and a theory of history involving creation and redemption through divine love. And it was in this formulation, sustained as it was by the universality and power of the church as an institution, that the postulate came to be known and accepted thereafter in the western world. Thus, although there had been various attempts from time to time both in Europe and in America to divest the postulate of its theological trappings and to return to a more secularized, and therefore more strictly Platonic, interpretation, none of them had succeeded to any considerable degree.

But, in whatever form it was understood, there can be no doubt of its central role in the development of American thought or of its effect upon American thinkers in their effort to rationalize and justify American social and political idealism. In search of a basis on which to defend the American experiment, exponents of the American "dream," as Gabriel has shown, were rarely satisfied with anything short of moral finality. It was not enough for them to be able to claim for the American experiment the sanction of utility—even though this sanction was in fact invoked—for utility depended upon circumstance and circumstances change. A more fundamental type of justification was demanded, one which would prove not only the usefulness of American institutions, but their eternal "rightness." And to this end the postulate of dualism, already at hand, seemed to provide the most adequate metaphysic. By assuming, in accordance with the postulate, an over-arching order of divine purpose and fixed moral laws, it became easy to claim for the American ideal—its faith in the individual, its reverence for constitutionalism, and even its later belief in the historic necessity of a program of democratic imperialism—both a supernatural prototype and an eternal sanction and verity. It is this postulate, in other words, which gave substance to Cotton Mather's "irradiated wilderness," to Jefferson's and Paine's "rights of man," and to Emerson's "Oversoul," as these various principles were invoked in defense of the American way of life. In the end, therefore, the postulate of dualism had become for America not only an article of its religious creed but the chief cornerstone of its social philosophy.

Although more difficult to describe, the postulates of fixity and atomism were of equal importance. Like the postulate of dualism, each of these also had had a long history in the western world preceding their implantation in America. The postulate of fixity, which resembles the postulate of dualism still further in also having sprung from Plato, is an assumption to the effect that the world is forever static with respect to its fundamental laws and principles of classification. More specifically, it holds that the world is composed of a fixed number of kinds or classes of objects, that any given object or form of life, whenever or wherever it occurs, will always belong to one of these classes and to no other, and that everything will therefore always manifest the general traits and behavior characteristics of a particular class. The view posits, in other words, a universe in which variation and change are definitely limited, and repetition and predictability become primary features.

The postulate of atomism, on the other hand, was first introduced into the modern world by Bacon and Descartes, and developed most fully in the seventeenth century by Locke and Newton, the former applying it in the fields of psychology, politics, and philosophy, the latter in the fields of physics and astronomy. Simply stated, the postulate is one holding that everything that exists, whether it be an idea, a person, an institution, or even an historical movement, is ultimately simple in nature, being always composed of a limited number of unanalyzable units of one form or another, and that to understand anything fully it is merely necessary to discover all the single units of which it is composed. It thus assumes the world to be of the nature of an aggregation, a loosely organized collection in which each object or event, although causally related to others, may nevertheless be fully understood without reference to the context in which it occurs.

Arid and abstract as these two postulates may seem when thus stated formally, they, no less than the postulate of dualism, formed part of the very warp and woof of American thought, and appear there historically under a myriad of guises. For example, it is the principle of fixity which underlay, among other things, the period's faith in the sameness of human nature everywhere, its belief in the existence of fixed institutional forms, and its conviction that excellence in art, science, and morals is a mere matter of adhering to a few simple rules or canons. The principle is even more clearly discernible in the scientific opinion of the age, where it continued to hold sway even in those fields where empirical evidence was already beginning to confute it. Thus, for example, although it had become increasingly difficult to employ fixed schemes of classification in biology and geology, and despite also the fact that Lamarck abroad and Wells and Leidy in this country had already broached tentative evolutionary hypotheses which denied the possibility of fixed, independent classes, most biologists of the day still postulated their existence.

Nor was the principle of atomism any less pervasive. It is revealed, for example, in the popular adherence to Locke's theory of mind as a set of separate faculties confronted by a mosaic of simple and clearly distinguishable sensations and in the capacity of this theory to maintain itself in the face of strenuous opposition from the Scotch "common sense" philosophy and transcendentalism. It is revealed, again, in the prevailing tendency of political and economic theorists to construe society as an aggregate of wholly independent individuals, to view government as a simple mechanism of checks and balances, and to conceive of the economic process as a mere exchange of unit-commodities. The postulate may even be detected in the religious attitude of the period where it operated under the guise of a radical form of congregationalism, holding that each congregation and each individual Christian stands in a direct and separate relationship to deity in total independence of each other. Indeed, it is probably not claiming too much to say that the postulate of atomism, as here defined, lay at the very heart of the doctrine of individualism, and that without its conditioning influence American individualism would never have assumed the extreme *laissez-faire* form that it did.

Other principles were basic to the American tradition in addition to the three just mentioned, but these, I believe, were among the most important. Certain it is, in any case, that they were foremost among those elements of the American tradition to be challenged by Hegelianism and Darwinism, and that it was through an attack upon these three in particular that the two foreign ideologies were to leave their most lasting marks upon American thought.

II

Hegel and Darwin began to be studied seriously in America at about the same time, namely, in the early 1860's. In the case of Darwin this virtually amounted to immediate recognition, since *The Origin of Species*, the first public statement of the Darwinian theory, had been published only in 1859. In the case of Hegel, however, the recognition was belated. Hegel had died in 1831 and long before that had been acclaimed a European thinker of the first rank. But aside from certain brief notices in the German-American press, and the interest of a few scholars, no widespread notice of his work had been taken in this country until 1859, the year Henry Brockmeyer undertook the translation of the "larger" *Logic* and, together with W. T. Harris, organized the St. Louis Philosophical Club. Brockmeyer, who was later to become lieutenant governor of Missouri, was a German immigrant who had arrived at Hegelianism by way of a study of New England transcendentalism, and it was he who first revealed the new philosophy to Harris.

Once introduced, however, Hegelianism no less than Darwinism attracted a great number of followers in all ranks and professions and, along with Darwinism, formed one of the poles around which many of the principal ideological controversies of the next forty years were to revolve. Although Darwinism achieved the greater notoriety because of its more obviously dramatic implications, Hegelianism also had a popular following—particularly among the German-Americans of the Middle West—and, so far as its ultimate effects were concerned, was to be no less important.

Hegel's central insight had been that man, nature, and history are all organic parts of a single world-process, and that apart from this process nothing could either exist or be properly understood. Striving to free philosophy from the consequences of the Cartesian dualism which had fixed a gulf between mind and values on the one side and physical nature on the other, and striving also to express the yearning of his generation for an expanding, illimitable universe capable of indefinite progress, Hegel had created an elaborate metaphysical system whose keynotes are organicism and process.

According to the first of these principles, everything that is, whether it be real or ideal, physical or mental, individual or social, stands in intimate and indissoluble association with everything else. Nothing is isolated or independent, and nothing understandable apart from its relation to the universe as a whole. And to prove this the case, Hegel actually set out to catalogue all the important phenomena of human existence and to show exactly what their interconnection is. In a remarkable series of works dealing with logic, psychology, art, science, history, philosophy, religion, and law, he attempted to bring all known facts within the compass of a single system and to show how, within this system, each fact contributed its own modicum of intelligibility and received in turn illumination from all the rest.

In line with the second principle, that of process, he also argued that everything that is, is always in process of change or mutation, and that nothing is permanent save process itself. Change, in other words, is held to be as universal as order, and although events always succeed each other in accordance with a plan implicit in the process of history itself, no particular object and no particular truth can be regarded as lasting in existence or value. Thus, in order to express cosmically the *Unruhe* and *Sehnsucht* of the romantic spirit, Hegel was driven into a reaffirmation of the ancient doctrine of Heraclitus that all beings have their being in change.

Whether he was ultimately successful in this ambitious speculative feat of fusing order and impermanency is a matter of dispute, and one with which we need not be concerned. It is merely necessary to note the two implications of this view which were to function most importantly in its impact upon American thought. One of these has to do with the relation of the individual to society and the other with the conception of progress.

Hegel identifies the world process with the restless surge-forward of the spirit of humanity which he refers to as "the world-reason," "the Absolute," and sometimes as "the spirit of history." Accepting the romantic premise that reality is ultimately spiritual in character, he describes world-history in general as the quest of the cosmic spirit for self-fulfillment through self-knowledge and self-expression. As vehicles of its purpose, this spirit is alleged to employ particular individuals, particular institutions, and the more ideal achievements of art, religion, and philosophy, but the latter have no importance in themselves. They have only the status of stages in a process, of acting as instruments to an end beyond themselves, which in this case is the march-forward of the process itself.

It does not follow from this, however, that the individual and the institution are thereby of equal worth. Although they are both aspects of one and the same process, they exist at different levels and exhibit different degrees of self-sufficiency. And since, according to Hegel, the individual, in particular, occupies the lower rank in this hierarchy, the greater value is to be ascribed to the institution, especially the institution of the state. He makes this quite clear in the *Phänomenologie des Geistes*, his first major work. There, in presenting what purports to be the true procession of forms through which the world-spirit must pass in its search for self-realization, the individual is represented as occupying a lower place than that occupied by any institution, however primitive the latter may be. This is maintained on the ground that the individual is produced, determined, and molded by his social environment, and that it is only in conforming to the patterns of group life that he may reach his own highest fulfillment. Thus, although institutions themselves fall short of perfection, particularly in comparison with the deeper cultural unities of art, religion, and philosophy, in comparison with the individual they are assumed to be superior. In the end, therefore, Hegel repudiates eighteenth-century individualism entirely and asserts once more the hegemony of the *Volk*.

Equally revolutionary from an eighteenth-century point of view is Hegel's conception of the logic of progress. Con-

ceding that progress indeed exists, he rejects utterly the optimistic conclusion of the French *philosophes* that its course
is ever direct or uneventful. In the movement of history from
lower to higher, it is never a matter of one stage giving way
immediately and peacefully to a higher one. Advance is possible, he contends, only at the price of struggle, and all roads
to perfection reveal themselves as roundabout. This is the
lesson he had learned from the epoch of the French Revolution
and which he sought to generalize in the law of dialectic, the
law decreeing that all things shall move in the triadic rhythm
of division, struggle, and reconciliation, and that nothing shall
be better than it is until it has first confronted opposition and
been transcended and purified in a higher synthesis. In other
words, death no less than life, conflict no less than cooperation,
make up the threads of history, and all progress is inherently
devious and tragic. As he himself once put it, the world-reason
is by nature both cunning and ruthless.

III

If Hegel's central insight gives us the unity of history,
Darwin's central insight gives us the unity of life, though
with less fanfare and drama. After many years of patiently
checking his data and after carefully reflecting upon the work
of his predecessors—some of whom were Americans—Darwin
had been finally led in 1859 to announce his own particular
formulation of the evolutionary hypothesis. As a general
theory, evolutionism was nothing strikingly new. But Darwin's version achieved both originality and force by virtue of
its greater simplicity and as a result of the fact that he had succeeded in marshaling an overwhelming mass of evidence in its
support.

According to the Darwinian conception of the hypothesis,
all forms of life—the human included—are genetically continuous. Each species is assumed to have developed out of one
that has existed before and each to go back ultimately, through
a graduated series of different forms, to the most primitive

type of unicellular organism. Also included in the hypothesis is the assumption that all species are inherently unstable and that none may be regarded as fixed and unchanging. Since each has a definite point of origin in time, and since many, as the study of fossils reveals, have already ceased to be, there is nothing to guarantee that any given species will continue to exist in any one form indefinitely or even to exist at all. Thus, Darwin envisages the whole of life as a single process in which various forms and functions continually emerge and pass away, and as one in which all the stages are linked together by the relation of birth and descent.

In explanation of this process, he appealed, not, as Hegel had done, to an a priori principle such as the dialectic, but to natural causes immanent in the species and the environment themselves. His problem, accordingly, was twofold: first, to discover natural causes capable of accounting for the origin of new species out of old ones; second, to find other natural causes able to explain why certain species survive and others perish. On the first of these questions, however, he had very little to say except to reiterate his conviction that here also physical conditions alone are operative and that their exact mechanism will some day be revealed. In regard to the second problem, on the other hand, he discovered what he believed to be a full and satisfactory solution in the principle of natural selection. This principle, whose original suggestion he owed to his early study of Malthus, located the conditions of development in the natural environment itself, holding that the environment automatically intervenes to preserve all life forms fitted to cope with it and to eliminate all those lacking in this capacity. In other words, it argues that survival is determined not by divine providence or by inner teleology, as Lamarck had supposed, but by the relentless struggle of individual with individual and of species with species. Hence, life becomes, on Darwin's view, not only continuous with respect to form and descent, but mechanically conditioned in every phase of its evolution by purely natural causes.

As in the case of Hegel, we need not be concerned with the
truth of this theory but only with such of its implications as
were to have the greatest impact on American thought. And
there are three of these in particular which should be noted.
In the first place, the theory involved the final triumph of the
mechanistic point of view. It implied that life and mind do
not constitute a separate realm of nature but, like everything
else, are phenomena of physical law, and that henceforth
there could be a science of life, mind, and society in precisely
the same sense in which there was a science of motion and of
light. There was no longer any need, in short, to take into
account such unscientific imponderables as the will of God,
chance, or human teleology.

By the same token, the theory also involved a radical revision of the attitude toward morals. Instead of interpreting
moral and legal codes as approximations of a supernaturally
grounded ideal—one that has been fixed eternally for man's
reverence and obedience—such codes must now be conceived
as human creations, as generalizations based merely on in-
stinct and desire. Darwin himself recognized this fact for he
explicitly argued that altruism, which he held basic to the
moral life, is not a matter of principle at all but·simply an
outgrowth of various instincts such as parental love and gre-
gariousness.

Finally, in the sphere of politics and of social theory generally, Darwinism, like Hegelianism, implied a shift of emphasis from the individual to the group or species. This was
inevitable because the mechanistic character of the Darwinian
theory denied freedom of will to the individual and also because it was the species, not the individual, which was now
supposed to count for more. Since it had been clearly shown
that in all lower animal species individuals were often sacrificed for the good of the species as a whole, it was difficult
not to presume the same principle operative in the human
species. Thus, Darwinism was committed in the end to an
extreme form of Malthusianism, one which could accept with

equanimity the destruction of particular individuals in the interest of the group as a whole.

IV

The revolutionary implications of the two new philosophies were not fully grasped at once by American thinkers. On the contrary, they were assumed at first to have a special relevance and validity for the American scene. This was a result of the operation of certain special conditions.

In the first place, both Hegelianism and Darwinism, each in its own way, proved a stimulus to American intellectual studies and for this reason were quickly hailed as great intellectual contributions. In the field of biology, for example, the significance of the evolutionary principle in particular was immediately grasped by such able biologists as Asa Gray of Harvard, and its extension to the related fields of psychology and sociology soon followed. Psychology, which up to that time had been dominated either by the intellectualist theories of Locke and of the Scotch realists or by the romantic intuitionism of transcendentalism, found in the new principle a basis for a fresh start, one which through its close linkage with biology was soon to open up such novel and rich branches of inquiry as physiological psychology, animal psychology, and comparative and genetic psychology. Similarly, under the influence of Herbert Spencer, one of Darwin's most eminent co-workers, the idea of an evolutionary sociology was planted in the minds of such men as William Graham Sumner and Lester Frank Ward, and quickly brought to fruition.

The intellectual acclaim of Hegelianism was no less great and immediate, especially in politics and philosophy, and to some extent also in economic theory. The fashion at that time of sending young men abroad to complete their training in German universities had introduced hundreds of young American scholars to at least the name of Hegel and in some instances had instilled in them a deep enthusiasm for his work. Although Hegelianism as such had been officially discredited in Germany after the revolution of 1848, its influence lingered on, particularly in philosophy and the social sciences, and this was communicated to many of the young Americans who came to study. Most prominent among these were the philosophers, George Sylvester Morris and Josiah Royce, who hailed Hegel's spiritism as a new justification of moral and social values; Theodore D. Woolsey, the political scientist, who saw in Hegel's organic conception of the state a much needed corrective of the Anglo-American view of the state as a contract between governor and governed; and finally, Richard T. Ely, the economist, who, having become interested in German nationalist economics, returned to America to become one of the founders of the American school of "welfare" economics.

The second condition which facilitated a ready acceptance of Hegelianism and Darwinism was the fact that they were first widely introduced during the period of the Civil War. In terms of the traditional American faith, the conflict between the North and South was even then viewed as a tragic and meaningless event. Here was patriot set against patriot, right against right; and however comforting the feeling on both sides that it was the enemy who had abandoned the faith, it was manifest that the fact of war itself was incompatible with the prevalent belief in a loving god and the complete adequacy of the Federal Constitution as a political instrument. To those Americans who felt the incompatibility deeply and who refused to take comfort in the repetition of platitudes, Hegelianism and Darwinism in different ways offered adequate solutions. To those already inclined to cynicism or despair, the Darwinism interpretation of war as another instance of the ever present struggle for existence seemed to provide overwhelming confirmation, and was readily accepted in this spirit. To those, on the other hand, who insisted on seeing in the struggle a deeper moral meaning, it was the Hegelian interpretation which had particular plausibility. On Hegel's theory that all life, even the life of a nation, must from time to time undergo the ordeal of revolution, and that this, far from signifying disintegration and decay, is really a sign of healthy, institutional growth, on this theory, to repeat, the war itself no longer appeared a purposeless struggle, but a trial necessary for national purification. This attitude was typical, for example, of many German-Americans, and particularly of the St. Louis Hegelians, some of whom even went so far as to claim a detailed parallel between Lincoln's violation of the Constitution in his conduct of the war and Hegel's thesis that once the state has been rent asunder its sovereignty must be reasserted on a new and higher basis.

A final factor which helped conceal the true import of the two philosophies was their initial use as a defense of conservative interests. Thus, Darwinism, especially as interpreted by Herbert Spencer, seemed at first a new way of justifying the reigning *laissez-faire* capitalism. The law of the survival of the fittest, which Darwin himself had intended as a mere description and not an endorsement of the conditions of survival, was now converted, through a confusion of thought, into a moral apology for economic aggrandizement. From the true premise that struggle is a tool for survival, defenders of the capitalist enterprise leaped unwarrantedly to the conclusion that struggle as such is desirable, and that the ruthless suppression of one's economic rivals is actually a social blessing in disguise. In much the same way, Hegelianism seemed at first adaptable to the purposes of Christian apologetics. Although Hegel himself was far from being an orthodox Christian or even a man of deep religious feeling, this fact was frequently forgotten, and his high but wholly incidental praise of religion as a great adventure of the human imagination thus came to be construed as a support of Christian revelation.

Once, however, the two philosophies were better understood and the full measure of their unorthodoxy perceived, the American reaction took a different form. In the first place, many writers were led to deny the two views all claim to truth whatever, and to denounce their implications as subversive both of religion and of democracy. Among the first to detect the threat to Christianity was the aging but still vigorous Charles Hodge of Princeton, who rejected evolutionism in favor of a completely literal interpretation of Genesis; while among the first to perceive the threat to democracy was William James, who, in a spirit equally confident, repudiated Hegelianism as destructive of both individuality and progress. It is significant that neither of these men took the trouble to examine disinterestedly the systems they were condemning, with the result that their strictures were often superficial and unconvincing. And since this was characteristic of extremists of their persuasion generally, neither religion nor democracy were at all adequately represented throughout the controversy that followed.

In contrast with these, there were the frank compromisers, those who sought after a *via media* which would allow equal validity to the old and to the new alike. This reaction was typical of thinkers who saw in Darwin and Hegel deep-rooted expressions of the age but who were themselves as yet unwilling to surrender the traditional beliefs entirely. It was this spirit, for example, which motivated such men as John Fiske, the historian, Asa Gray, the biologist, and James McCosh, the philosopher, in their attempt to reconcile science with religion; and it was this which underlay Louis Agassiz' famous effort to harmonize the new doctrine of evolution with the old theory of fixed species.

But the most interesting and most important reaction of all was that which accepted the central doctrines of Hegel and Darwin without question and sought to fuse the two philosophies into a new basis for social criticism. At first sight, this proposal might have appeared unfeasible in view of the obvious differences between the two thinkers. Where Hegel rested his conclusions on pure reason alone, Darwin sought to rely only on experience and observation. Where Hegel transformed history into an adventure of the spirit, Darwin interpreted it as an interplay of natural forces. And where Hegel posited a goal or limit for the historic process purely ideal in character, viz., the self-realization of spirit, the logic of Darwin envisages only the survival of the fittest irrespective of all questions of value or worth. But underneath these divergencies there is a fundamental unity of thesis which becomes apparent if the two views are contrasted with the earlier American tradition, particularly when the latter is considered in respect to what I have described as its three basic postulates. For where the American faith accepted, as we have seen, the premises of dualism, fixity, and atomic individualism, the systems of Hegel and of Darwin denied these premises out of hand, each affirming the unity of the world process rather than its diversities, each insisting upon the fluxlike character of the process, and each exalting the institution and the group over the individual. There was, in short, a broad but genuine sense in which the influence of Hegel and that of Darwin were able to reinforce each other and to offer a common opposition to the previous pattern of American thought. And this is what actually occurred in the thinking of a number of influential critics who happened to be subjected to both influences.

For the most part, these were thinkers who saw in the growing evils of industrialism—already plainly visible by the midcentury—a practical refutation of the older individualism, and who believed that nothing short of a radical revision of the established creed could either explain the new development or arrest its progress. The fusion is implicit, for example, in the work of Thorstein Veblen and to some extent in the later writings of William Graham Sumner, for in the case of each of these thinkers a serious attempt was made to unite the evolutionary view of Darwin with the cultural and institutional approach of Hegel and to employ these in a searching critique of American democracy. But it is most clearly illustrated, perhaps, in the instrumentalist philosophy of John Dewey, since here the debt to Hegel and Darwin is plainly manifest, while Dewey's subsequent emergence as the foremost contemporary critic of American traditionalism reveals how deep an impression the two influences when thus fused were to make on American thought.

V

Dewey first began to study Hegel and Darwin critically[1] during his years as a graduate student at Johns Hopkins University in the early 1880's. As an undergraduate at the University of Vermont he had been trained in the Scottish intuitional philosophy, but this, by his own admission, was to have little effect on his later development. The Scotch philosophy was then—as it always had been—orthodox and rigid in attitude, and incapable therefore of satisfying his youthful craving for a philosophical synthesis in which science and religion, the individual and society—the two great dualisms of the day—could be organically related within a single system. Consequently, when he enrolled at Hopkins in 1884, he was ripe for conversion to a new point of view.

At that time, Johns Hopkins was the most important center of graduate studies in America, and while there Dewey studied under two of its most distinguished teachers: G. Stanley Hall, a pioneer student of adolescent psychology, and George Sylvester Morris, one of the ablest of the early expositors of Hegel in America. In Hall's seminar Dewey first became familiar with the principles and the methods of evolutionary and experimental psychology, and in Morris' seminar with the ramifications of the idealistic epistemology. But although the influence of Hall was to be the more lasting, it was Morris, the Hegelian, who had the greatest immediate effect. Under Morris' guidance, Dewey began to read not only Hegel but the English followers of Hegel, particularly Thomas Hill Green and Edward Caird. And this, together with Morris' own dynamic teaching, was enough to tip the scales. Dewey himself became an ardent Hegelian and went

[1] For an excellent history of Dewey's intellectual development, see Morton G. White's monograph, *The Origin of Dewey's Instrumentalism.* I have leaned heavily on this account throughout.

on to write and teach in the accepted Hegelian manner for the next fifteen years.

Eventually, however, and at first imperceptibly, his point of view underwent a drastic change. Originally, he had been receptive to evolutionism and evolutionary psychology only to the extent that they seemed to confirm the Hegelian position. This is made clear, for example, in the manner in which he refers to Darwinism in his earliest books and articles. But gradually the situation was reversed. Under the influence of a growing concern with the practical problems of education and social reform, Darwinism assumed a new significance. Since Darwin's naturalistic and genetic method provided a more direct approach to the problem of social control than did the dialectic of Hegel, it, accordingly, began to receive the greater emphasis. And this process, once initiated, continued. As his interest in social questions deepened over the years, the earlier point of view receded farther and farther into the background, until it eventually gave way to an entirely new position, one which although retaining many of the Hegelian insights was predominantly naturalistic and evolutionary in tone.

The central feature of this new philosophy, as it was later elaborated, is its radical humanism, its contention that man rather than God or nature is the chief end and agent of creation. As opposed to materialism, which reduces history to the mechanical interplay of physical causation, and to supernaturalism, which sees in it the actualization of divine providènce, instrumentalism interprets history as primarily the sphere of human endeavor, the region in which human intelligence and will are omnicompetent, and in which, accordingly, man has full power both to plan and to control his own future. Man is thus held to be neither the victim of blind circumstance nor the darling of the gods, but a creative force in his own right.

But this power of man to control his own destiny is not interpreted by Dewey as proving either that man is anything more than a part of the natural process or that the exercise of this power is mainly an individual matter—two implications which the earlier American philosophy, as I have described it, would certainly have insisted upon.

In the first place, Dewey, like Darwin, views man as one animal among others. He holds that there is nothing divine in the origin of the human species and no essential mystery about its nature. Man's intelligence, which is his most distinctive trait, is described as a natural function of the body, no more and no less peculiar than the functions of breathing and eating. It is held to be a tool which the human species has happened to evolve in the course of its struggle for survival, and which comes into play whenever the organism is blocked in its activity by the environment. As Dewey has often put it, intelligence is nothing but a habit, a habit of stopping to review in imagination all the possible ways of acting in a given situation and of finally choosing that one action which promises to satisfy the greatest number of needs and impulses then present.

In the second place, Dewey also argues that the control of nature accruing to man by virtue of his intelligence is properly a function of institutional rather than of individual enterprise. Although he recognizes that society does not exist apart from the individual and that social action reduces ultimately to cooperative individual action, he, like Hegel, places his main emphasis upon the institution and upon the fact that the individual is largely the product of his social environment. Thus according to Dewey, it is the institution rather than the individual that makes history, and thus also it is only by working in and through institutions that man may actually acquire that control over nature which the factor of intelligence renders possible. It is because of this, for example, that Dewey has constantly argued the necessity for fluid institutional forms capable of continuous adjustment to the changing needs of men, and it is for this reason also that he has consistently employed the methods of social, rather than of individual, psychology in his approach to all practical problems.

Instrumentalism thus breaks with the American tradition

at two vital points and in a manner expressive of the influences brought to bear upon its creator as a young man. In place of the older dualism it would substitute an evolutionary monism which in many of its particulars reflects the evolutionary naturalism of Darwin; while in place of the older individualism, it defends an institutionalism reminiscent of Hegel. Its most revolutionary break with the past, however, and the point at which it promises to transform the character and structure of American life most radically is to be found in its use of the Darwinian and Hegelian conception of history as a new ground for asserting moral and political relativism.

Although Dewey rejects Darwin's and Hegel's historical determinism, he nonetheless subscribes to their view that history is ever changing and that the validity of all things, whether natural or man made, is limited to the particular historical context in which they arise. All things, he argues, even ideals and fundamental institutions, have been evolved only as the result of special needs in special circumstances, and when these needs and circumstances change—as they inevitably do—new ideals and new institutions must emerge to take their place. This means, concretely, that no truth, no moral or political principle, may be regarded as absolute, and that a sound social philosophy requires the same antitraditional, experimental attitude that is to be found in the natural sciences. In short, by construing the conception of process in as extreme a form as possible, instrumentalism affirms the doctrine that nothing is permanent save change itself, and boldly accepts the relativistic implications of this view for human conduct and moral theory.

This becomes clear in Dewey's evaluation of the American scene and in his frequent pronouncements on the American tradition. Thus he has constantly criticized the conservative tendency to confuse means with ends and has sharply opposed any disposition to treat American political forms as final. He has no sympathy, for example, with those who regard the Federal Constitution as sacrosanct, holding, instead, that if the

Constitution is to survive as an efficient instrument of the democratic will, it must be so flexibly interpreted as to render it continually sensitive to changing social conditions. Nor has he stopped with proclaiming the relativity of political methods. Probing still deeper, he has even come to challenge the permanency of political ends, for example, the belief in inherent individual rights. This follows from the kind of world view the emphasis upon process implies. In a universe in which everything is part of the natural process, there may be particular interests but not universal rights. For rights in the Christian-Platonic sense, which is the sense in which they have always been understood, imply a region of fact over and above the natural process, one that is grounded in "natural law" or divine will rather than upon physical phenomena. Similarly, in a world in which nothing is permanent, nothing, not even interests, will eternally "inhere" in anything else. Interests as well as situations change, and what is to the interest of one generation need not be to the interest of another.

The fact that Dewey thus strikes at the very root and foundation of the traditional American faith is not always clearly recognized, even by Dewey himself. This is partly because Dewey personally happens to embody many of the qualities and virtues which the American ethos has always cherished. But it is also because his repeated advocacy of democracy as a still viable political method has often been mistaken for a defense of democracy as a permanent way of life, although only the former of these may be consistently held within the instrumentalist framework.

This confusion is nowhere more evident than in the assumption by some of Dewey's followers that instrumentalism as applied socially is really nothing new, but only a continuation and development of the tradition of American democratic revolutionism, particularly as this was expressed in Jefferson. They point, for example, to the fact that instrumentalism and Jeffersonianism are in complete agreement in their faith in the potentialities of an educated electorate, in their distrust of tradition, and in their conviction that the welfare of the people as a whole is the chief end and purpose of government. In other words, on this view the basic difference between the two philosophies would consist principally in the fact that the one has had the advantage of a century of scientific progress while the other has not.

In reality, however, the difference cuts much deeper. For while it is true that Jeffersonianism is in a very real sense revolutionary, it is revolutionary only within limits and to a degree far less extreme than instrumentalism. Thus, although it has always been suspicious of rigid institutional forms and recognizes the importance of flexibility in the tools of government, it has never extended that scepticism to include the goals of government. It has always accepted certain moral and political truths as self-evident—for example, that all men are and ought to be free and equal—and has ever insisted that these are universally valid and desirable for all men. But it is precisely at this point that Jeffersonianism and instrumentalism are irreconcilably opposed. For the latter, having rejected the principle of fixity as such, must, as we have seen, deny not only the possibility of fixed means but the possibility of fixed goals as well. Ideals no less than methods must be regarded as inherently fallible and be kept pliable, even to the point of complete surrender, if government and policy are to be genuinely efficient. In other words, instrumentalism unlike Jeffersonianism stands committed to the view that although the democratic way of life has proved satisfactory thus far, there is no guarantee that it will continue to do so in the future when present material and social conditions have changed.

In the end, therefore, Dewey's philosophy, far from representing a logical development of what was implicit in the American tradition to begin with, is actually an innovation, a radical reinterpretation of that tradition in monistic, relativistic, and institutional terms.

VI

In instrumentalism, therefore, both as a philosophy and as a social program, it is possible to trace at least one important consequence of the confluence of Hegelianism and Darwinism in American thought. For although there are other paths which have led to instrumentalism besides the one followed by Dewey, and other factors in the American scene which have helped promote the relativism and collectivism for which instrumentalism stands, it is Dewey who has given these doctrines their clearest contemporary expression and with whose name their success is most prominently associated. The rise of instrumentalism, in short, while not wholly attributable to the influence of Hegel and Darwin is at least in large part so attributable.

And as such, it reveals that influence to have been very great. For instrumentalism has by now developed into something far more important than an esoteric system of thought professed only in the university lecture hall. Through Dewey's great prestige as a leader of American education and his position as a defender of many liberal causes, it has become the underlying philosophy of thousands of public-school teachers and of influential sections of liberal opinion everywhere. It has been able to enlist the support of such distinguished figures as Sidney Hook in philosophy, Horace M. Kallen in art, P. W. Bridgman in physics, and Thurman W. Arnold in law and government. And this is to mention only a few of the many outstanding individuals upon whom its effects have been pronounced. It represents therefore a dominant contemporary attitude now actively at work shaping and controlling American policy.

Whether this new attitude is to be welcomed or deplored, and whether it will finally succeed in supplanting the more traditional American attitudes completely, are questions falling outside the proper scope of this paper. It is merely necessary to note that whatever its ultimate consequences may be, its present effects are likely to be felt for years to come. For it is difficult to believe that any philosophy could attain so firm a hold upon the popular imagination or break so radically with the past without leaving some permanent mark upon the course of our national development.

PART II
CRITICAL BIBLIOGRAPHIES

THE *following bibliographical essays duplicate in form and content bibliographies distributed in connection with a student conference on foreign influences held at Princeton during 1942-1943. Thus, the section in each essay entitled "The Problem" describes briefly the problems of the session in which the bibliography was used; the section entitled "General Reference Works" lists the works to which the students were there referred for general background material; while the section headed "Special Topics" describes problems assigned for individual reports together with the works to be consulted in their preparation.*

IMMIGRATION
BETWEEN 1800 AND 1924*

I. THE PROBLEM

THE principal migrations to the United States have been from northwest and southeast Europe; from the West Indies, Canada, and Mexico in the western hemisphere; and from China, Japan, and the Philippine Islands in the Orient. These different migrations have varied widely, each exhibiting distinctive characteristics of its own in regard to motivation, progress, and effect (Topics 1-4). Equally varied, moreover, has been the American reaction to this migration. In some instances, the migration has been feared and condemned, leading to the emergence of organized nativist movements such as the Ku Klux Klan (Topic 5) and, in the case of the Negro and the Oriental, to the adoption of policies of cultural and social segregation (Topic 6). In other instances, the attitude has been friendly, motivated by the traditional idealization of America as the haven of the poor and oppressed. On the whole, however, the opponents of immigration have generally prevailed, particularly in recent decades. After the theory of the "melting pot" had been found wanting even by many of its original adherents (Topic 7), immigration legislation became increasingly restrictive until finally in 1924 the quota system was introduced and the entrance of immigrants in effect banned altogether (Topic 8).

II. GENERAL REFERENCE WORKS

GENERAL HISTORY OF IMMIGRATION. The most brilliant and penetrating studies of the history of immigration to America are those found in Marcus Lee Hansen's *The Atlantic Migration, 1607-1860* (Cambridge, Mass. 1940. 391 pp.) and *The Immigrant in American History* (Cambridge, Mass. 1940. 230 pp.), while the best source book on the subject is

* See also Chapter II, "The Americanization of the Immigrant," on page 39.

[175]

Edith Abbott's *Historical Aspects of the Immigration Problem: Select Documents* (Chicago. 1926. 881 pp.). Competent accounts are also to be found, however, in John R. Commons' *Races and Immigrants in the United States* (New York. 1907, 1915, and 1920. 242 pp.), and George M. Stephenson's *A History of American Immigration, 1820-1924* (Boston. 1926. 316 pp.). On immigrant backgrounds and "contributions" see *Immigrant Backgrounds* (New York. 1927. 269 pp.), edited by Henry Pratt Fairchild, and Carl Wittke's *We Who Built America: The Saga of the Immigrant* (New York. 1939. 547 pp.), while, for conditions of immigrant travel in the middle of the nineteenth century and for the history of immigrant legislation, see Friedrich Kapp's *Immigration and the Commissioners of Emigration of the State of New York* (New York. 1870. 241 pp.) and Roy L. Garis' *Immigration Restriction: A Study of the Opposition to and Regulation of Immigration into the United States* (New York. 1927. 376 pp.). For statistical studies see: Stella H. Sutherland's *Population Distribution in Colonial America* (New York. 1936. 353 pp.); William J. Bromwell's *History of Immigration to the United States* (New York. 1856. 225 pp.), a statistical analysis of immigration between 1819 and 1855; Warren S. Thompson's and P. K. Whelpton's *Population Trends in the United States* (New York. 1933. 415 pp.), a statistical survey relating to the twentieth century; and Walter F. Wilcox's (ed.) *International Migrations* (New York. 1929 and 1939. 2 vols.), the best statistical source book on migration as a world phenomenon. For a bibliography on immigration see Ralph W. Janeway's *Bibliography of Immigration in the United States, 1900-1930* (Columbus, Ohio. 1934. 132 pp.).

HISTORY OF PARTICULAR EUROPEAN GROUPS. The material on particular immigrant groups is voluminous but frequently of indifferent quality. Only the more familiar items are listed here. On BRITISH immigration, the two best books are William A. Carrothers' *Emigration from the British Isles* (London. 1929. 328 pp.) and Stanley C. Johnson's *A History of Emigration from the United Kingdom to North America, 1763-1912* (London. 1913. 387 pp.) but neither treats in any great detail of the emigration to the United States. See also William Cunningham's *English Influence on the United States* (New York. 1916. 168 pp.). For the FRENCH immigration, Howard Mumford Jones' *America and French Culture, 1750-1848* (Chapel Hill. 1927. 615 pp.) offers the most rounded account but valuable material is also found in Charles W. Baird's *History of the Huguenot Emigration to America* (New York. 1885. 2 vols.), Frances S. Childs' *French Refugee Life in the United States, 1790-1800: An American Chapter of the French Revolution* (Baltimore. 1940. 229 pp.), T. W. Clarke's *Émigrés in the Wilderness* (New York. 1941. 247 pp.); Gilbert J. Garraghan's *The Jesuits of the Middle United States* (New York. 1938. 3 vols.), and J. G. Rosengarten's *French Colonists and Exiles in the United States* (Philadelphia. 1907. 234 pp.). On the GERMAN migrations to America, Albert B. Faust's *The German Element in the United States* (Boston and New York. 1909. 2 vols.) still remains the standard work although now somewhat dated. It is adequately supplemented, however, as regards the earlier German migration by W. A. Knittle's *Early Eighteenth Century Palatine Emigration* (Philadelphia. 1937. 320 pp.) and by many articles in the *Publications and Proceedings of the Pennsylvania German Society* (1891-). For the German immigration of the middle and late nineteenth century see John A. Hawgood's *The Tragedy of German America: The Germans in the United States of America during the Nineteenth Century and After* (New York. 1940. 334 pp.). For bibliographical material see Emil Meynen's exhaustive *Bibliography on German Settlements in Colonial North America* (Leipzig. 1937. 636 pp.).

The best account of the IRISH immigration is William F. Adams' *Ireland and Irish Emigration to the New World from 1815 to the Famine* (New Haven. 1932. 444 pp.), but histories of the early Irish settlements and of the Irish impact on American life are also to be found in Thomas D. McGee's *History of the Irish Settlers in North America* (Boston. 1851. 5th rev. ed. 1852. 240 pp.), John F. Maguire's *The Irish in America* (London. 1868. 653 pp.), Oscar Handlin's *Boston's Immigrants, 1790-1865* (Cambridge, Mass. 1941. 287 pp.), and Francis P. Dewees' *The Molly Maguires: The Origin, Growth and Character of the Organization* (Philadelphia. 1877. 380 pp.). On the SCOTCH-IRISH, the most authoritative histories are: Henry J. Ford's *The Scotch Irish in America* (Princeton. 1915. 607 pp.) and Charles A. Hanna's *The Scotch Irish; or the Scot in North Britain, North Ireland, and North America* (New York. 1902. 2 vols.).

For the ITALIAN immigration, Giovanni Schiavo's *The Italians in America Before the Civil War* (New York. 1934. 399 pp.) deals with the period before the Italian migration assumed the proportions of a mass movement, Robert F. Foerster's *The Italian Emigration of our Times* (Cambridge, Mass. 1919. 556 pp.) is an authoritative treatment of that immigration at its tide, while John H. Mariano's *The Italian Contribution to American Democracy* (Boston. 1921. 317 pp.) and the Federal Writers' Project, *The Italians of New York* (New York. 1938. 241 pp.), describe the Italians in New York City.

The SCANDINAVIAN migration, particularly that of the Swedes and Norwegians, is excellently described in Kendric C. Babcock's general survey, *The Scandinavian Element in the United States* (Urbana, Ill. 1914. 223 pp.); but George M. Stephenson's *The Religious Aspects of Swedish Immigration: A Study of Immigrant Churches* (Minneapolis. 1922. 542 pp.), Nels Hokanson's *Swedish Immigrants in Lincoln's Time* (New York. 1942. 259 pp.), and Theodore C. Blegen's monumental studies, *Norwegian Migration to America, 1825-1860* (Northfield, Minn. 1931. 413 pp.) and *Norwegian Migration to America: The American Transition* (Northfield, Minn. 1940. 655 pp.) are also noteworthy.

On other European migrations to America see Malcolm M. Vartan's *The Armenians in America* (Boston. 1919. 142 pp.); Thomas Capek's *The Czechs (Bohemians) in America* (Boston. 1920. 293 pp.); Henry Pratt Fairchild's *Greek Immigration to the United States* (New Haven. 1911. 278 pp.); Peter Wiernik's *History of the Jews in America from the Period of the Discovery of the New World to the Present Time* (New York. 1931. 465 pp.); William Thomas' and Florian Znaniecki's *The Polish Peasant in Europe and America* (New York. 1918-1920. 2 vols.), one of the best studies, to date, on an immigrant group; Donald R. Taft's *Two Portuguese Communities in New England* (New York. 1923. 375 pp.); Jerome Davis' *The Russian Immigrant* (New York. 1922. 219 pp.); John Paul von Grueningen's (ed.) *The Swiss in the United States* (Madison, Wis. 1940. 153 pp.); and Philip K. Hitti's *The Syrians in America* (New York. 1924. 139 pp.).

HISTORY OF PARTICULAR ORIENTAL GROUPS. Mary R. Coolidge's *Chinese Immigration* (New York. 1909. 531 pp.) is one of the older but still one of the best studies on the Chinese in America. On the Filipinos, see Bruno Lasker's *Filipino Immigration to Continental United States and to Hawaii* (Chicago. 1931. 445 pp.), and on the Japanese: Yamato Ichihashi's *Japanese in the United States: A Critical Study of the Problems of the Japanese Immigrants and their Children* (Stanford University. 1932. 462 pp.) and Edward K. Strong's *The Japanese in California* (Stanford University. 1933. 188 pp.).

HISTORY OF PARTICULAR GROUPS FROM THE WESTERN HEMISPHERE. For the French-Canadian immigration see Bessie B. Wessel's *An Ethnic Survey of Woonsocket, Rhode Island* (Chicago. 1931. 290 pp.) and for the Mexican: Emory S. Bogardus' *The Mexican in the United States* (Los Angeles. 1934. 128 pp.) and Manuel Gamio's *Mexican Immigration to the United States: A Study of Human Migration and Adjustment* (Chicago. 1930. 262 pp.).

IMMIGRANT BIOGRAPHIES. For lists of immigrant biographies see Maurice R. Davie's *World Immigration* (New York. 1936. 588 pp.), pp. 563-567 and William C. Smith's *Americans in the Making* (New York. 1939. 454 pp.), pp. 433-437. For a list of immigrant biographies and fiction dealing with the immigrant see Davie, *op. cit.*, pp. 567-571. For books containing brief immigrant biographies see: Louis Adamic's *From Many Lands* (New York. 1940. 350 pp.), Hannibal G. Duncan's *Immigration and Assimilation* (Boston. 1933. 890 pp.), Manuel Gamio's *The Mexican Immigrant: His Life Story* (Chicago. 1931. 288 pp.), and Hamilton Holt's *The Life Stories of Undistinguished Americans As Told by Themselves* (New York. 1906. 299 pp.).

HISTORY OF THE AMERICAN NEGRO AND HIS INFLUENCE. Benjamin G. Brawley's *A Short History of the American Negro* (New York. 1913. Rev. ed. 1939. 288 pp.) and Ina C. Brown's *The Story of the American Negro* (New York. 1936. 208 pp.) are among the better briefer and more popular accounts. For more detailed studies see Lorenzo Greene's *The Negro in Colonial New England* (New York. 1942. 404 pp.), Ulrich B. Phillips' *American Negro Slavery* (New York. 1918. 196 pp.), William E. B. Du Bois' *Black Folk, Then and Now: An Essay in the History and Sociology of the Negro Race* (New York. 1939. 401 pp.), and particularly the same author's *Black Reconstruction: An Essay Toward a History of the Part which Black Folk Played in the Attempt to Reconstruct Democracy in America, 1860-1880* (New York. 1935. 746 pp.). See also the two monographs of the U.S. Bureau of the Census: *Negro Population, 1790-1915* (Washington. 1918. 884 pp.) and *Negroes in the United States, 1920-1932* (Washington. 1935. 845 pp.). For additional material see the *Journal of Negro History* (1916-), and Monroe N. Work's *A Bibliography of the Negro in Africa and America* (New York. 1928. 698 pp.).

III. SPECIAL TOPICS

1. EUROPEAN IMMIGRATION: "OLD TYPE." For the German and French immigrations as instances of the "old" immigration and for their contrasting influences upon American institutions, see A. B. Faust's, *The German Element in the United States* (Boston and New York. 1909. 2 vols.), particularly Volume II, pp. 1-27, 122-250, 250-293, 377-475 and Howard M. Jones' *America and French Culture, 1750-1848* (Chapel Hill. 1927. 615 pp.), particularly pp. 15-172 and 291-572. For the background of the older Irish immigration, consult W. F. Adams' *Ireland and Irish Immigration to the New World* (New Haven. 1932. 444 pp.), which emphasizes conditions in Ireland and the process of immigration. No good study of English emigration to the United States exists but S. C. Johnson's *A History of Emigration from the United Kingdom to North America, 1763-1912* (London. 1913. 387 pp.) and the relevant selections from Edith Abbott's *Historical Aspects of the Immigration Problem* (Chicago. 1926. 881 pp.) may be used. T. C. Blegen's *Norwegian Migration to America* (Northfield, Minn. 1931. 413 pp.) is an excellent case study of the Scandinavian group.

2. EUROPEAN IMMIGRATION: "NEW TYPE." The Italians, Russians, and Polish may be treated as typical instances of the "new" immigration and illustrate clearly the characteristic differences between the "old" and the "new" immigrations generally. On this topic, consult Robert F. Foerster's *The Italian Emigration of Our Times* (Cambridge, Mass. 1919. 556 pp.), particularly pp. 320-411, Jerome Davis' *The Russian Immigrant* (New York. 1922. 213 pp.) and Thomas and Znaniecki's *The Polish Peasant in Europe and America* (New York. 1927. 2,250 pp.), particularly Vol. II, pp. 1467-1822. A general treatment of the "new" immigration, emphasizing the characteristic social conditions and problems of assimilation faced after the 1880's may be found in Peter Roberts' *The New Immigration* (New York. 1912. 386 pp.). Emily G.

Balch's *Our Slavic Fellow Citizens* (New York. 1910. 536 pp.) is a general discussion. A case study of new world adjustment and conflict with other immigrant groups is made in Bessie B. Wessel's *An Ethnic Survey of Woonsocket, Rhode Island* (Chicago. 1931. 290 pp.).

3. ORIENTAL IMMIGRATION. The course of Oriental immigration and its effect on American life are represented most graphically in the Chinese and Japanese immigrations, which are covered adequately in Mary R. Coolidge's *Chinese Immigration* (New York. 1909. 531 pp.), particularly pp. 3-145 and 337-497, and Yamato Ichihashi's *Japanese in the United States* (Stanford University. 1932. 426 pp.), particularly pp. 1-14, 47-106, 207-400. For additional information on Oriental immigration, see B. Lasker, *Filipino Immigration to Continental United States and to Hawaii* (Chicago. 1931. 445 pp.). Problems in oriental adjustment to American society are discussed in S. L. Gulick's *The American Japanese Problem* (New York. 1914. 349 pp.) and T. Lyenga's and K. Sato's *Japan and the California Problem* (New York. 1921. 249 pp.). B. Schrieke's *Alien Americans* (New York. 1936. 208 pp.) shows how economic conflict translates itself into race conflict.

4. NEW WORLD IMMIGRATION. The early importation of the Negroes as slaves from the West Indies and the later French-Canadian and Mexican immigrations are discussed as distinctive types of the New World immigration in the following works: Ulrich B. Phillips' *American Negro Slavery* (New York. 1918. 196 pp.), Robert C. Dexter's "The French-Canadian Invasion" (*The Alien in Our Midst*, edited by Madison Grant and C. S. Davison. New York. 1930. pp. 70-79), William Wood's "The French Canadians" (*Immigrant Backgrounds*, edited by H. P. Fairchild. New York. 1927. Chapter III), and Manuel Gamio's *Mexican Immigration to the United States* (Chicago. 1930. 262 pp.). Exhaustive statistical material on Canadian-American migration will be

found in L. E. Truesdall's *The Canadian Born in the United States. An Analysis of the Statistics of the Canadian Element in the Population of the United States, 1850-1930* (New Haven. 1943. 263 pp.). For further material on Mexican immigration consult E. S. Bogardus, *The Mexican in the United States* (Los Angeles. 1934. 126 pp.) and Manuel Gamio, *The Mexican Immigrant* (Chicago. 1931. 288 pp.). The history of White-Indian relations is told in Helen Hunt Jackson's *A Century of Dishonor* (Boston. Rev. ed. 1885. 514 pp.).

5. NATIVISM. Nativism in America has been expressed most dramatically in the "Know-Nothing" movement, in the American Protective Association, and most recently in the Ku Klux Klan. For Know-Nothingism see Ray A. Billington's *The Protestant Crusade, 1800-1860* (New York. 1938. 514 pp.). The political aspects of the movement are discussed in G. M. Stephenson's "Nativism in the Forties and Fifties, with Special Reference to the Mississippi Valley" (*Mississippi Valley Historical Review*, IX [1922], pp. 185-202) and in A. C. Cole's "Nativism in the Lower Mississippi Valley" (*Proceedings of the Mississippi Valley Historical Association*, VI [1912-1913], pp. 258-275). Although there is no adequate study of the American Protective Association, Humphrey J. Desmond's *The A. P. A. Movement* (Washington, D.C. 1912. 102 pp.) discusses the movement in general, while a shorter account, with some additional material, may be found in Gustavus Myers' *History of Bigotry in the United States* (New York. 1943. 495 pp.), especially pp. 219-247. Emerson H. Loucks' *The Ku Klux Klan in Pennsylvania* (New York. 1936. 213 pp.) is a case study of recent nativism. J. M. Mecklin's *The Ku Klux Klan* (New York. 1924. 244 pp.) is a general appraisal.

6. THE SEGREGATION OF THE NEGRO. Since his emancipation, the Negro has made little progress (in comparison with other groups) in being assimilated. Because of this segregation

he has evolved characteristic attitudes of his own and a characteristic class structure within the caste into which he has been forced. For an excellent analysis of this attitude and class structure in their relation to American society as a whole, read Alison Davis' *Deep South: A Social Anthropological Study of Caste and Class* (Chicago. 1941. 558 pp.) and W. E. B. Du Bois' *Souls of the Black Folk* (Chicago. 1903; 17th ed. 1931. 264 pp.). The extent to which the Negro has been physically assimilated, however, is estimated with spectacular results by Melville Herskovits in *The American Negro: a Study in Racial Crossing* (New York. 1928. 92 pp.). John Dollard's *Caste and Class in a Southern Town* (New Haven. 1937. 502 pp.) is a social psychological study of Negro and white attitudes as developed within the caste structure.

7. THE MELTING POT MISTAKE. For the history and theory of "The Melting Pot," and an account of its failure to work, see Henry P. Fairchild's *The Melting Pot Mistake* (Boston. 1926. 266 pp.) and Edward A. Ross' *The Old World in the New* (New York. 1914. 304 pp.). For arguments in favor of the "ethnic federation" theory of assimilation see Isaac B. Berkson's *Theories of Americanization* (New York. 1920. 226 pp.). Other theories of adjustment are discussed in: Philip Davis (ed.), *Immigration and Americanization* (Boston. 1920. 770 pp.), Carol Aronovici, *Americanization* (St. Paul. 1919. 48 pp.), A. A. Costa, "Americanization and Reaction" (*Living Age*, CCCV [1920], pp. 67-71). These discussions published at the end of the World War are also useful in indicating the issues uppermost in the minds of Americans as the question of immigration restriction was being debated.

8. AMERICAN IMMIGRATION LEGISLATION. The history of immigration legislation from 1800 on and the social forces of which it was the result are described in Julius Drachsler's *Democracy and Assimilation* (New York. 1920. 275 pp.), M. R. Davie's *A Constructive Immigration Policy* (New

Haven. 1923. 46 pp.), and in R. L. Garis' *Immigration Restriction* (New York. 1927. 376 pp.). The Report of the Immigration Commission (the Dillingham Report) is too extensive to be used effectively, but a summary of its findings, with discussions and criticisms, will be found in *The Survey* for 1910-1911 and 1923, XXV, pp. 571-604, and XLVII, pp. 815-821. See also the chapters in G. M. Stephenson's *A History of American Immigration* (Boston. 1926. 316 pp.) which deal with various proposals for immigrant restriction.

THE PATTERN OF ASSIMILATION*

I. THE PROBLEM

THE process of assimilation in America has rarely, if ever, followed a completely peaceful course. The influx of immigrants and of alien viewpoints alike has often created social problems of a peculiar and sometimes critical nature. Some of these problems have arisen at the purely ideological level and have consisted mainly in a clash of ideas. Instances of this are to be found in the conflict between liberal American and conservative German Lutheranism early in the nineteenth century (Topic 1), and in the influence of British and Allied propaganda upon American public opinion between 1914 and 1917 (Topic 2). Other problems created, however, are of a more personal and intimate type and are experienced by certain individuals in the form of a sense of "rootlessness" or of being "at odds" with members of the older generation. Whenever either of these occurs, we have the phenomenon of the "marginal man" (Topic 3) or of the "second generation immigrant" (Topic 4). Still other problems may arise which affect the pattern of group life as a whole, as is illustrated, for example, in the development of the alien subcommunity (Topics 5 and 6), in the evolution of educational policies of exclusion or indoctrination (Topic 7), and in the general increase of crime and juvenile delinquency (Topic 8).

II. GENERAL REFERENCE WORKS

THE ACCULTURATION OF THE IMMIGRANT. The most recent and most lucid analysis of the problem of immigrant assimilation is that given in William Carlson Smith's *Americans in the Making* (New York. 1939. 454 pp.), while the best collection of case studies on the problem is that found in Edith Abbott's *Immigration: Select Documents and Case Records*

* See also Chapter III, "The Problem of Ethnic and National Impact from a Sociological Point of View," on page 57.

(Chicago. 1924. 809 pp.). Other standard treatments which review the problem as a whole are: Maurice R. Davie's *World Immigration: With Special Reference to the United States* (New York. 1936. 588 pp.) and Henry Pratt Fairchild's *Immigration: A World Movement and Its American Significance* (New York. 1913. Rev. ed. 1933. 520 pp.) which describe the causes, course, and effects of immigration; J. W. Jenks' and W. J. Lauck's *The Immigration Problem: A Study of American Immigration Conditions and Needs* (New York. 1911. 6th ed., revised and enlarged by Rufus D. Smith, 1926. 717 pp.) which provides an excellent analysis of the reports of the Immigration Commission; and T. J. Woofter's *Races and Ethnic Groups in American Life* (New York. 1933. 247 pp.), a statistical study of the principal ethnic patterns in America during the twentieth century. For works mainly concerned with the effects of the process of assimilation upon the immigrant himself see: Grace Abbott's *The Immigrant and the Community* (New York. 1917. 303 pp.) which analyzes the problem of adjustment and the need for a sympathetic treatment of the immigrant; Lawrence Guy Brown's *Immigration: Cultural Conflicts and Social Adjustments* (New York. 1933. 419 pp.) which discusses the attitude of the immigrant in relation to his social environment; and B. Schrieke's *Alien Americans: A Study of Race Relations* (New York. 1936. 208 pp.), a notable study by a Dutch anthropologist particularly concerned with the Negro, Mexican, Chinese, and Japanese groups. Other texts dealing with the problem of minority groups are: Donald Young's *American Minority Peoples: A Study in Racial and Cultural Conflicts in the United States* (New York. 1932. 621 pp.); F. J. Brown's and J. F. Roucek's *Our Racial and National Minorities* (New York. 1937. 877 pp.); Robert E. Park's and Herbert A. Miller's *Old World Traits Transplanted* (New York. 1921. 307 pp.); and Carey McWilliams' *Brothers Under the Skin* (Boston. 1943. 325 pp.). For various theories of Americanization see Isaac B. Berkson's *Theories of Americaniza-*

tion: A Critical Study with Special Reference to the Jewish Group (New York. 1920. 226 pp.). For a typical study of the assimilation of a particular group see Phyllis H. Williams' *South Italian Folkways in Europe and America* (New Haven. 1938. 216 pp.).

THE ACCULTURATION OF THE NEGRO. Studies of the Negro in American life are numerous and in recent years have achieved an extraordinarily high scholarly level. Of the most recent general surveys of the problem, Charles S. Johnson's *The Negro in American Civilization* (New York. 1930. 538 pp.) is one of the best, as is also Johnson's and W. D. Weatherford's *Race Relations: Adjustment of Whites and Negroes in the United States* (Boston. 1934. 590 pp.), while *The Negro's Progress in Fifty Years* (Publication of the Am. Acad. of Political and Social Science. Philadelphia. 1913. 224 pp.) briefly reviews the historical background.* On special phases of the subject, the following studies are particularly notable: Melville J. Herskowits' *The Anthropometry of the American Negro* (New York. 1930. 283 pp.) describes the submergence of typically Negroid traits through the process of miscegenation; Charles S. Johnson's *Patterns of Negro Segregation* (New York. 1943. 332 pp.) lists and analyzes the various types of Negro segregation, while Paul E. Baker's *Negro-White Adjustment* (New York. 1934. 267 pp.) critically evaluates the various methods employed in promoting interracial harmony; Robert R. Moton's *What the Negro Thinks* (New York. 1929. 267 pp.) is now somewhat dated but still valuable in presenting the Negro's reaction to his place in American life; Frazier E. Franklin's *The Negro Family in the United States* (Chicago. 1939. 686 pp.) is an excellent analysis of the effect of the Negro's social status upon

* To this should be added Gunnar Myrdal's *An American Dilemma: The Negro Problem and Modern Democracy* (New York. 1944. 2 vols.), a survey which was published too late to be included above but which is too important to be omitted from any bibliography on the subject. This work represents a summary of the findings of a noted Swedish sociologist and is especially valuable as expressing the point of view of a foreign observer.

his domestic life. Carter G. Woodson's *The Rural Negro* (New York. 1930. 265 pp.) and T. J. Woofter's *Negro Problems in Cities* (New York. 1928. 284 pp.) describe the status of the Negro in rural and urban districts, respectively. The latter author's *Negro Migration* (New York. 1920. 195 pp.) and Louise V. Kennedy's *The Negro Peasant Turns Cityward* (New York. 1930. 271 pp.) are concerned with the Negro migration to northern cities which began with the first World War.

A number of excellent studies have been made of the Negro problem in particular localities. Of these, one of the latest and best is Roi Ottley's *'New World A-Coming': Inside Black America* (Boston. 1943. 364 pp.), a study of Negro life in Harlem, but equally noteworthy are Allison Davis' *Deep South: A Social Anthropological Study of Caste and Class* (Chicago. 1941. 558 pp.) and John Dollard's *Caste and Class in a Southern Town* (New Haven. 1937. 502 pp.) both of which are studies of Negro life in typical southern communities. Of lesser importance but still valuable is *The Negro in Chicago: The Study of Race Relations and a Race Riot* (Chicago. 1932. 672 pp.), the report of the Chicago Commission on Race Relations growing out of the Chicago race riots of 1919.

For further material on these and other phases of the problem see: Jerome Dowd's *The Negro in American Life* (New York. 1926. 611 pp.), the U.S. Census Bureau's *Negroes in the United States, 1920-1932* (Washington. 1935. 845 pp.), E. B. Reuter's *The American Race Problem* (New York. 1927. 448 pp.), and Edgar T. Thompson's (ed.) *Race Relations and the Race Problem* (Durham, N.C. 1939. 338 pp.).

III. SPECIAL TOPICS

1. THE CRISIS IN NINETEENTH CENTURY AMERICAN LUTHERAN THEOLOGY. The impact of German Lutheran doctrine upon Lutheran dogma and church government in America during the nineteenth century may be taken as typi-

cal of the effects which foreign ideas have frequently had upon American institutional life, and may be considered, therefore, as a case study in relation to this problem. The two best books bearing directly on the subject are: Vergilius Ferm's *The Crisis in American Lutheran Theology* (New York. 1927. 409 pp.) and Carl Mauelshagen's *American Lutheranism Surrenders to the Forces of Conservatism* (Athens, Ga. 1936. 252 pp.). Both books should be read. For additional informa-tion regarding Lutheran dogma and the history of the American Lutheran church, consult Henry E. Jacobs' *A History of the Evangelical Lutheran Church in the United States* (New York. 1893. American Church History, Vol. IV. 539 pp.) and the same author's article, "Lutheranism," in Vol. VIII of *Hastings' Encyclopedia of Religion and Ethics* (New York, 1916. 13 vols.). See also "Lutherans" by G. Froboss and J. B. Clark in Vol. VII of *The New Schaff-Herzog Encyclopedia of Religious Knowledge* (New York. 1910. 12 vols.).

2. BRITISH WAR PROPAGANDA IN AMERICA, 1914-1917. Another case study in the institutional effects of foreign ideas in America is found in the effects of British propaganda upon American public opinion during the first World War. This case study differs from that treated in Topic 1 in that it constitutes an instance of impact which was deliberately contrived and engineered to suit the ends of a foreign power. Probably the best book on the subject is Horace Peterson's *Propaganda for War: the Campaign against American Neutrality* (Norman, Okla. 1939. 357 pp.) and the next best, James D. Squires' *British Propaganda at Home and in the United States from 1914 to 1917* (Cambridge, Mass. 1935. 113 pp.). For a fuller account of America's entry into the war see Walter Millis' *The Road to War: America, 1914-1917* (Boston. 1935. 466 pp.) and for a fuller treatment of atrocity propaganda see James M. Read's *Atrocity Propaganda, 1914-1919* (New Haven. 1941. 319 pp.). For America's own propaganda efforts after entering the war see James R.

Mock's *Words that Won the War: the Story of the Committee on Public Information, 1917-1919* (Princeton. 1939. 372 pp.).

3. THE MARGINAL MAN. "Cultural marginality" is one of the most striking by-products of the process of assimilation and one which has only recently been isolated for special study. The concept of the marginal man was first given prominence by R. E. Park in "Human Migration and the Marginal Man" (*American Journal of Sociology*, XXXIII [May, 1928], pp. 881-893); "The Mentality of Racial Hybrids" (*American Journal of Sociology*, XXVI [January, 1931], pp. 534-551); and in "Behind Our Masks" (*Survey Graphic*, LVI [May 1, 1926]). The best treatment of the subject, however, is to be found in E. V. Stonequist's *The Marginal Man: a Study in Personality and Culture Conflict* (New York. 1937. 228 pp.) and this should be read in conjunction with the articles by Park. For further treatment see various essays included in E. B. Reuter's *Race Mixture: Studies in Intermarriage and Miscegenation* (New York. 1931. 224 pp.) and the same author's *The Mulatto in the United States* (Boston. 1918. 417 pp.).

4. THE SECOND-GENERATION IMMIGRANT. The literature on the characteristic attitudes and problems of the second-generation immigrant is voluminous, but the following works may be mentioned as representative: John H. Mariano's *The Italian Contribution to American Democracy* (Boston. 1921. 317 pp.); Louis Adamic's "Thirty Million New Americans" (*Harpers*, XLIX [November, 1934], pp. 284-294); Read Lewis' "Immigrants and Their Children" (*Social Work Year Book*. 1935); Abram Myerson's "The Conflict Between the Old and the New Generation" (*The Family*, III [November 7, 1922], pp. 163-165) and "Descendants of the Foreign Born" (*Annals*, CLI [September, 1930], pp. 149-153); Thaddeus Sleszynski's "The Second Generation of Immigrants in the Assimilation Process" (*Annals*, XCIII

[January, 1921], pp. 156-161); William C. Smith's "Changing Personality Traits of Second Generation Orientals in America" (*American Journal of Sociology*, XXXIII [May, 1938], pp. 922-929); Pauline Young's "The Reorganization of Jewish Family Life in America" (*Social Forces*, VII [December, 1928], pp. 238-244). For further material on the second-generation Oriental see Edward K. Strong's *The Second-Generation Japanese Problem* (Stanford University. 1934. 292 pp.). For statistics on the second-generation immigrant generally see Niles Carpenter's *Immigrants and their Children, 1920* (Washington. 1927. 431 pp.).

5. THE GHETTO. Racial or immigrant groups are often denied full access to urban life and are forced to live in "Ghettos" or "Black Belts," where they may develop a group life independent of the larger community. Chicago and New York Jewish settlements may be considered examples in point, and in this connection Louis Wirth's *The Ghetto* (Chicago. 1928. 306 pp.) and K. Bercovici's "The Greatest Jewish City in the World" (*The Nation*, CXVII [September 12, 1923], pp. 259-261) provide some interesting comparisons and contrasts. For further information on immigrant urban acculturation see K. H. Claghorn's "The Foreign Immigrant in New York City" (*U.S. Industrial Commission Reports*. Washington. 1900-1902. XV, pp. 449-492), *Hull House Maps and Papers* (New York. 1895. 230 pp.) for material on Chicago, and Robert A. Woods' *The City Wilderness* (Boston. 1898. 319 pp.) for material on Boston.

6. THE RURAL IMMIGRANT. The concentration of immigrant groups in rural communities sets up characteristic conflict situations of types different from those found in the urban environment, and they are handled in different ways by the immigrant groups concerned. For a description of these conflicts and of the contrasting methods by which they have been met, see *Rural Community Types* (Univ. Illinois Studies in the Social Sciences, XVI [December, 1928], 184 pp.) by

E. T. Hiller, F. E. Corner, and W. L. East, and pp. 1511-1574 of *The Polish Peasant in Europe and America* (New York. 1918-1920. 2 vols.) by W. I. Thomas and F. Znaniecki. These offer three rural groups for contrast. For additional material see K. H. Claghorn's "Agricultural Distribution of Immigrants" (*U.S. Industrial Reports*. Washington. 1900-1902. XV, pp. 492-646).

7. THE NEGRO AND THE EDUCATIVE PROCESS. The educative process in its several forms normally prepares the individual for a responsible position in society. The Negro, however, as a member of a subordinate caste faces special disabilities and handicaps in his quest for a formal education. Realizing the importance of education in the emancipation of the Negro from caste bondage, many obstacles have been placed in the way of granting him full educational opportunities. These obstacles together with their effect upon the Negro himself are adequately discussed in Carter G. Woodson's *The Miseducation of the Negro* (Washington. 1933. 207 pp.), W. E. B. Du Bois' *The Negro Common School* (Atlanta Univ. Publication. VI [1901], 120 pp.), and Charles H. Thompson's "The Status of Education *of* and *for* the Negro in the American Social Order" (*Journal of Negro Education*, VIII [July, 1939], pp. 489-510). Additional references may be found in other issues of the *Journal of Negro Education* and in the "Bibliography of Negro Education" (*U.S. Commissioner of Education's Report for 1893-94*. I, pp. 1038-1061). For comparison of the Negro's plight with that of other unassimilable groups see Herschel T. Manuel's *The Education of Mexican and Spanish Speaking Children in Texas* (Austin, Tex. 1930. 173 pp.) and Marian Svensrud's "Attitudes of the Japanese Towards their Language Schools" (*Sociology and Social Research*, XVII, pp. 259 f.).

8. THE IMMIGRANT, THE NEGRO, AND CRIME. For material on the incidence of crime and juvenile delinquency among the foreign born see the *Report on Crime and the Foreign Born*

(Washington. 1931. 416 pp.) by the National Commission on Law Observance and Enforcement; and for material analyzing the causes of immigrant crimes see: Raymond Abrashkin's "Listen to the Friends and Neighbors of Two Young Killers" (*PM's Sunday Picture News*, October 25, 1942, pp. 1-8), E. B. Crook's "Cultural Marginality in Sex Delinquency" (*American Journal of Sociology*, XXXIX [January, 1934], pp. 493-500), K. H. Claghorn's "Immigration and Pauperism" (*Annals*, XXIV [July, 1904], pp. 187-195), and Louis Wirth's "Culture Conflict and Misconduct" (*Social Forces*, IX [June, 1931], pp. 484-492). For material on the Negro in relation to crime, read relevant chapters in E. B. Reuter's *The American Race Problem* (New York. 1927. 448 pp.) and in Jesse Spirer's *Negro Crime* (Comp. Psych. Monographs. June, 1940. 64 pp.).

THE ECONOMIC IMPACT*

I. THE PROBLEM

ALMOST all European schools of economic theory have had prominent American representatives and have affected the development of American economic theory. Although the economic peculiarities of the American continent precluded the acceptance of European speculation in an unmodified form, such diverse theories as British Mercantilism, French Physiocracy, the classical-liberal school of Smith, Ricardo, and Malthus, the nationalist theory of Friedrich List, and the Austrian school of Böhm-Bawark have all, in succession, left their mark (Topic 1). Equally vital, however, has been the effect of foreign groups and immigrants upon our economic institutions. From the beginning of the country, the immigrant and Negro have played a central role in the cultivation of the land, in the westward push, and in laying the basic foundations of the American economy. It was the Germans, for example, who first opened up the farming country of central and western Pennsylvania and of many sections in the South and Middle West and who are in part responsible for the diversified economy of these regions today (Topic 2). It was Negro labor which made and still makes possible the great southern crops of cotton, tobacco, and rice (Topic 5); Mexican and Oriental labor which made possible the large-scale truck-farming of California (Topics 4 and 6); and Italian muscle which has furnished the power for the building and construction industry in the Northeast (Topic 3). Nor has the immigrant's contribution been limited to that of providing unskilled labor. Immigrant groups have contributed skills which have been crucial in the evolution of American manufacturing (Topic 2), have played an indispensable role in the growth of trade unions (Topic 8), and have been in

* See also Chapter IV, "Ethnic and National Factors in the American Economic Ethic," on page 67.

large part responsible for such significant economic experiments in this country as the cooperative movement (Topic 9), people's banks (Topic 10), and social insurance (Topic 11).

II. GENERAL REFERENCE WORKS

GENERAL HISTORY OF FOREIGN INFLUENCES UPON AMERICAN ECONOMIC INSTITUTIONS. There are no works which deal directly and comprehensively with the general history of alien impacts upon our economic institutions. Carl Wittke's *We Who Built America* (New York. 1940. 547 pp.) is probably the most comprehensive treatment but is inadequate in being little more than a compilation of facts, and in failing to cover the English and the Negro impacts. John R. Commons' *Races and Immigrants in America* (New York. 1907 and 1920. 242 pp.) presents a brilliant interpretation of the economic role of the alien in American history but fails to consider each alien group in detail. For still more summary treatments see: Chester W. Wright's *Economic History of the United States* (New York. 1941. 1,120 pp.), E. C. Kirkland's *A History of American Economic Life* (New York. 1932. 767 pp.), and Louis Hacker's *The Triumph of American Capitalism: The Development of Forces in American History to the End of the Nineteenth Century* (New York. 1940. 460 pp.). Wright and Kirkland include good descriptive bibliographies.

LABOR. Louis Adamic's *Dynamite: The Story of Class Violence in America* (New York. 1931. 452 pp.) describes the role of such outstanding alien labor leaders as Most, Sacco, and Vanzetti. Isaac A. Hourwich's *Immigration and Labor: The Economic Aspects of European Immigration to the United States* (New York. 1912. 544 pp.) and Charles H. Wesley's *Negro Labor in the United States: 1850-1925* (New York. 1927. 343 pp.) describe the roles of the immigrant and the Negro, respectively, in American labor. See also P. A. Sorokin's "Leaders of Labor and Radical Movements in the United States and Foreign Countries" (*American Journal of*

Sociology, XXXIII, pp. 382-411), Sterling D. Spero's *The Black Worker: The Negro and the Labor Movement* (New York. 1931. 509 pp.), and scattered references in John R. Commons' *History of Labor in the United States* (New York. 1917-1918. 4 vols.) and in the same author's *Documentary History of American Industrial Society* (New York. 1910-1911. 10 vols.). Commons' history, which stops at 1880, may be supplemented by Selig Perlman's *History of Trade Unionism in the United States* (New York. 1922. 313 pp.) and N. J. Ware's *Labor Movement in the United States, 1860-1895* (New York. 1929. 409 pp.).

AGRICULTURE. On the immigrant see E. de S. Brunner's *Immigrant Farmers and their Children: With Four Studies of Immigrant Communities* (New York. 1929. 277 pp.), R. C. Loehr's "Influence of English Agriculture on American Agriculture, 1775-1825" (*Agricultural History*, XI, pp. 3-15), E. F. Meade's "The Italian on the Land: A Study in Immigration" (*U.S. Bureau of Labor Reports*, XIV, pp. 475-533), R. A. Allen's "Mexican Peon Women in Texas" (*Sociology and Social Research*, XVI, pp. 131 ff.), P. S. Taylor's "Mexican Labor in the United States" (*University of California Publications in Economics*, VI, VII, XII, XIII), E. E. Anthony's "Filipino Labor in Central California" (*Sociology and Social Research*, XVI, pp. 441 ff.). On the Negro see Ulrich B. Phillips' *American Negro Slavery* (New York. 1918. 529 pp.) and *Life and Labor in the Old South* (Boston. 1929. 375 pp.). For scattered references to both immigrant and Negro see *Household Manufactures in the United States, 1640-1840* (Chicago. 1917. 413 pp.) by R. M. Tryon, *History of Agriculture in the Northern United States, 1620-1860* (Washington. 1925. 512 pp.) by Percy W. Bidwell and John D. Falconer, and *History of Agriculture in the Southern United States, 1620-1860* (Washington. 1933. 2 vols.) by Lewis C. Gray. For a short history of American agriculture see the U.S. Department of Agriculture's Yearbook for 1940, *Farmers in a Changing World*, pp. 111-326, and for additional works on the same subject, E. E. Edwards' *A Bibliography of the History of Agriculture in the United States* (Dept. Agric. Misc. Pub. No. 84. 1930).

INDUSTRY AND FINANCE. On the immigrant in industry see Herman Feldman's *Racial Factors in American Industry* (New York. 1931. 318 pp.), Harry Jerome's *Migration and Business Cycles* (New York. 1926. 256 pp.), W. M. Leiserson's *Adjusting Immigrant and Industry* (New York. 1924. 356 pp.), Peter Roberts' *Anthracite Coal Communities: A Study of the Demography, the Social, Educational, and Moral Life of the Anthracite Region* (New York. 1904. 387 pp.), W. T. Kataoka's "Occupations of Japanese in Los Angeles" (*Sociology and Social Research*, XIV, pp. 53 ff.), and Frank J. Warne's *The Slav Invasion and the Mine Workers* (Philadelphia. 1904. 211 pp.). On the Negro, in the same connection, see *The Negro Wage Earner* (Washington. 1930. 353 pp.) by Lorenzo Greene and Carter G. Woodson, *The Southern Urban Negro as a Consumer* (New York. 1932. 323 pp.) by Paul K. Edwards, and *Negro Labor in the United States: 1850-1925* (New York. 1927. 343 pp.) by Charles H. Leslie. For general histories of American manufactures, transportation, commerce, currency, and finance, see: V. S. Clark's *History of Manufactures in the United States* (New York. 1929. 3 vols.); B. H. Meyer's *History of Transportation in the United States before 1860* (Washington. 1917. 678 pp.); Emory R. Johnson's *History of Domestic and Foreign Commerce of the United States* (Washington. 1915. 2 vols.); A. B. Hepburn's *History of Currency in the United States* (New York. 1924. 573 pp.), Richard A. Lester's *Monetary Experiments: Early American and Recent Scandinavian* (Princeton. 1939. 316 pp.); and D. R. Dewey's *Financial History of the United States* (New York. 12th ed. 1939. 600 pp.).

HISTORY OF FOREIGN INFLUENCES UPON AMERICAN ECONOMIC THEORY. As in the case of economic institutions, there are no works which deal directly and comprehensively with foreign impacts upon American economic theory. There does not even exist a history of American economic theory as such. Some material, however, may be found in the following: E. V. Willis' "Political Economy in the Early American College Curriculum" (*South Atlantic Quarterly*, XXIV [1925], pp. 131 ff.), E. R. A. Seligman's "The Early Teaching of Economics in the United States" (*Economic Essays in Honor of John Bates Clark*. Edited by J. H. Hollander. New York. 1927. 368 pp.), and F. A. Fetter's "The Early History of Political Economy in the United States" (*Proc. Am. Phil. Soc.*, LXXXVIII, 1, pp. 51-60) cover the early teaching of economics in the United States and list some of the textbooks, foreign and domestic, then in use. Suranyi-Unger's *Economics in the Twentieth Century* (Translated from the German by N. D. Moulton. New York. 1931. 397 pp.) traces the development of present day American economic theory to its roots in the past (both in America and abroad) and indicates its philosophical affinities. Edmund Whittaker's *A History of Economic Ideas* (New York. 1940. 766 pp.), John Kells Ingram's *A History of Political Economy* (London. Rev. ed. 1923. 315 pp.) and L. H. Haney's *History of Economic Thought* (New York. Rev. ed. 1922. 677 pp.) treat of American economists and of the development of American economic theory but do so in a summary fashion. Probably the most readable of the general histories of economic theory are *A History of Economic Doctrines from the Time of the Physiocrats to the Present Day* (Boston. 2nd ed. 1915. 672 pp.) by Charles Gide and Charles Rist, and *Philosophy and Political Economy in Some of their Historical Relations* (London. 1927. 424 pp.) by James Bonar, but neither treat to any considerable degree of American developments.

On EARLY COLONIAL THEORY, see Edgar A. Johnson's *American Economic Thought in the Seventeenth Century* (London. 1932. 292 pp.), the sections on New England in R. H. Tawney's *Religion and the Rise of Capitalism* (New York. 1926. 337 pp.), and the bibliography on pp. 792-798 of Perry Miller's and T. H. Johnson's anthology, *The Puritans* (New York. 1938. 846 pp.).

On the PHYSIOCRATIC INFLUENCE AND SCHOOL, see Gilbert Chinard's long introduction to his *Correspondence of Jefferson and Du Pont de Nemours* (Baltimore. 1931. 293 pp.), John Taylor's *An Inquiry into the Principles and Policy of the Government of the United States* (Fredericksburg, Va. 1814. 656 pp.) and Eugene T. Mudge's *The Social Philosophy of John Taylor of Caroline: A Study in Jefferson Democracy* (New York. 1939. 227 pp.). For a short exposition and critique of the physiocratic theory, see Henry Higgs' *The Physiocrats* (London. 1897. 158 pp.).

On the EARLY ECONOMIC NATIONALISTS, see Alexander Hamilton's *Report on Manufactures* (1791), and, for the historical influences upon Hamilton, J. T. Morse's *The Life of Alexander Hamilton* (Boston. 1876. 2 vols.) and Harold Hutcheson's *Tench Coxe: A Study in American Economic Development* (Baltimore. 1938. 227 pp.). For the sources and best exposition of the "American School," see Henry Carey's *Principles of Social Science* (Philadelphia. 1858-1859. 3 vols.), Abraham D. Kaplan's *Henry Charles Carey: A Study in American Economic Thought* (Baltimore. 1931. 96 pp.), and K. W. Rowe's life of Henry Carey's father, *Mathew Carey: A Study in American Economic Development* (Baltimore. 1933. 140 pp.). For an early statement of the *laissez-faire* point of view, see President Van Buren's Message to Congress, Sept. 4, 1837 (*Messages and Papers of the Presidents* [New York. 1897-1927. 20 vols.], III, pp. 344 ff.).

On the UTOPIANS and their foreign sources, see *History of American Socialism* (Philadelphia. 1870. 678 pp.) by John Humphrey Noyes who himself led the communist experiment at Oneida, New York; Charles Nordhoff's *The Communistic Societies of the United States* (New York. 1875. 439 pp.) which includes illustrations; and *Where Angels Dared to Tread* (New York. 1941. 381 pp.) by V. F. Calverton. The last mentioned volume includes new material on the Utopians and is popularly written. On the New Harmony settlements of the Rappites and Owenites see G. B. Lockwood's *New Harmony Movement* (New York. 1905. 404 pp.) and G. D. H. Cole's short biography, *Robert Owen* (London. 1925. 267 pp.). For the Brook Farm experiment both in its transcendental and Fourierist phases see J. T. Codman's *Brook Farm* (Boston. 1894. 335 pp.) and Lindsay Swift's *Brook Farm: Its Members, Scholars, and Visitors* (New York. 1900. 303 pp.).

On the European backgrounds of American SOCIALISM and COMMUNISM, see Morris Hillquit's *History of Socialism in the United States* (New York. 1903. 371 pp.), James Oneal's *American Communism* (New York. 1927. 256 pp.), P. T. Brissenden's *The I.W.W.* (New York. 1919. 432 pp.); and, for the European complements of these movements, H. W. Laidler's *History of Socialist Thought* (New York. 1927. 712 pp.).

For brief summaries of the influence of the British Classical school, the German Historical and Nationalist school, and the Austrian school upon American economic theory after the Civil War, see R. H. Gabriel's *The Course of American Democratic Thought* (New York. 1940. 452 pp.) and T. Suranyi-Unger's *Economics in the Twentieth Century* (New York. 1937. 397 pp.). For other phases of the same period, see: Sidney Sherwood's *Tendencies in American Thought* (Baltimore. 1897. 42 pp.) which describes the native influences at work upon American economic theory, and Joseph Dorfman's *Thorstein Veblen and his America* (New York. 1934. 556 pp.) which provides similar material from the life of one of America's greatest economists; Francis A. Walker's *Discussions in Economics and Statistics* (New York. 1899. 2 vols.) which expresses American criticisms of the *laissez-faire* point of view at that time; and both G. R. Geiger's *The Philosophy of Henry George* (New York. 1933. 581 pp.) and

Henry George's own *Progress and Poverty* (New York. 1881. 512 pp.) for the single-tax school.

III. SPECIAL TOPICS

1. EUROPEAN INFLUENCES UPON AMERICAN THEORY. This is an extremely broad and complex problem but for a brief summary of the interrelated histories of European and American theory regarding economic individualism, the distribution of wealth, economic reform, and economic nationalism, read Edmund Whittaker's *A History of Economic Ideas* (New York. 1940. 766 pp.), Chapters III-VI, Frank A. Fetter's "The Early History of Political Economy in the United States" (*Proc. Am. Phil. Soc.*, LXXXVII, 1, pp. 51-60), and Ralph Gabriel's *The Course of American Democratic Thought* (New York. 1940. 452 pp.), Chapters XIX and XXIII. For early experiments in monetary theory, read R. A. Lester's *Monetary Experiments: Early American and Recent Scandinavian* (Princeton. 1939. 316 pp.), Chapters I-VII; and for the impact of evolution upon American theory, read Thorstein Veblen's *The Place of Science in Modern Civilization* (New York. 1919. 509 pp.), Chapters I-IV and X-XIII.

2. THE GERMAN CONTRIBUTION. For the general effect of German immigration upon American agriculture, manufacturing, and commerce see the chapters on economic and material developments in Volume II of A. B. Faust's *The German Element in the United States* (Boston. 1909. 2 vols.). For its particular effects in various localities see Chapter II of *The Pennsylvania Germans* (Princeton. 1942. 299 pp.) edited by Ralph Wood, and relevant chapters in R. L. Biesele's *History of German Settlements in Texas* (Austin, Texas. 1930. 259 pp.), and J. A. Russell's *The Germanic Influence in the Making of Michigan* (Detroit. 1927. 415 pp.).

3. THE ITALIAN CONTRIBUTION. For the economic significance of the Italian immigration in general see R. F. Foerster's

The Italian Emigration of Our Times (Cambridge, Mass. 1919. 556 pp.), and for the Italian immigrant's role in the American agricultural system in particular, read Emily F. Meade's "The Italian on the Land" (*U.S. Bureau of Labor Reports*, No. 70. XIV, pp. 475-533). For additional bibliography see W.P.A. Federal Writers' Project, *The Italians of New York* (New York. 1938. 241 pp.).

4. THE SPANISH-MEXICAN CONTRIBUTION. For a history of the Spanish and Mexican agrarian economy in colonial California, see R. G. Cleland's *The Cattle on a Thousand Hills* (San Marino. 1941. 327 pp.), and for Mexican labor and agriculture in the United States today, read Paul S. Taylor's "Mexican Labor in the United States" (*University of California Publications in Economics*, VI, pp. 1-235). For additional information see Katherine Coman's *Economic Beginnings of the Far West* (New York. 1912. 2 vols.) and Emory Bogardus' *The Mexican in the United States* (Los Angeles. 1934. 128 pp.).

5. THE NEGRO CONTRIBUTION. The role of the Negro in southern agriculture before the Civil War is described in Ulrich B. Phillips' *American Negro Slavery* (New York. 1918. 529 pp.) and in the same author's *Life and Labor in the Old South* (Boston. 1929. 375 pp.). For the Negro worker both North and South since the Civil War, consult Charles H. Wesley's *Negro Labor in the United States: 1850-1925* (New York. 1927. 343 pp.).

6. THE ORIENTAL CONTRIBUTION. Material relating to the place and function of the Oriental worker and entrepreneur in the economy of the West Coast, where this impact has been principally felt, may be obtained from relevant chapters in E. T. Bunje's *The Story of Japanese Farming in California* (Unpublished ms. 1937. 234 pp.), Eliot Mear's *Resident Aliens on the American Pacific Coast* (Chicago. 1928. 545 pp.), and *California and the Oriental* (California State Board of Control. 1920. 231 pp.), particularly Sections 1 to 6, and

from R. K. Das' *Hindustani Workers on the Pacific Coast* (Berlin. 1923. 126 pp.).

7. THE IMMIGRANT AND THE RAILROAD. Immigration to America and the western expansion of the railroad have been interrelated phenomena in the history of the United States. The early railroads frequently promoted immigration while the immigrants, in turn, often provided the labor for the building of the railroad and the communities or the colonies from which the railroad drew its traffic. Paul Wallace Gates' *The Illinois Central Railroad and Its Colonization Work* (Cambridge, Mass. 1934. 374 pp.) and J. B. Hedges' *Henry Villard and the Railways of the North West* (New Haven. 1930. 224 pp.), trace the pattern of this interrelationship in its more general outlines. For additional material see bibliography, pp. 351-352, in Gates (*op. cit.*).

8. THE IMMIGRANT AND THE NEGRO IN THE TRADE UNION MOVEMENT (1860-1896). In contrast to the Negro who is often deliberately excluded from membership in trade unions, the immigrant has consistently played a prominent part in the history of the American labor movement. Many of the early labor leaders were foreign born, and it has been the foreign born element at large in the unions which has so often been responsible for their class conscious and leftist tendencies, particularly in the formative period, 1860 to 1896. For the role of the immigrant during this period read the relevant sections in Volume II of *The History of Labor in the United States (1860-1896)* (New York. 1917-1918. 4 vols.) edited by John R. Commons, Louis Adamic's *Dynamite: The Story of Class Violence in America* (New York. 1931. 452 pp.), and P. A. Sorokin's "Leaders of Labor and Radical Movements in the United States and Foreign Countries" (*American Journal of Sociology*, XXXIII, pp. 382-411). For the role of the Negro, see Sterling D. Spero's *The Black Worker: The Negro and the Labor Movement* (New York. 1931. 509 pp.).

9. THE COOPERATIVE MOVEMENT. The form assumed by the cooperative movement in the United States, and its European—particularly British—backgrounds are briefly described in Ellis Cowling's *Cooperatives in America: Their Past, Present and Future* (New York. 1938. 208 pp.), Jacob Baker's *The Cooperative Enterprise* (New York. 1937. 266 pp.), Maxwell S. Stewart's *Cooperatives in the U.S.—A Balance Sheet* (Public Affairs Pamphlet, No. 32. 1939. 32 pp.) and in R. S. Vaile's collaborative study, *Consumer Cooperatives in the North Central States* (Minneapolis. 1941. 431 pp.). For further material on early cooperative experiments in this country and abroad, see Charles Gide's *Communist and Cooperative Colonies* (New York. 1931. 223 pp.) and George J. Holyoake's *The History of Cooperation* (New York. 1906. 2 vols.).

10. COOPERATIVE BANKING. A special form of the cooperative movement in the United States has been people's banks, the idea of which is European in origin. For accounts of the typical organization of people's banks, their American and European beginnings, and their significance for American economic institutions, material may be drawn from D. S. Tucker's *The Evolution of People's Banks* (Columbia University Studies in History, Economics and Public Law, No. 102. New York. 1922. 272 pp.) and R. F. Bergengren's *Cooperative Banking* (New York. 1923. 370 pp.).

11. THE EUROPEAN BACKGROUNDS OF SOCIAL INSURANCE. The idea of social insurance which has grown rapidly in the United States in recent years has roots both in American trade union practice and in social insurance experiments abroad. For a description of the form social insurance has taken in this country and its European antecedents, see Abraham Epstein's *Insecurity: A Challenge to America; A Study of Social Insurance in the United States and Abroad* (New York. 2nd ed. 1933. 939 pp.). Other materials, historical and explanatory, may be found in Part III of Barbara N. Armstrong's *Insuring*

the Essentials (New York. 1932. 717 pp.), in the Social Security Board's *Social Security in America* (Washington. 1937. 592 pp.), in the Industrial Relations Counselors' *An Historical Basis for Unemployment Insurance* (Minneapolis. 1934. 296 pp.), and in Bryce M. Stewart's *Unemployment Benefits in the United States: The Plans and Their Setting* (New York. 1930. 727 pp.). For additional material, see Helen Baker's *Social Security: Selected List of References* (Princeton. 1939. 28 pp.).

THE POLITICAL IMPACT*

I. THE PROBLEM

AMERICAN political theory and practice have been affected in many ways by different national and ethnic groups. In regard to theory, we have been particularly influenced by the English and the Germans. It was English common law and theory (Topic 1) and the English church tradition (Topic 2) which determined the main lines of our early constitutional theory. It was Darwinism, spreading from England to America in the middle and late nineteenth century, which introduced into constitutional debate, first, a new defense for *laissez-faire* individualism (Topic 3) and, later, a strong positivistic and pragmatic tendency (Topic 4). And it was the infiltration of German political ideas during the same period which accounts for the recent trend of American theory toward "Statism" (Topic 5). Nor have such influences been restricted to the plane of theory. For example: it was the German liberal element in this country which once led the way in Civil Service reform, and the British Civil Service System which provided the model for that reform (Topic 6); it was the Irish-Americans who, until just recently, were the group most prominently associated with the growth and success of machine politics (Topic 7), and it has been the Negro, who, just by virtue of his exclusion from political activity, has been the occasion of fundamental malformations in the pattern of that activity (Topic 8).

II. GENERAL REFERENCE WORKS

There is no general history of ethnic and national impact upon American political theory and practice, but there are many works dealing with special phases of that history and almost all historical studies of American politics refer to the European backgrounds.

* See also Chapter V, "The Immigrant and American Politics," on page 84.

GENERAL WORKS ON AMERICAN GOVERNMENT AND POLITICS. Andrew C. McLaughlin's *Constitutional History of the United States* (New York. 1935. 833 pp.) and Henry C. Hockett's *Constitutional History of the United States* (New York. 1939. 3 vols.) provide a briefer and a more extended account, respectively, of constitutional history. Charles Beard's *American Government and Politics* (New York. 1922. 772 pp.) and *The American Leviathan* (New York. 1930. 824 pp.) analyze the American theory of government. Edward S. Corwin's *The President, Office and Powers* (New York. 1940. 476 pp.), and *The Doctrine of Judicial Review* (Princeton. 1914. 177 pp.), Louis Boudin's *Government by Judiciary* (New York. 1932. 2 vols.), Ralph V. Harlow's *The History of Legislative Methods in the Period Before 1825* (New Haven. 1917. 269 pp.), and Joseph P. Chamberlain's *Legislative Processes, National and State* (New York. 1936. 369 pp.) are all standard items dealing with the history and organization of the separate branches of government. For a popularized account see Ernest Sutherland Bates' *The Story of Congress* (New York. 1936. 468 pp.) and *The Story of the Supreme Court* (New York. 1936. 377 pp.). *The Constitution Reconsidered* (New York. 1938. 434 pp.), edited by Conyers Read, contains excellent essays on the background and history of the American Constitution and on its influence abroad.

For histories of American political theory see Charles E. Merriam's *A History of American Political Theories* (New York. 1924. 364 pp.) and *American Political Ideas; 1865-1917* (New York. 1920. 481 pp.), Raymond G. Gettel's *History of American Political Theories* (New York. 1925. 511 pp.), and E. R. Lewis' *History of American Political Thought from the Civil War to the World War* (New York. 1937. 561 pp.). For a history of political theory in general see William A. Dunning's *A History of Political Theories from Rousseau to Spencer* (New York. 1920. 446 pp.) and

George H. Sabine's *A History of Political Theory* (New York. 1937. 797 pp.).

EARLY PURITAN AND COLONIAL PERIOD. G. P. Gooch's *History of English Democratic Ideas in the 17th Century* (Cambridge, England. 1898. 363 pp.) gives the English background. Perry Miller's *The New England Mind: The Seventeenth Century* (New York. 1939. 528 pp.) provides a detailed account of the New England theocratic theory, and Thomas C. Hall's *The Religious Background of American Culture* (Boston. 1930. 348 pp.), Part I, relates this theory to later constitutional development. Roscoe Pound's "Puritanism and the Common Law," (*American Law Review*, XLV [1911], pp. 811-829) and Paul S. Reinsch's "English Common Law in the Early Colonies" (*Univ. Wisconsin Bulletin*, II [1899], 4) discuss the influence of the English legal tradition, while Richard B. Morris' *Studies in the History of American Law with Special References to the 17th and 18th Centuries* (New York. 1930. 287 pp.) canvasses in detail the types of law in force in the colonies.

CONSTITUTIONAL PERIOD. The literature on the background of the ideas implicit in the Revolution and in the Constitution is enormous, but among the more standard items the following may be mentioned: Carl Becker's *The Declaration of Independence* (New York, 1922. 286 pp.) is a brilliant study of the sources of that great document. Charles Beard's *An Economic Interpretation of the Constitution of the United States* (New York. 1923. 330 pp.) argues that the motivation of the Framers was primarily one of economic self-interest. Andrew C. McLaughlin's *The Foundations of American Constitutionalism* (New York. 1932. 176 pp.) and Alice M. Baldwin's *The New England Clergy and the American Revolution* (Durham. 1928. 222 pp.) discuss the religious influence. J. B. Thayer's "The Origin and Scope of the American Doctrine of Constitutional Law" (*Legal Essays*. Boston. 1908. 402 pp.) is a compact but excellent summary. Benjamin F. Wright's *American Interpretation of Natural Law*

(Cambridge. 1931. 360 pp.) describes the growing interest in the concept of natural law up to the revolutionary and early national periods and its subsequent decline. Howard Mumford Jones' *America and French Culture, 1750-1848* (Chapel Hill. 1927. 615 pp.) is an inadequate but still the best general account of the French influences during this period.

LATER PERIOD. Merle Curti's "The Great Mr. Locke: America's Philosopher, 1783-1861" (*Huntington Library Bulletin*, XI [April, 1937], pp. 107-155) describes the continuing influence of Locke in popular thought down to the Civil War. Chapter IV of the second volume of A. B. Faust's *The German Element in the United States* (Boston. 1909. 2 vols.) and John A. Hawgood's *The Tragedy of German-America* (New York. 1940. 334 pp.), together with the excellent bibliographies appended in each case, provide an introduction to the study of the German political influence after 1848, but no comprehensive treatment of the subject as yet exists in English. Marcus Lee Hansen's *The Immigrant in American History* (Cambridge. 1940. 230 pp.) contains suggestive material on the general political contribution of the immigrant, and Harold Fields' *The Refugee in the United States* (New York. 1938. 229 pp.) describes the status and attitude of the recent political refugee. Matthew Josephson's *The Robber Barons: The Great American Capitalists, 1861-1901* (New York. 1934. 474 pp.), *The Politicos, 1865-1896* (New York. 1938. 760 pp.), and *The President Makers: The Culture of Politics and Leadership in an Age of Enlightenment, 1896-1919* (New York. 1940. 584 pp.) describe the political and economic forces abroad in America from the Civil War to the first World War.

III. SPECIAL TOPICS

1. THE AMERICAN INFLUENCE OF COKE AND LOCKE. G. F. Macdonell's article on Sir Edward Coke in the *Dictionary of National Biography* (XI, pp. 229-244) summarizes the great

jurist's theory against the background of his life and times, while Locke's theory is best summarized in the second of his *Two Treatises on Government* (1690). E. S. Corwin's "The 'Higher Law' Background of American Constitutional Law" (*Selected Essays in Constitutional Law*. Association of American Law Schools. Chicago. 1938. I, pp. 1-67) and "The Basic Doctrine of American Constitutional Law" (*ibid.*, I, pp. 101-127) trace the influence of Coke and Locke on the American theory of natural right, vested interest, and judicial review.

2. THE RELIGIOUS BACKGROUND OF AMERICAN CONSTITUTIONAL LAW. As may be seen from Topic 1, American constitutional law, in its earlier phase, was rooted both in English common law and in English political theory of the fifteenth, sixteenth, and seventeenth centuries. A further source, however, is to be found in the thought and practice of the English church. The Puritan evolution toward a congregational form of church government, the Levellers' insistence upon the separation of church and state, and the "Federal" theology's emphasis upon "covenant" or contract as the basic type of religious and social relationship, all anticipate important and fundamental elements in American constitutional law. The character of these anticipations, particularly as manifested in early New England theology, and the extent to which later constitutional development may actually be attributed to them are discussed in the following works: Alice M. Baldwin's *The New England Clergy and the American Revolution* (Durham. 1928. 222 pp.), Andrew C. McLaughlin's *The Foundations of American Constitutionalism* (New York. 1932. 176 pp.) and Ernest Sutherland Bates' *American Faith; Its Religious, Political and Economic Foundations* (New York. 1940. 479 pp.), Books I, II, III. For further material see Perry Miller's *The New England Mind; The Seventeenth Century* (New York. 1939. 528 pp.), particularly Chapters IV and IX; Benjamin F. Wright's *American Interpretations of Natural Law* (Cambridge. 1931. 360 pp.); Richard B.

Morris' *Studies in the History of American Law with Special Reference to the 17th and 18th Centuries* (New York. 1930. 287 pp.); relevant parts of G. P. Gooch's *History of English Democratic Ideas in the 17th Century* (Cambridge, England. 1898. 363 pp.); and William S. Carpenter's *The Development of American Political Thought* (Princeton. 1930. 191 pp.), particularly Chapter I.

3. THE INFLUENCE OF SPENCER ON AMERICAN CONSTITUTIONAL LAW. Darwin's theory of evolution was probably the greatest, single intellectual influence brought to bear upon nineteenth-century America. The doctrine that man is basically an animal and the human race merely one phase in an evolutionary process characterized by change and the struggle for survival was so radical and far-reaching in its implications that almost every sphere of human thought and activity was affected. One result of this influence was an attempt by such conservative thinkers as Herbert Spencer and John Fiske to convert the doctrine into a new justification for political and economic *laissez faire*, and it was under this particular guise, in fact, that evolutionism first made itself felt in American political theory. Once the implications of Spencer's interpretation were grasped, corporation lawyers were quick to employ it in arguments before the Federal Courts and in this way succeeded in introducing it into constitutional debate. For material both on the background of the influence and in the exact form that influence took, see Hugh Eliot's "Herbert Spencer" (*Dictionary of National Biography*, 2nd Supplement, Vol. III, pp. 360-369), James Truslow Adams' "John Fiske" (*Dictionary of American Biography*, Vol. VI); Herbert Spencer's *The Man Versus the State* (Ed. by Albert J. Nock. Caldwell. 1940. 213 pp.); John Fiske's *The Destiny of Man Viewed in the Light of His Origins* (Boston. 1884. 121 pp.), Benjamin R. Twiss' *Lawyers and the Constitution; How Laissez-Faire Came to the Supreme Court* (Princeton. 1942. 271 pp.), and *The Age of Enterprise* (New York. 1942. 394

pp.) by Thomas C. Cochran and William Miller. For further material on Spencer and Fiske see David Duncan's *Life and Letters of Herbert Spencer* (London. 1906. 284 pp.) and John S. Clark's *The Life and Letters of John Fiske* (Boston. 1917. 2 vols.). For a critical evaluation of Spencer's and Fiske's philosophy see Arthur K. Rogers' *English and American Philosophy since 1800* (New York. 1922. 468 pp.) and *Morals in Review* (New York. 1927. 456 pp.), and D. G. Ritchie's *The Principles of State Interference; Four Essays on the Political Philosophy of Mr. Herbert Spencer, J. S. Mill, and T. H. Green* (London. 1891. 172 pp.).

4. EVOLUTIONARY SCIENCE AND POLITICAL PRAGMATISM. The genuinely revolutionary implications of Darwinism for political theory in general and for American political theory in particular were developed, not by the apologists for *laissez faire,* but by the supporters of scientific positivism and pragmatism, two schools of thought which came into prominence in the last decades of the nineteenth century. Holding (1) that moral and political principles evolve and are as relative as the species itself, (2) that mind and knowledge function primarily as tools for survival, and (3) that science alone has learned how to utilize these tools properly, this group of thinkers has been led to deny validity to the concepts of natural right and of natural law, and to argue, instead, that human happiness is a matter of satisfying existing human needs and of using scientific methods to determine both what these needs are and how best they may be satisfied. The influence may be studied best, perhaps, in the works of its two chief American representatives, John Dewey and the late Mr. Justice Holmes. For an understanding of just what the political philosophies of the two men are and in just what sense their philosophies represent an abrupt and revolutionary departure from the American political philosophy of the past, see Sidney Hook's *John Dewey, an Intellectual Portrait* (New York. 1939. 242 pp.); John Dewey's *The Influence of Darwin on Philosophy and Other Essays*

(New York. 1910. 309 pp.), Essay I; Joseph Ratner's *Intelligence in the Modern World: John Dewey's Philosophy* (New York. 1939. 1,077 pp.), Chapters IV, VII, XIV (761-783); Oliver Wendell Holmes Jr., "The Path of the Law," "Law in Science and Science in Law," "Ideals and Doubt," and "Natural Law" in *Collected Legal Papers* (New York. 1920. 316 pp.); and Oliver M. Blackburn's *The Political Philosophy of Oliver Wendell Holmes Jr.* (Unpublished Princeton Senior Thesis in Politics. 1942.) For further material on Dewey see Ratner's extended, critical introduction to the volume mentioned above; also, *The Philosophy of John Dewey* (Evanston. 1939. 708 pp.), edited by Paul A. Schilp, and *John Dewey, The Man and His Philosophy* (Cambridge. 1930. 181 pp.), edited by Henry W. Holmes. For additional material on Holmes see *Holmes-Pollock Letters, 1874-1932* (Cambridge. 1941. 2 vols.); also, *The Dissenting Opinions of Mr. Justice Holmes* (New York. 1929. 314 pp.) and *Representative Opinions of Mr. Justice Holmes* (New York. 1931. 319 pp.), both edited by Alfred Lief; and Francis Biddle's biography, *Mr. Justice Holmes* (New York. 1942. 214 pp.). For other American expressions of political pragmatism see Thurman W. Arnold's *The Symbols of Government* (New Haven. 1935. 278 pp.), Mr. Justice Cardozo's *The Nature of the Judicial Process* (New Haven. 1921. 180 pp.), Roscoe Pound's "Scope and Purpose of Sociological Jurisprudence" (*Harvard Law Review*. XXIV, pp. 59-88 and XXV, pp. 140 ff.), and Edgar Kemler's *The Deflation of American Ideals* (Washington. 1941. 184 pp.).

5. THE GERMAN INFLUENCE ON THE AMERICAN CONCEPTION OF THE STATE. When the Constitution was framed, and for many years thereafter, American political theory tended to assume that liberty is inherent in the individual and that the state was founded and exists for the sole purpose of protecting that liberty. Toward the end of the nineteenth century, however, this notion was challenged. In certain quarters it then

came to be held that liberty is not inherent in the individual but is derived from the state, and that the powers of the state itself must be understood to include not only the protection of individual rights but the promotion of the general welfare as well. This marked the influence of Germanic conceptions and, in particular, the influence of such German-born theorists as Francis Lieber, and such students of German political theory as Theodore Woolsey and John W. Burgess. For the sources of this influence and for its workings in subsequent American political theory see Francis C. Wilson's *The Elements of Modern Politics* (New York. 1936. 716 pp.), Chapter XXI; Francis Lieber's *Manual of Political Ethics* (Philadelphia. 2nd ed. 1881. 2 vols.), Vol. I, Bk. II, Chapters 1, 3, 4, 5, 6, 9; Theodore Woolsey's *Political Science; or the State Theoretically Considered* (New York. 1886. 2 vols.), Part II, Chapter I; Woodrow Wilson's *The State: Elements of Historical and Practical Politics* (Boston. 1889. 686 pp.), Chapters XV, XVI, and F. D. Roosevelt's Address before the Commonwealth Club. San Francisco (1932) and Message to Congress, January 6, 1937. For further information on Lieber see his *On Civil Liberty and Self Government* (Philadelphia. 1859. 629 pp.), *The Life and Letters of Francis Lieber* (Boston. 1882. 439 pp.), edited by Thomas S. Perry, and Lewis R. Harley's *Francis Lieber; His Life and Political Philosophy* (New York. 1899. 213 pp.). For a brief but thorough survey of the German background of Statism in Hegel and his followers, see relevant chapters in G. H. Sabine's *A History of Political Theory* (New York. 1937. 797 pp.).

6. CIVIL SERVICE REFORM AND EXPERT ADMINISTRATION: CARL SCHURZ. The ideal of civil service reform and of efficiency in government represents a phase in our political development in which foreign influence has been very great. Many of the basic principles upon which that ideal was based were derived in the first instance from a study of the British Civil Service system undertaken by Dorman B. Eaton, and much of

the early support for the idea was drawn from the liberal German element in this country under the leadership of Carl Schurz. As Secretary of the Interior under Hayes, Schurz introduced notable reforms in the administration of government personnel, in the conduct of Indian affairs, and in the formulation of a national conservation policy. For the reforms of Schurz, stressing in what sense they represented genuine innovations in governmental administration see Carl R. Fish's *The Civil Service and its Patronage* (Cambridge. 1904. 280 pp.), pp. 105-229; Oswald Garrison Villard's "Carl Schurz" (*Dictionary of American Biography*, XVI, pp. 466-470); Frederic Bancroft's and William A. Dunning's "Sketch of Carl Schurz's Political Career, 1869-1906" (*The Reminiscences of Carl Schurz*, by Carl Schurz. New York. 1908. Vol. III, pp. 313-455); and relevant parts (see the index, Vol. VI) of Carl Schurz's *Speeches, Correspondence, and Political Papers* (New York. 1913. 6 vols.). For further material on Schurz see his *Reports* as Secretary of the Interior; Matthew Josephson's *The Politicos, 1865-1896* (New York. 1938. 760 pp.) which describes the party politics of Schurz's period; and E. Bruncken's *German Political Refugees in America, 1815-1860* (Chicago. 1904. 59 pp.) which describes the class of immigrants to which Schurz belonged. For general material on the history and organization of the Civil Service, both here and abroad, see: Herman Finer's *The Theory and Practice of Modern Government* (New York. 1932. 2 vols.), Part VIII, for a brief survey of modern civil service systems; Darrel H. Smith's *The United States Civil Service Commission* (Baltimore. 1928. 153 pp.) and Lewis Mayers' *The Federal Service: A Study of the Personnel Administration of the United States Government* (New York. 1922. 607 pp.) for a briefer and a more extended account, respectively, of the U.S. Civil Service; and Emmeline W. Cohen's *The Growth of the British Civil Service, 1780-1939* (London. 1941. 221 pp.) for a brief account of the history and development of the British Civil Service. Dorman B. Eaton's *Civil Service in*

Great Britain: A History of Abuses and Reforms and their Bearing upon American Politics (New York. 1880. 469 pp.) is the famous study from which American proponents of civil service reform drew so many of their criticisms and arguments.

7. THE IRISH AND MACHINE POLITICS. The Irish of Boston, New York, and Chicago are here chosen as typical of those immigrant groups upon whose support the political machine has so often been built and for whom, in turn, the machine has provided the quickest and easiest way to control and modify American institutions. For the Irish in the political life of Boston see Marcus Lee Hansen's *The Immigrant in American History* (Cambridge. 1940. 230 pp.), Chapter V, and Oscar Handlin's *Boston's Immigrants, 1795-1865* (Cambridge. 1941. 289 pp.). For additional material on the Irish in Boston consult William G. Bean's "Puritan vs. Celt, 1850-1860" (*The New England Quarterly*, VII, pp. 70 ff.); Arthur B. Darling's *Political Changes in Massachusetts, 1824-1848* (New Haven. 1938. 392 pp.), which traces the rise and decline of Jacksonian democracy in Massachusetts between the dates indicated; Chapters II, III, and VI in each of the two volumes of sociological studies edited by Robert A. Woods: *The City Wilderness* (Boston. 1899. 319 pp.) and *Americans in Process* (Boston. 1902. 389 pp.), which deal with the status and influence of the immigrant in Boston at the turn of the century; and Joseph Dinneen's novel, *Ward Eight* (New York. 1936. 329 pp.). For the Irish in New York see Caroline F. Ware's *Greenwich Village, 1920-1930. A Comment on American Civilization in the Post War Years* (Boston. 1935. 496 pp.), particularly Chapters V, VI, IX, and X, and Roy V. Peel's *The Political Clubs of New York* (New York. 1935. 360 pp.), particularly Chapters III and XXIII. For additional material on Tammany Hall consult Gustavus Myer's *The History of Tammany Hall* (New York. 1917. 2nd ed. 414 pp.) and Max R. Werner's *Tammany Hall* (New York.

1928. 586 pp.). For the Irish in Chicago see relevant sections of Harold F. Gosnell's *Machine Politics: Chicago Model* (Chicago. 1937. 229 pp.) and, for additional information, relevant passages of Charles E. Merriam's informal but informative *Chicago: A More Intimate View of Urban Politics* (New York. 1929. 305 pp.). For an excellent fictional treatment of the Irish in Chicago see James T. Farrell's trilogy, *Studs Lonigan* (1935). For general background material on the Irish see William F. Adams' *Ireland and Irish Emigration to the New World from 1815 to the Famine* (New Haven. 1932. 444 pp.) and Ina Ten Eyck Firkins' bibliography, "Irish in the United States" (*Bulletin of Bibliography*. Boston. 1916. Vol. IX, pp. 22-24). For background material on machine politics see Harold Zink's *City Bosses in the United States: A Study of Twenty Municipal Bosses* (Durham. 1930. 371 pp.) and Frank R. Kent's popularly written *The Great Game of Politics* (New York. 1924. 322 pp.).

8. THE NEGRO AND THE EXERCISE OF THE FRANCHISE. The disenfranchisement of the Negro in wide areas of the South today is at once symbolic of our failure to realize the democratic ideal in general and a mark or measure of the extent to which this failure has resulted in specific malformations of our political institutions. For an analysis of the causes of this failure and an account of some of its more characteristic results see Lewinson's *Race, Class and Party: A History of Negro Suffrage and White Politics in the South* (New York. 1932. 302 pp.), Harold F. Gosnell's *Negro Politicians: the Rise of Negro Politics in Chicago* (Chicago. 1935. 404 pp.), and the cases cited in Edward S. Corwin's *The Constitution and What it Means Today* (Princeton. 7th ed. 1941. 227 pp.), pp. 202-205 and 207-209. For a general history of the reconstruction period, consult: J. G. Randall's *The Civil War and Reconstruction* (New York. 1937. 959 pp.), W. A. Dunning's *Reconstruction, Political and Economic: 1865-1877*

(New York. 1907. 378 pp.), and William E. B. Du Bois'
Black Reconstruction (New York. 1935. 746 pp.), the last of
which is written from a somewhat Marxian point of view.
George Fort Milton's *The Age of Hate: Andrew Johnson
and the Radicals* (New York. 1930. 787 pp.) is an excellent
account of national politics during Johnson's administration,
and Gilbert T. Stephenson's *Race Distinctions in American
Law* (New York. 1910. 388 pp.), although old, is a useful
summary of discriminatory southern legislation after 1865.
For the reconstruction period in Virginia see June P. Guild's
Black Laws of Virginia (Richmond. 1936. 249 pp.) which
summarizes Virginia's Negro legislation down to the present;
Charles C. Pearson's *The Readjustor Movement in Virginia*
(New Haven. 1917. 191 pp.) which defends the conservative
opposition to the political union of blacks and whites under
Mahone, and James H. Johnson's "The Participation of Negroes in the Government of Virginia from 1877 to 1888"
(*Journal of Negro History*, XIV [1929], pp. 251-272)
which defends that union. For the reconstruction period in
other regions see Alrutheus A. Taylor's *The Negro in the Reconstruction of Virginia* (Washington. 1926. 300 pp.), *The
Negro in South Carolina During the Reconstruction* (Washington. 1924. 341 pp.), and *The Negro in Tennessee, 1865-
1880* (Washington. 1941. 306 pp.). Edward R. Turner describes the gradual emancipation of the Negro in Pennsylvania
before the Civil War in his *The Negro in Pennsylvania—
Slavery—Servitude—Freedom, 1639-1861* (Washington.
1911. 314 pp.). For other discussions of note on the subject,
see *The Journal of Negro History, passim.*

THE ARTISTIC
AND LITERARY IMPACT*

I. THE PROBLEM

ALTHOUGH many American artists and writers have been self-consciously and even belligerently nationalistic (Topic 1), our art and literature have, on the whole, been extremely sensitive to foreign influences. Thus, in literature, the British influence has been both great and constant. It has been British literature, for example, to which so many of our more popular writers in the past have turned for their models, and it has been the British, again, who have so often been the first to "discover," and to encourage, important new American talent. In the fine arts, too, the foreign influence has been great although more diverse in point of origin. Thus, so long as American artists felt it necessary to go abroad to study (and this was true until just recently), English, Italian, German, and French studios became, at various times, principal and determining factors in our artistic development. And even today, when foreign study is no longer held to be essential and when many of our artists have become more nationalistic than ever before, such influence continues in the shape of a newly awakened interest in the art of the American Indian, and in the art of Mexico, Central America, and South America.

In general, these influences have been of two major types. In the first place there is the influence of the "cultural island," the foreign community in America which remains relatively isolated, and in which, as a result, the literary tradition and those of the major and minor arts continue to be rooted in the tradition of the homeland rather than in that of the adopted country. Of these the Pennsylvania Germans (Topic 2), the French in New Orleans (Topic 3), and the Spanish in the Southwest and California have been notable examples. One effect of the existence of such islands has been the purely nega-

---

* See also Chapter VI, "Foreign Influences in American Art," on page 99, and Chapter VII, "The American Expatriate," on page 126.

tive one of creating within the main literary and artistic streams of our culture minor streams which although *in* America are not, in a full sense, *of* America, and which, therefore, require for their study and appreciation a radically different critical apparatus. Another such effect is the slow diffusion of literary, artistic, and architectural forms originating within the islands into the surrounding American culture, as illustrated, for example, in the spread of the Pennsylvania German style of barn. But, in literature, the effect has been even more varied, leading, in one instance, to the creation of the bilingual writer (Topic 4) and, in the other, to the literary exploitation of the life of the cultural islands by native American writers (Topic 5).

The second type of foreign influence to consider is that which originates, not within the cultural island, but abroad, and whose effect may assume any one of three forms: (1) that which merely reinforces or reformulates, in a slightly different way, native art forms already in use; (2) that which acts to provide vehicles of expression for native points of view which hitherto have not been clearly or adequately expressed; and (3) that which serves to introduce both a new attitude and a new set of art forms to express it. The influence of the Düsseldorf school upon our painting and the influence of the French naturalist school upon our literature (Topic 8) are instances of the first sort of influence, since the effect of each was merely to underline and develop certain realistic techniques already being employed by native artists and writers. The influences in art of neoclassicism (Topic 6), and of the Gothic revival (Topic 7), represent the second form of influence, since both of these were imported to express cultural and social needs which had hitherto lacked adequate artistic expression. The influences of aestheticism (Topic 9), and of Post-Impressionism (Topic 10) are examples of the third variety of influence from abroad, that in which new ideas as well as new vehicles of expression are introduced. Finally, in the phenomenon of expatriation (Topic 11) the influence may assume any one or all of these three forms.

II. GENERAL REFERENCE WORKS

Although the non-American influences upon our art and literature have been very great, no over-all history of these influences exists. Such studies as do exist are largely concerned with individual influences upon particular artists and writers, and make little or no attempt at generalization. Most of the following standard items, however, touch upon the subject in some form or other.

ART. Suzanne La Follette's *Art in America* (New York. 1929. 361 pp.) is not illustrated, but is otherwise the best short critical account; *Art in America, A Complete Survey* (New York. 1939. 162 pp.), by H. Cahill and A. Barr and *The American Spirit in Art* (New Haven. 1927. 354 pp.) by F. J. Mather, C. R. Morey, and W. J. Henderson are both well illustrated surveys; M. C. Cheney's *Modern Art in America* (New York. 1939. 190 pp.) discusses the more recent movements in painting and sculpture but is somewhat superficial. For histories of painting see S. Isham and R. Cortissoz's *The History of American Painting* (New York. Rev. ed. 1942. 608 pp.) which is copiously illustrated but descriptive rather than critical in treatment. For the history of sculpture see Lorado Taft's *The History of American Sculpture* (New York. Rev. ed. 1930. 622 pp.) which is the only general history of its sort; also A. Adams' *The Spirit of American Sculpture* (New York. Rev. ed. 1929. 196 pp.). For architecture consult S. F. Kimball's *American Architecture* (Indianapolis. 1928. 262 pp.), an excellent survey but somewhat "antimodern" in point of view; T. Tallmadge's *The Story of Architecture in America* (New York. Rev. ed. n.d. 322 pp.), a survey, with few illustrations, by a professional architect, Lewis Mumford's suggestive, but often superficial, history of the social backgrounds of American architecture, *Sticks and Stones* (New York. 1924. 247 pp.); and T. F. Hamlin's *The*

American Spirit in Architecture (New Haven. 1926. 353 pp.) which is essentially a picture book. For an introduction to the minor arts and crafts see S. G. Williamson's survey, *The American Craftsman* (New York. 1940. 239 pp.), and for the history of American collections see R. Brimo's *L'évolution du goût aux Etats-Unis* (Paris. 1938. 207 pp.).

LITERATURE. Among the better general histories, *The Cambridge History of American Literature* (New York. 1917-1921. 4 vols.) is adequate on the early periods, but otherwise uneven in quality, while V. L. Parrington's *Main Currents of American Thought* (New York. 1927-1930. 3 vols.), the most brilliant of the interpretative studies, was never finished. On humor see W. Blair's *Native American Humor* (New York. 1937. 573 pp.) and Constance Rourke's excellent *American Humor* (New York. 1931. 324 pp.). On the history of periodicals and newspapers see F. L. Mott's *History of American Magazines, 1741-1885* (New York. 1930-1938. 3 vols.), and the same author's *American Journalism, 1690-1940* (New York. 1941. 772 pp.). On the American language, H. L. Mencken's *The American Language* (New York. 4th ed. 1938. 769 pp.) is a fairly dependable, popular account. On special periods and origins, Moses Coit Tyler's *History of American Literature, 1607-1765* (New York. 1879. 2 vols.), though dated, contains material not easily obtainable elsewhere; Van Wyck Brooks' *The Flowering of New England, 1815-1865* (New York. 1936. 550 pp.) and *New England: Indian Summer, 1865-1915* (New York. 1940. 557 pp.) present a detailed, highly impressionistic account of the New England writers between the dates specified, in which nostalgia sometimes gets the better of critical perceptions; F. O. Matthiessen's *American Renaissance* (New York. 1941. 678 pp.) provides a brilliant study and interpretation of the writers and thinkers of the middle years of the nineteenth century; Oscar Cargill's *Intellectual America: Ideas on the March* (New York. 1941. 777 pp.) is confused in its classifications but remains the most detailed and compendious account of American writers from the Civil War on. Alfred Kazin's *On Native Grounds* (New York. 1942. 541 pp.) is the most able account of recent and contemporary figures.

III. SPECIAL TOPICS

1. NATIONALISM IN AMERICAN ART AND LITERATURE. Since the founding of the Republic, American writers and artists have stressed the importance of creating a national art and literature. Most have believed such a nationalist tradition desirable but there has been a sharp division of opinion regarding the form this tradition should take. According to one school —for example, that represented by James Russell Lowell— American art and literature should merely develop further the European tradition, utilizing both European themes and styles for this purpose. According to another school—for example, that represented by Emerson—American artists and writers should break with the European tradition entirely and strive to express what is purely indigenous to the American scene. Between these two extremes controversy has moved back and forth for over a hundred years and has assumed multiple forms. A quick survey of the subject, however, may be had from the following: P. Boswell's *Modern American Painting* (New York. 1940. 166 pp.), pp. 33-62; A. Burrough's *Limners and Likenesses* (Cambridge, Mass. 1936. 246 pp.), pp. 190-221; Harry Hayden Clark's "Nationalism in American Literature" (*Univ. Toronto Quart.*, II, pp. 492-519); Thomas Craven's *Modern Art* (New York. 1934. 378 pp.), pp. 311-345; Ralph Waldo Emerson's *The American Scholar* (1837); Alfred Kazin's *On Native Grounds* (New York. 1942. 541 pp.), Chapter 16; S. M. Kootz's *New Frontiers in American Painting* (New York. 1943. 63 pp.), pp. 10-15; F. O. Matthiessen's *American Renaissance* (New York. 1941. 678 pp.), particularly the parts dealing with Greenough, Thoreau, Mount, and Eakins; Harold Stearns' *Civilization in the United States* (New York. 1922. 577 pp.), the preface and pp. 179-197, 227-241; and Louis Sullivan's *Kinder-*

garten Chats (Washington. 1934. 391 pp.), especially pp. 123-126, 129-133, 167-170, 181-187, 209-212.

For further material on the same subject the following also are helpful: W. E. Channing's "Remarks on National Literature" (*Works*. Boston. 1890. pp. 124-138), W. C. Bryant's review of Catherine M. Sedgwick's *Redwood* (*William Cullen Bryant*. Ed. by Tremaine McDowell. New York. 1935. pp. 177-183), and Herman Melville's "Hawthorne and His Mosses" (*The Apple-Tree Table and Other Sketches*. Princeton. 1922. pp. 53-86) are all earlier discussions of nationalism in literature, while Van Wyck Brooks' *America's Coming of Age* (New York. 1915. 183 pp.), and Randolph Bourne's *The History of a Literary Radical* (New York. 1920. 343 pp.) provide more recent discussions of that topic. For nationalism in art, F. O. Matthiessen's *American Renaissance* (New York. 1841. 678 pp.) and Greenough's essays on art included in H. T. Tuckerman's *A Memorial of Horatio Greenough* (New York. 1853. 245 pp.) discuss and express the influence of the Emersonian tradition, while the following in large degree describe the particular influence of the same tradition in the "Chicago School" of architecture: H. Morrison's *Louis Sullivan* (New York. 1935. 391 pp.); Louis Sullivan's *The Autobiography of an Idea* (New York. 1924. 330 pp.); the January, 1938, issue of *The Architectural Forum* which is devoted to Frank Lloyd Wright; Frank Lloyd Wright's *An Autobiography* (New York. 1932. 371 pp. and New York. Rev. ed. 1943. 581 pp.) and *Modern Architecture* (Princeton. 1931. 115 pp.); C. Bragdon's *Architecture and Democracy* (New York. 1918. 213 pp.); and F. Gutheim's *Frank Lloyd Wright on Architecture* (New York. 1941. 275 pp.). For the frontier spirit in painting see works of Caleb Bingham illustrated in A. Christ-Janer's *George Caleb Bingham* (New York. 1940. 171 pp.) and for recent midwestern regionalistic nationalism see the following: T. H. Benton's autobiography, *An Artist in America* (New York. 1937. 276 pp.), Thomas Craven's anti-European *Mod-*

ern Art (New York. 1934. 378 pp.), the articles on Benton, Wood, and Curry in P. Boswell's *Modern American Painting* (New York. 1940. 166 pp.), and the material on Wood, Curry, and Benton in the May, 1942, April, 1941, and February, 1943, issues of *Demcourier*.

2. THE PENNSYLVANIA GERMANS. The Pennsylvania Germans represent one of the oldest of our cultural islands and also that type of island which at an early date loses contact with the continuing traditions of the homeland and goes on either to develop these traditions in its own way or to freeze them into static forms from which little or no deviation is permitted. Since this particular group was originally of peasant stock and came principally because of religious persecution, its loyalty to many of the main streams of German culture was tenuous, even at first, and, in any case, soon disappeared. The result has been a literary and artistic tradition which has remained faithful to the cultural forms originally imported, and which has made its most characteristic contributions in farm architecture and the minor arts, and in literature of the periodical and newspaper variety. For background and for the literary achievements of the group, see Ralph Wood's (ed.) *The Pennsylvania Germans* (Princeton. 1942. 299 pp.), while for its achievement in the arts, read F. Fetherolf's *The Art and Architecture of the Pennsylvania German* (Unpublished Princeton Senior Thesis in Art. 1935. 64 numbered leaves), T. J. Wertenbaker's *The Founding of American Civilization: The Middle Colonies* (New York. 1938. 367 pp.), Chapters VIII and IX, and the same author's *The Old South* (New York. 1942. 364 pp.), Chapter V. For additional material, consult A. B. Faust's very factual and uninspiring account of the literature of the group in Volume IV (pp. 572-590) of *The Cambridge History of American Literature*. For a popularly written, but well illustrated, description of the Pennsylvania Dutch country today see Elmer C. Stauffer's "In the Pennsylvania Dutch Country" (*National Geographic*, LXXX, pp. 37-74).

3. THE FRENCH CULTURE IN NEW ORLEANS. In contrast
to the Pennsylvania Germans, the French in New Orleans
strove for many years to promote and sustain contact with the
French homeland. They sent their sons back to France to be
educated, imported and imitated French literature and art,
and built their homes and conducted their social life as much
as possible in the French manner. If, in the end, their effort
to transplant and vivify French culture on these shores failed,
it was no fault of their own but the result of circumstances
over which they had no control. However, before they failed,
they succeeded in setting a Gallic stamp upon the architecture,
the minor arts, and the literature of the New Orleans region
which has endured down to the present. For the background
and the literature of the group read: "Ante-Bellum New
Orleans" in Grace King's *New Orleans: The Place and the
People* (New York. 1911. 402 pp.); the introduction to
E. L. Tinker's *Les ecrits de langue française en Louisiane*
(Paris. 1932. 502 pp.); the references to the theater and
opera in H. M. Jones' *America and French Culture* (Chapel
Hill. 1927. 615 pp.); and the accounts of Charles Gayarre in
Grace King's *Creole Families of New Orleans* (New York.
1921. 465 pp.), and of Alfred Mercier in Tinker (*op. cit.*,
pp. 351-369). For the arts see N. C. Curtis' "Architecture
of Old New Orleans" (*The Architectural Record*, XXX, pp.
85-98); and the pictures in both N. C. Curtis' *New Orleans:
Its Old Houses, Shops and Public Buildings* (Philadelphia.
1933. 267 pp.), and I. W. Ricciuti's *New Orleans and Its En-
virons: The Domestic Architecture, 1727-1870* (New York.
1938. 160 pp.). For additional material on the literary
achievements of the group see Ruby Van Allen Caulfield's
The French Literature of Louisiana (New York. 1929. 282
pp.), Lewis P. Waldo's *The French Drama in America in the
18th Century and Its Influence on the American Drama of
That Period* (Baltimore. 1942. 269 pp.), and Edward J.
Fortier's account in *The Cambridge History of American
Literature* (Vol. IV, pp. 590-598). For a description of

Creole families and Creole life today see the W.P.A. *Guide to New Orleans* (Boston. 1938. 430 pp.).

4. THE BILINGUAL WRITER. The bilingual writer is one who writes in two languages, or whose work through translation exists in two languages, and thereby may contribute to both. The bilingual writer, of course, is not a purely American phenomenon, nor is he always the product of the cultural island, although he may be and often is. For material on three outstanding American bilingualists see Bernhard A. Uhlendorf's *Charles Sealsfield: Ethnic Elements and Natural Problems in His Works* (Chicago. 1922. 243 pp.), particularly pp. 7-34; Charles Sealsfield's *The Cabin Book: or, Sketches of Life in Texas*, translated by C. F. Mersch (New York. 1844. 155 pp.), particularly pp. 1-96; George L. White's "H. H. Boyesen: A Note on Immigration" (*American Literature*, XIII, pp. 363-371); Theodore Jorgensen and Nora O. Solum's *Ole Edvart Rölvaag* (New York. 1939. 446 pp.), particularly Chapters VI and XIV; and O. E. Rölvaag's *Giants in the Earth* (1927). For further material on Sealsfield see Otto Heller and Theodore H. Leon's *Charles Sealsfield: Bibliography of His Writings, Together with a Classified and Annotated Catalogue of Literature Relating to His Works and Life* (Washington University Studies. St. Louis. 1939. 88 pp.).

5. LITERARY EXPLOITATION OF THE CULTURAL ISLAND. One of the most striking literary by-products of the cultural island is the interest its life arouses in native American writers, and the use to which it is often put as literary material. Among the most notable instances of this type of exploitation are the novels of George Cable dealing with the Creoles of New Orleans, the novels of Willa Cather dealing with the Czechs and Germans of the Middle West, and the novels of Harvey Fergusson dealing with the Spaniards and Mexicans of the Southwest. For specific examples see George W. Cable's *Old Creole Days* (1879); Willa Cather's *O Pioneers!* (1913) and

My Antonia (1918); and both the introduction and the first novel, *Blood of the Conquerors* (1921), in Harvey Fergusson's trilogy, *Followers of the Sun* (1936). For material on the life of Cable see Lucy Cable Bikle's *George W. Cable: His Life and Letters* (New York. 1928. 328 pp.), and for material on the lives of Cather and Fergusson see S. J. Kunitz's *Living Authors* (New York. 1931. 466 pp.).

6. NEOCLASSICISM IN ART. Neoclassicism was an international style in architecture and sculpture, and to some degree in painting, which developed during the late eighteenth century, and which became for a time the dominant American style. Spreading to this country from England and France, it was even more popular here than elsewhere because it was felt to express both the spirit of our republican institutions and (in the South) the ideal of a democracy based upon a substratum of slavery. Its basic forms, as the name suggests, were classic in inspiration, though they were used with a romantic nostalgia for antiquity. Discussions of various phases of the movement will be found in S. F. Kimball's *American Architecture* (Indianapolis. 1928. 262 pp.), pp. 69-117; H. Major's *Domestic Architecture of the Early American Republic: The Greek Revival* (Philadelphia. 1926. 96 pp.); T. F. Hamlin's "The Greek Revival in America and Some of Its Critics" (*The Art Bulletin*, XXIV, pp. 244-258); and Lorado Taft's *The History of American Sculpture* (New York. 1930. 622 pp.), pp. 15-91 and 131-149. For further material on architecture see S. F. Kimball's *Domestic Architecture of the American Colonies and of the Early Republic* (New York. 1922. 314 pp.), pp. 145-261, dealing with the Roman revival; H. M. Pierce Gallagher's *Robert Mills* (New York. 1935. 233 pp.), the biography of one of the outstanding classic revivalist architects; and R. Newton's *Town and Davis* (New York. 1942. 315 pp.), the history of an early firm which often worked in the neoclassic style. For material on sculpture consult C. R. Post's *A History of European and American Sculpture* (Cam-

bridge, Mass. 1921. 2 vols.), Vol. II, pp. 107-112. For material on painting see Cahill and Barr's *Art in America, A Complete Survey* (New York. 1939. 162 pp.), pp. 31-37, and W. L. Nathan's "Thomas Cole and the Romantic Landscape" in *Romanticism in America* (G. Boas, ed. Baltimore. 1940. 202 pp.), pp. 24-63.

7. THE GOTHIC REVIVAL. Like neoclassicism, the Gothic revival was a European movement with romantic connotations which owed its success in America at least in part to the fact that it could embody, or seemed able to embody, attitudes for which American art up to that time had failed to provide an adequate expression. One such attitude was that of high-church Episcopalianism—a movement even then particularly appealing to the American *nouveaux riches* among others—and one which with its romantic leanings could find nothing congenial either in the Renaissance spirit of the Georgian, or in the sublime simplicity of the neoclassic styles. The Gothic with its high degree of structural articulation also appealed to the American love of technical problems and played a part in influencing some of the early designers of metal-frame skyscrapers. See for the English background of the school, K. Clark's *The Gothic Revival* (New York. 1929. 308 pp.), and for the movement in the United States both A. Addison's *Romanticism and the Gothic Revival* (New York. 1938. 187 pp.), Chapter VI, and the relevant essays in *Romanticism in America* (G. Boas, ed. Baltimore. 1940. 202 pp.). For further material, consult: E. M. Upjohn's *Richard Upjohn: Architect and Churchman* (New York. 1939. 243 pp.), R. A. Cram's *My Life in Architecture* (Boston. 1936. 325 pp.), and C. H. Whitaker's *Bertram Grosvenor Goodhue* (New York. 1925. 50 pp.), all of which deal with architects who have worked in some phase of the Gothic revival style. Consult, also, R. Newton's *Town and Davis* (New York. 1942. 315 pp.), the history of an early firm

which often used the Gothic style, and *The Work of Cram and Ferguson* (New York. 1929), a book of plates.

8. NATURALISM IN AMERICAN LITERATURE. American literature and art has never been without its realistic strain, although this strain at times has been completely submerged by the "genteel" and "polite" tradition. Accordingly, when American writers such as Frank Norris began to study and imitate Zola and other great apostles of French naturalism they were doing little more than widening the scope and redefining the purpose of techniques and attitudes already implicit in the American tradition. For a general survey of the movement see Oscar Cargill's *Intellectual America* (New York. 1941. 777 pp.), pp. 48-175; Alfred Kazin's *On Native Grounds* (New York. 1942. 541 pp.), pp. 10-16, Chapter XIII, and the sections on Norris, Crane, Dreiser, and London; Herbert Edwards' "Zola and the American Critics" (*American Literature*, IV, pp. 114-129); while for particular examples of the naturalistic novel see Stephen Crane's *Maggie: A Girl of the Street* (1896), William Faulkner's *As I Lay Dying* (1930), and James T. Farrell's *The Young Manhood of Studs Lonigan* (1934).

There have been various types of naturalism in art, of which perhaps the most "scientific" in intent has been the movement, particularly important in painting, known as Impressionism. For the European background of Impressionism consult W. Weisbach's *Impressionismus, ein Problem der Malerei* (Berlin. 1910-1911. 2 vols.), and for Impressionism in the United States, Cahill and Barr's *Art in America* (New York. 1939. 162 pp.), pp. 84-88, F. J. Mather's *Homer Martin* (New York. 1912. 76 pp.), A. Adams' *Childe Hassam* (New York. 1938. 144 pp.), G. P. du Bois' *Ernest Lawson* (New York. 1932. 56 pp.), all of which contain biographical and pictorial material on outstanding American Impressionists with, however, little critical content.

9. AESTHETICISM. Aestheticism, or "art for art's sake," was originally a phenomenon of the "fin-de-siecle" in England and France, to which two countries it was primarily confined. It had, however, certain repercussions in America, and these are discussed in Oscar Cargill's *Intellectual America* (New York. 1941. 777 pp.), pp. 176-229, 418-456, 473-516; Alfred Kazin's *On Native Grounds* (New York. 1942. 541 pp.), pp. 51-72; Lewis E. Gates' "Impressionism and Appreciation" (1900), reprinted in Norman Foerster's *American Critical Essays, XIXth and XXth Centuries* (World's Classics. Oxford. 1930. 520 pp.), pp. 186-211; Bernard Smith's *Forces in American Criticism* (New York. 1939. 401 pp.), pp. 266-285; James Huneker's *Painted Veils* (1920); and J. M. Whistler's "Ten O'clock" (*The Gentle Art of Making Enemies*. London. 1890. 292 pp.). For examples of aestheticism in American novels see Harold Frederic's *The Damnation of Theron Ware* (1896), and James Branch Cabell's *Jurgen* (1919).

10. POST-IMPRESSIONISM. Along with aestheticism, Post-Impressionism in art and Symbolism in literature have been European movements for which there were no real equivalents among native American traditions and which, accordingly, have appealed to relatively few American artists and writers. For the theory and purpose of the movement, see, for the European background, G. Lemaitre's *From Cubism to Surrealism in French Literature* (Cambridge, Mass. 1941. 247 pp.); and for the movement in America, Cahill and Barr's *Art in America, A Complete Survey* (New York. 1939. 162 pp.), pp. 92-100, S. M. Kootz's *New Frontiers in American Painting* (New York. 1943. 63 pp.), *passim*, and S. Giedion's *Space, Time, and Architecture* (Cambridge, Mass. 1941. 601 pp.), pp. 350-432. For additional material on the movement see H. R. Hitchcock and P. Johnson's *The International Style* (New York. 1932. 240 pp.) and the following catalogues of exhibitions at the Museum of Modern Art:

Cubism and Abstract Art (New York. 1936. 249 pp.), *Fantastic Art, Dada, Surrealism* (New York. 1936. 248 pp.), *Modern Architecture* (New York. 1932. 199 pp.), and *Bauhaus, 1919-1928* (New York. 1938. 224 pp.). For the Symbolist movement in literature both in France and in America see Edmund Wilson's *Axel's Castle* (New York. 1931. 319 pp.).

11. THE AMERICAN EXPATRIATE. The effect of European culture on American writers has at various times in our history been exerted directly without having to traverse the Atlantic. During certain periods, more than in others, the writer or artist found it impossible to live and work in his native land. He might, at the extreme, expatriate himself completely as Henry James and T. S. Eliot finally did, becoming British subjects, or he might merely spend many months of each year in Europe, moving from one congenial and beautiful spa or city to another, as did Mark Twain—oddly enough—in his later years. In colonial times many Americans went to Edinburgh or London for their higher education and some of these men lingered in the old country or returned there to be Englishmen. In the early years of the Republic, when copyright difficulties made writing an uncertain profession at home and artists had not yet learned how to earn a living in a democratic society, such men as Irving and Cooper and Willis, Copley, West, and Allston lingered abroad for years or settled there permanently.

It was in the period after the Civil War, however, that the most notable and symptomatic exodus of American writers and artists took place. The flight of such painters as Whistler, Sargent, Edwin Abbey, and Mary Cassatt, of such writers as Bret Harte, Henry James, Edith Wharton, Logan Pearsall Smith, and George Santayana, is a phenomenon whose causes are social as well as personal.

In studying this phenomenon the writings of Henry James are of the first importance since his imagination dwelt constantly on what happens when American innocence and curiosity encounter the maturity and pessimism of Europe. See especially his *William Wetmore Story and his Friends* (Boston. 1903. 2 vols.), a study of a remarkable mid-century group of English and American expatriates in Italy; *Nathaniel Hawthorne* (New York. 1879. 177 pp.); *The American Scene* (New York. 1907. 442 pp.); the short story, "The Jolly Corner"; and the unfinished novel, *The Ivory Tower* (1917). Consult, for the early years, Hawthorne's *Our Old Home* (1863), his observations on England; and *Passages from the French and Italian Notebooks*, edited in 1871 by Mrs. Hawthorne. The ties which connect Hawthorne, James, and T. S. Eliot are discussed in F. O. Matthiessen's *American Renaissance* (New York. 1941), pp. 292-305 and 351-368. Additional information can be found in Van Wyck Brooks' *The Pilgrimage of Henry James* (New York. 1925. 170 pp.), and in his *New England: Indian Summer* (New York. 1940. 557 pp.), Chapters XIII and XIX (on James); and XII and XVII (on Henry Adams). See also Edith Wharton's *A Backward Glance* (New York. 1934. 385 pp.); Logan Pearsall Smith, *Unforgotten Years* (Boston. 1939. 296 pp.); and George Santayana, *The Genteel Tradition at Bay* (New York. 1931. 74 pp.).

For accounts of the expatriate generation of the 1920's, whose heaven was Paris, see Malcolm Cowley's *Exile's Return* (New York. 1934. 308 pp.) and H. E. Stearns, *The Street I Know* (New York. 1935. 411 pp.).

THE RELIGIOUS
AND PHILOSOPHIC IMPACT*

I. THE PROBLEM

FROM the point of view of American religion and philosophy, the nineteenth and twentieth centuries represent a period of extraordinary ferment. It was during this period, for example, that each of the two disciplines finally declared their independence of each other after centuries of close union. It was during this period also that each began to grow more sensitive to the growing challenge of science and to the specific needs and demands of the social milieu in which they existed. Finally, it was during this period that the interchange of ideas with European theologians and philosophers increased tremendously in scope and complexity.

The foreign influences felt, however, as a result of this interchange differ little in general type from the kind of influences we have been concerned with thus far. Thus, we find that the British, French, and German influences have predominated, and that while some influences have tended to reinforce (Topics 1 and 8), others have tended to obstruct (Topics 2 and 3) previously established native traditions. We also find that some of these influences have been mediated through the immigrant (Topic 6), others through the normal diffusion of ideas (Topics 4 and 8), and that they have affected American life at both the level of practice (Topic 6) and the level of theory (Topic 7). For immediate purposes, however, it will be convenient to disregard the above classification entirely and to consider these influences only in the light of their tendency to support or to destroy fundamental elements in the American tradition. And from this point of view, we discover that they were preponderantly antitraditional in implication and effect. Thus, European romanticism, whose influence was felt

---

* See also Chapter VIII, "Hegel, Darwin, and the American Tradition," on page 146.

most directly in New England transcendentalism (Topic 1), in the St. Louis Movement, and in American Neo-Hegelianism (Topic 2), was basically humanistic rather than supernatural in orientation, while the ultimate effect of science, showing itself most clearly in the development of positivism (Topic 3) and of evolutionism (Topic 4), was to encourage scepticism, or, at the very least, the demand that religious faith be grounded on and given meaning in terms of natural processes. And the same secularistic tendencies are to be observed in the practicalism of pragmatism (Topic 5) and in the humanitarianism of religious humanism (Topic 7). The sole exceptions to this general trend are found in the spreading influence of Roman Catholicism in the middle of the nineteenth century (Topic 6) and in the resurgence, more recently, of traditional Catholicism in Neo-Thomism and of traditional Protestantism in the so-called "crisis" theology of Karl Barth (Topic 8).

II. GENERAL REFERENCE WORKS

As in the case of political and economic theory and of art and literature, there is no over-all treatment of foreign influence in American philosophy and religion, but the following works, dealing with the general history of these disciplines in America, discuss this influence incidentally in greater or less degree.

PHILOSOPHY. Woodbridge Riley's *American Thought* (New York. 1915. Rev. ed. 1922. 438 pp.) is by far the best general history, but it is too condensed and too little concerned with the relationship of American philosophy to American social history. Among other general histories, H. G. Townsend's *Philosophical Ideas in the United States* (New York. 1934. 293 pp.) is sketchy and at points obscure; A. K. Rogers' *English and American Philosophy Since 1800* (New York. 1922. 468 pp.) is an excellent critical history from a technical point of view but focuses on individuals rather than movements and neglects the social background almost entirely; *Philosophy in America from the Puritans to James* (New York. 1939. 570 pp.) by P. R. Anderson and M. H. Fisch is an anthology but contains competent, brief comments and carefully selected bibliographies on the great periods and movements. For other over-all accounts see M. M. Curtis' "An Outline of Philosophy in America" (*Western Reserve Univ. Bull.*, II [March, 1896], pp. 3-18); Noah Porter's "On English and American Philosophy" (Supplement to English translation of F. Überweg's *History of Philosophy*. 1901. Vol. II, pp. 442-460); Gustav E. Muller's *Amerikanische Philosophie* (Stuttgart. 1938. 303 pp.); and E. G. L. van Becelaere's *La philosophie en Amerique depuis les origines jusqu'à nos jours (1607-1900)* (New York. 1904. 180 pp.). For the history of the teaching of philosophy see Benjamin Rand's "Philosophical Instruction in Harvard University from 1636 to 1906" (*Harvard Graduates Magazine*, XXXII [1929], pp. 296-311), and G. S. Hall's "On the History of American College Text-books and Teaching in Logic, Ethics, Psychology, and Allied Subjects" (*Proc. Am. Ant. Soc.*, ns IX [1894], pp. 137-174). Merle Curti's *The Growth of American Thought* (New York. 1943. 848 pp.) is a general intellectual history with some emphasis upon American philosophy, religion and science, and is especially valuable for its critical bibliographies.

On the colonial period, Perry Miller's *The New England Mind: The Seventeenth Century* (New York. 1939. 528 pp.) is the most detailed and authoritative account of early Puritanism; Woodbridge Riley's "Philosophers and Divines, 1720-1789" (*Cambridge History of American Literature*, Vol. I, Chapter V) and Herbert and Carol Schneider's *Samuel Johnson, President of King's College: His Career and Writings* (New York. 1929. 4 vols.) contain valuable material on the later colonial period; while Woodbridge Riley's *American Philosophy: The Early Schools* (New York. 1907. 595 pp.), although often pedestrian in style, is the most thorough and able history of the colonial period as a whole. For the deistic movement of the early nationalist period see Herbert M. Morais' *Deism in Eighteenth Century America* (New York. 1934. 203 pp.), Eugene P. Link's *Democratic-Republican Societies, 1790-1800* (New York. 1942. 256 pp.), describing the political ramifications of the movement, and G. A. Koch's excellent *Republican Religion: The American Revolution and the Cult of Reason* (New York. 1933. 334 pp.).

On the period, 1800-1865, Merle Curti's "The Great Mr. Locke: America's Philosopher; 1783-1861" (*Huntington Library Bulletin*, XI [April, 1937], pp. 107-155) is the definitive history of the continuing influence of Locke; James McCosh's *The Scottish Philosophy: Biographical, Expository, Critical, from Hutcheson to Hamilton* (New York. 1875. 481 pp.) presents the background, both here and abroad, of the so-called "Princeton School"; Robert Blakey's "Metaphysical Writers of the United States of America" (Vol. IV, Chapter V, of his *History of the Philosophy of Mind*. London. 1850) catalogues and reviews briefly the work of the principal academic philosophers of the period; Woodbridge Riley's "La philosophie francaise en Amerique; I, De Voltaire à Cousin; II, Le positivisme" (*Revue philosophique*, LXXXIV [1917], pp. 393-428, and LXXXVII [1919], pp. 369-423) traces the French influence in general, while R. L. Hawkins' *Auguste Comte and the United States (1816-1853)* (Cambridge, Mass. 1936. 147 pp.) and *Positivism in the United States (1853-1861)* (Cambridge, Mass. 1938. 243 pp.) trace the influence of French positivism in particular. For the French influence also, see Adrienne Koch's *The Philosophy of Thomas Jefferson* (New York. 1943. 208 pp.). James Murdock's *Sketches of Modern Philosophy, Especially among the Germans* (Hartford, Conn. 1842. 201 pp.) and O. B. Frothingham's *Transcendentalism in New England* (New York. 1876. 395 pp.) deal with the European backgrounds of transcendentalism. For a general survey of the philosophic ideas current in America at the time see Alexis de Tocqueville's *Democracy in America* (Ed. by John Bigelow. New York. 1904. 2 vols.),

Vol. II, Chapter I, and Henry Adams' *History of the United States of America* (New York. 1890. 9 vols.), Vol. IX, Chapters VIII-X.

On the period from 1865 to the present, R. B. Perry's *Philosophy of the Recent Past: An Outline of European and American Philosophy since 1860* (New York. 1926. 230 pp.) is the most extensive but also one of the most superficial of the general histories of the period and is not nearly so useful as such briefer accounts as Morris R. Cohen's "Later Philosophy" (*Cambridge History of American Literature*, III, pp. 226-265, with bibliography in Vol. IV) and Frank Thilly's "La philosophie Americaine contemporaine" (*Revue de metaphysique et de morale*, XVI [1908], pp. 607-634). Also valuable on the period as a whole are G. Stanley Hall's "Philosophy in America" (*Mind*, IV [1879], pp. 549 ff.), A. C. Armstrong's "Philosophy in American Colleges" (*Educational Review*, XIII [1897], pp. 10-22), and Josiah Royce's "Systematic Philosophy in America in the Years 1893, 1894, and 1895" (*Archiv für Systematische Philosophie*, III [1897], pp. 245-266). On the post-Civil War Hegelian movement, William Schuyler's "German Philosophy in St. Louis" (*Educational Review*, XXXIX [May, 1905], pp. 450-467) is one of the most concise accounts of the early midwest Hegelians and is superior, in fact, to the more diffuse account in Denton J. Snider's *The St. Louis Movement* (St. Louis. 1920. 608 pp.); while G. W. Cunningham's *The Idealistic Argument in Recent British and American Philosophy* (New York. 1933. 547 pp.) describes and evaluates (in technical terms) the thought of the more prominent later American Hegelians. *Contemporary Idealism in America* (New York. 1932. 326 pp.), edited by Clifford Barret, offers a defense of Idealism by various contemporary writers and includes an essay by R. F. A. Hoernlé describing the recent resurgence of Idealism in America. There is no good history of pragmatism, but John Dewey's "The Development of American Pragmatism" (*Philosophy and Civilization*. New York. 1931. 334 pp.) briefly describes the origins of the movement; George H. Mead's "The Philosophies of Royce, James, and Dewey in their American Setting" (*International Journal of Ethics*, XL, pp. 211-231) describes the thought and development of the two foremost American pragmatists; William James' *Pragmatism* (New York. 1907. 309 pp.) is the best exposition and defense of the pragmatic philosophy; while Arthur O. Lovejoy's "The Thirteen Pragmatisms" (*The Journal of Philosophy*, V [1908], pp. 6-12 and 29-39) constitutes a rigorous and searching critique of it. There is also much valuable material on the background of the movement in Ralph Barton Perry's *The Thought and Character of William James* (Boston. 1935. 2 vols.). The best account of the development of twentieth-century realism is W. P. Montague's "The Story of American Realism" (*Philosophy*, XII, 46, pp. 140-150 and 155-161). For contemporary American philosophers see *Contemporary American Philosophy* (New York. 1930. 2 vols.) edited by R. Adams and W. P. Montague and *American Philosophy Today and Tomorrow* (New York. 1935. 518 pp.) edited by H. M. Kallen and Sidney Hook, both of these volumes containing the "credos" and "vitas" of "older" and "younger" contemporary thinkers respectively. T. V. Smith's *The Philosophic Way of Life in America* (New York. 2nd ed. rev. 1942. 258 pp.) is a lively interpretation of the great American philosophers of the past fifty years. For a general account of European philosophic movements parallel to those in America see Harald Höffding's *A History of Modern Philosophy* (London. 1900. 2 vols.), Rudolf Metz's *A Hundred Years of British Philosophy* (New York. 1938. 828 pp.), J. T. Merz's *History of European Thought in the Nineteenth Century* (Edinburgh. Rev. ed. 1912-1928. 4 vols.), and G. H. Mead's *Movements of Thought in the Nineteenth Century* (Chicago. 1938. 518 pp.).

RELIGION. On the general history of American Christianity, W. W. Sweet's *The Story of Religion(s) in America* (New York. 1930. Rev. ed., 1939. 571 pp.), although compact, is the best recent survey, while Peter Mode's *Source Book and Bibliographical Guide for American Church History* (Menasha, Wis. 1921. 735 pp.) provides full bibliographical data. Other general surveys are: Leonard W. Bacon's *A History of American Christianity* (New York. 1897. 429 pp.), G. J. Garraghan's *The Jesuits of the Middle United States* (New York. 1938. 3 vols.), and G. Sherwood Eddy's *The Kingdom of God and the American Dream* (New York. 1941. 319 pp.). For the history of bigotry, see Gustavus Myers' *History of Bigotry in the United States* (New York. 1943. 504 pp.).

On the colonial period, F. H. Foster's *A Genetic History of the New England Theology* (Chicago. 1907. 568 pp.) is the standard work but Thomas C. Hall's *The Religious Background of American Culture* (Boston. 1930. 348 pp.), Joseph Haroutunian's *Piety versus Moralism: The Passing of the New England Theology* (New York. 1932. 329 pp.), and Sanford H. Cobb's *The Rise of Religious Liberty in America* (New York. 1902. 541 pp.) are also useful. Ernest Sutherland Bates' *American Faith* (New York. 1940. 470 pp.) is one of the better popular surveys of the period with emphasis upon the social significance of the different forms of church government. On the deistic tendencies of the time see the references to deism given above under PHILOSOPHY.

On the period from 1800 to 1865, S. L. Wolff's "Divines and Moralists, 1783-1860" (*Cambridge History of American Literature*, II, pp. 196-223 and 524-539) and E. F. A. Goblet d'Alviella's *The Contemporary Evolution of Religious Thought in England, America, and India* (New York. 1886. 344 pp.), Part II, are accounts and interpretations from the orthodox and the liberal points of view respectively. There is also valuable material in Williston Walker's *The Creeds and Platforms of Congregationalism* (New York. 1893. 604 pp.) and in certain of the essays in *Unitarianism: Its Origin and History* (Boston. 1890. 394 pp.), a compilation of sixteen essays by Unitarian clergymen. Albert Post's *Popular Free*

Thought in America, 1825-1850 (New York. 1943. 258 pp.) summarizes the continuing influence of the Enlightenment.

On the period from 1865 to the present, the best general account is Winfred E. Garrison's *The March of Faith: The Story of Religion in America since 1865* (New York. 1933. 332 pp.), but Ambrose W. Vernon's "Later Theology" (*Cambridge History of American Literature*, III, pp. 201-225; with bibliography in Vol. IV) is a helpful briefer account. For the rise of humanism and the impact of science see Sidney Warren's *American Free-thought, 1860-1914* (New York. 1943. 257 pp.) and Stow Persons' *The Free Religious Movement in America, 1867-1893* (Unpublished Yale Doctoral Dissertation. 1940. 205 pp.); and for contemporary tendencies, *American Philosophies of Religion* (Chicago. 1936. 370 pp.), by H. N. Wieman and B. E. Meland.

III. SPECIAL TOPICS

1. TRANSCENDENTALISM. The transcendentalist movement in New England was the first, and certainly the most indigenous, expression of American romanticism. Originating in a reaction against the sensationalistic and atomistic philosophy of Locke (then the dominant American philosophy), it went on to affirm the characteristic romantic doctrines of the unity of man with God and of nature with man, and to argue for the existence of a type of knowledge different from and superseding knowledge based on authority or reason. In a very real sense the movement was grounded upon native traditions: the mysticism which had been implicit in Calvinism from the beginning and the passionate belief in the supreme worth and potency of the individual, a belief nurtured both by the ideals of the Revolution and by the conditions of frontier life. But although the impetus and central doctrines of the movement were thus grounded in America's own past, its language and mode of expression was the language of Oriental mysticism and of German romanticism. This was a result, in part, of the fact that Emerson and other leaders of the group were stu-

dents both of Oriental philosophy and of the German idealism as it was interpreted by Coleridge and Carlyle in England and by Cousin in France. But it was also the result, in part, of the fact that the English and American philosophic vocabulary of the time was unsuitable for expressing the central convictions of the group. For this reason, therefore, transcendentalism became a native movement with a foreign name, an American voice expressing itself in an Oriental and (particularly) German idiom. But the foreign influence did not stop here. Since no language can be adapted to new expressive purposes without subtly altering both the language itself and that which is to be expressed in it, so here the use of alien conceptions introduced certain modifications, certain new inflections, giving to transcendentalism a twist it might not otherwise have had. For general material on the background of the movement and for its expression in American writers, see Woodbridge Riley's *American Thought* (New York. 1922. 438 pp.), Chapters II and VI; Merle Curti's "The Great Mr. Locke: America's Philosopher, 1783-1861" (*Huntington Library Bulletin*, XI [April, 1937], pp. 107-155); O. B. Frothingham's *Transcendentalism in New England* (New York. 1876. 395 pp.); James Marsh's introduction to his edition of Coleridge's *Aids to Reflection* (1829); Theodore Parker's "Transcendentalism" (*The World of Matter and the Spirit of Man*. Boston. 1907. 428 pp.); and Ralph Waldo Emerson's *Nature* (1836). For further material see George Santayana's "The Genteel Tradition in American Philosophy" (*Winds of Doctrine*. New York. 1913. 215 pp.) and J. H. Muirhead's *The Platonic Tradition in Anglo-Saxon Philosophy* (New York. 1931. 446 pp.). On the German influence in particular see René Wellek's "The Minor Transcendentalists and German Philosophy" (*New England Quarterly*, XV [December, 1942], pp. 652-680) and "Emerson and German Philosophy" (*ibid.*, XVI [March, 1943], pp. 41-62). The British influence is discussed in F. T. Thompson's "Emerson and Carlyle" (*Studies in Philology*, XXIV [1927], pp. 438-453) and "Emerson's Indebtedness to Coleridge" (*ibid.*, XXIII [1926], pp. 55-76), as well as in William Girard's "De l'influence exercée par Coleridge et Carlyle sur la formation du transcendentalisme" (*Univ. Calif. Publ. in Modern Philology*, IV [1916], pp. 404-411). On the Oriental influence see A. B. Christy's *The Orient in American Transcendentalism: A Study of Emerson, Thoreau, and Alcott* (New York. 1932. 382 pp.). E. W. Todd's "Philosophical Ideas at Harvard College, 1817-1837" (*New England Quarterly*, XVI [March, 1943], pp. 63-90) describes the Scotch influence at Harvard as a "bridge" between Lockeanism and transcendentalism. Ronald Vale Wells' *Three Christian Transcendentalists* (New York. 1943. 230 pp.) traces the influence of Coleridge upon James Marsh, that of Cousin upon Caleb Sprague Henry, and that of the German writers on Frederic Henry Hedge.

2. AMERICAN NEO-HEGELIANISM. American philosophical romanticism did not disappear with transcendentalism. It lived on after the Civil War, reemerging first in the St. Louis movement (1859-1880) and, slightly later, in the so-called American Neo-Hegelian school (1890-1917). In this later phase, however, it assumed a new and characteristically different form. For one thing, the German influence became more direct and more marked. Where transcendentalism had absorbed little more than the vocabulary of German romanticism, and this only indirectly through British and French sources, the St. Louis group and the Neo-Hegelians studied German philosophy for its own sake and at first hand. Again while the earlier thinkers drew principally upon the work of Jacobi, Fichte, and Schelling, the initiators of the German romantic movement, the later thinkers drew their inspiration from Hegel, whose system represents the culmination of German romanticism. Finally, and most importantly for our purpose here, while the transcendentalists could and did fuse a faith in the unity of nature with a faith in the importance of

the individual without undue risk of inconsistency, this was not possible in the case of the Neo-Hegelians since Hegel's system, with its explicit exaltation of the community over the individual, was thoroughly anti-individualistic in tone and import. Thus, where the influence of the early German romantics had been absorbed into the American pattern with relative ease and a minimum of shock, the influence of Hegel raised many difficulties and seemed to face the Neo-Hegelians with the choice of surrendering either their traditional faith in individualism or their new found faith in Hegel. As it turned out, however, they were unwilling to accept either alternative. Individualism in some form or another they could not forego and Hegelianism they would not, for not only did Hegel himself seem to them the greatest thinker of the modern world, but to those of the group who, like Royce, were sensitive to the social evils of the day, Hegel's system with its emphasis upon the rights of the community seemed to offer the only sound basis for the criticism and correction of *laissez-faire* individualism. In other words, what the group wanted and set out to develop was a type of Hegelianism which could justify an insistence upon the social responsibility of the individual and yet, in the process of doing so, did not entirely submerge the individual himself. J. H. Muirhead's "How Hegel Came to America" (*Philosophical Review*, XXXVII, pp. 226-240); Josiah Royce's *The Spirit of Modern Philosophy* (Boston. 1892. 519 pp.), Chapter VII; R. H. Gabriel's *The Course of American Democratic Thought* (New York. 1940. 452 pp.), Chapter XXI; R. B. Perry's *Shall Not Perish From the Earth* (New York. 1940. 159 pp.), Chapter II; and Royce's *The Philosophy of Loyalty* (New York. 1908. 409 pp.) describe and illustrate (in the case of Royce) how the group sought to solve this problem and the degree to which they were successful. For material on the St. Louis group see William Schuyler's "German Philosophy in St. Louis" (*Educational Review*, XXIX [May, 1905], pp. 450-467); C. M. Perry's *The St. Louis Movement in Philosophy:*

Some Source Material (Norman, Okla. 1930. 148 pp.);
Francis B. Hermon's *The Social Philosophy of the St. Louis
Hegelians* (New York. 1943. 112 pp.); and the essays by
Perry, Dodson, and Townsend in Edwin L. Schaub's *William
Torrey Harris, 1835-1935* (Chicago. 1936. 136 pp.). For
further material on the Neo-Hegelians see R. M. Wenley's
The Life and Work of George Sylvester Morris (New York.
1917. 332 pp.); J. W. Buckham's and G. M. Stratton's
George Holmes Howison: Philosopher and Teacher (Berke-
ley, Calif. 1934. 418 pp.); F. J. McConnell's *Borden Parker
Bowne* (New York. 1929. 291 pp.); and the essays on James
Edwin Creighton in the *Philosophical Review*, Vol. XXXIV,
pp. 211-261, and in the *Journal of Philosophy*, Vol. XXII,
pp. 253-264. For the group as a whole, and for Royce in particular, see George Santayana's *Character and Opinion in the
United States* (New York. 1920. 233 pp.).

3. SCIENTIFIC POSITIVISM AND SCEPTICISM. One of the
most important and lasting effects of nineteenth-century
natural science upon philosophy and religion was the development of scientific positivism. This was the belief (1) that
science alone can give truth, (2) that the object of science is
to describe rather than explain, i.e., is to deal only with the
"how" of things, not with their "why," and (3) that hence
religion and traditional philosophy, which had always attempted to get behind the phenomena of experience and to
explain their "why," must be rejected as vain and nonsensical
speculation. The view was first developed in France by Auguste Comte, but it quickly spread, first to England where it
was taken up by John Stuart Mill, Karl Pearson, and others,
and then to America, where its earliest and probably most distinguished representative was Chauncey Wright, a young
American physicist and disciple of Mill. In America, as elsewhere, however, the import of the position was not immediately apparent because of the technical language in which it
was couched. Nevertheless, it gradually gained ground among

the students of science, and in the end was productive of subtle changes in the whole American attitude. Among other things, for example, it turned the interest of American philosophy more and more in the direction of scientific problems, and in particular led to an increased concern with the nature of scientific method. Another result was Peirce's famous doctrine of "fallibilism," according to which all knowledge is inherently fallible, and still another, Henry Adams' search for a mechanical formula to describe the processes of history. It even had repercussions at the level of popular thought, for, although imperfectly understood, it there strengthened the case for religious agnostics and atheists like Robert Ingersoll. For a view of the implications of the movement, both here and abroad, see Karl Pearson's *The Grammar of Science* (London. 1892. 493 pp.), Chapters I and III; Charles S. Peirce's *The Philosophy of Peirce: Selected Writings* (Edited by Justus Buchler. New York. 1940. 386 pp.), Chapters II and III; Henry Adams' "Letter to the History Teachers" (Brooks Adams, ed., *The Degradation of the Democratic Dogma*. New York. 1919. 317 pp.); and Robert Ingersoll's "The Gods" (*The Works of Robert G. Ingersoll*. Dresden Edition. New York. 1907. 12 vols., Vol. I, pp. 7-90). For further material on Peirce and Adams see Justus Buchler's *Charles Peirce's Empiricism* (New York. 1939. 275 pp.); Henry Adams' "The Rule of Phase in History" (*op. cit.*); and *The Education of Henry Adams* (New York. 1918. 519 pp.). For the impact of science on academic philosophy during the nineteenth century see Chapter VII of H. G. Townsend's *Philosophical Ideas in the United States* (New York. 1934. 293 pp.), and for the triumph of positivism among the scientists themselves see Muriel Rukeyser's *Willard Gibbs* (Garden City, N.Y. 1942. 465 pp.).

4. EVOLUTIONISM AND THE IDEAL OF A SCIENTIFIC METAPHYSIC AND A SCIENTIFIC RELIGION. The most spectacular effect of nineteenth-century natural science upon philos-

ophy and religion was not the growth of positivism but the new impetus given to the belief in the possibility of a scientifically based metaphysic and religion by the development of the theory of evolution. This belief, which ran counter to the positivist contention that metaphysics and religion as such are scientifically meaningless, was not particularly new, going back, as it did, to Descartes' attempt to ground philosophy upon mathematics and physics. But it gained a new lease on life at this time and was given a new twist as a result of the enthusiasm initially created by Darwin's formulation of the evolutionary hypothesis. To such thinkers as Herbert Spencer in England and John Fiske, his disciple, in America, evolution was not merely descriptive but explanatory, and explanatory not merely of the facts of heredity but of society, morals, religion, and, indeed, of everything. And on this assumption, accordingly, they set out to interpret the world completely in terms of an evolutionary process. The resulting metaphysic, however, was more notable for its historical effect than for its intrinsic value. Superficial, vague, and mechanical in its conclusions, evolutionism as a specific philosophic system scarcely outlasted the generation which created it. Its effects on other fields, however, were extensive and profound. In literature, e.g., it reinforced the trend toward naturalism in such writers as Jack London, and accounts at least in part for the popular taste for novels of the type of Edgar Rice Burrough's *Tarzan*. In economics and politics, on the other hand, it provided (as we saw earlier) a new justification for *laissez-faire* capitalism. But its most important influence, probably, was upon religion. Here its effect was threefold: (1) in the case of certain thinkers (e.g., Haeckel, and, later, Bertrand Russell), it led to the rejection of religion as such, and to the adoption, instead, of an evolutionary type of naturalism; (2) in the case of other thinkers, it led to an effort to reconcile science and theology (as in Asa Gray and James McCosh) and, more radically, even to an attempt to base religion upon science (as in Fiske and F. E. Abbot); (3) finally, in the case of still others (e.g., William Jennings Bryan), it led to the rejection of the scientific account altogether and to a defense of the most narrow type of religious fundamentalism. All three types of attitude were prominently represented in America, but of the three, the second is probably the most significant and is considered both as regards its genesis and outcome in E. B. Poulton's "Charles Darwin" (*Encyclopaedia Britannica*, 13th ed. Vol. VII, pp. 840-843); Harald Höffding's *History of Modern Philosophy* (London. 1900. 2 vols.), Vol. II, pp. 438-451; E. F. A. Goblet d'Alviella's *The Contemporary Evolution of Religious Thought in England, America, and India* (New York. 1886. 344 pp.), pp. 209-221; Stow Persons' *The Free Religious Movement in America, 1867-1893* (Unpublished Yale Doctoral Dissertation. 1940. 205 pp.); Asa Gray's *Natural Science and Religion* (New York. 1880. 111 pp.); Francis Ellingwood Abbot's *Scientific Theism* (Boston. 1885. 219 pp.). For further material see John W. Draper's *History of the Conflict Between Science and Religion* (New York. 1875. 373 pp.) and Andrew D. White's *A History of the Warfare of Science with Theology in Christendom* (New York. 1896. 2 vols.) which attempt to summarize the principal issues involved; John Fiske's *Through Nature to God* (Boston. 1899. 194 pp.) which develops the Spencerian thesis that religion and science are merely two different approaches to the same problem; and the symposium on *Law and Design in Nature* (*North American Review*, CXXVIII [1879] pp. 537-562) by Simon Newcomb, Noah Porter, James Freeman Clarke, and James McCosh which illustrates both the vacuity typical of so much of the controversy and the different degrees of compromise it effected.

5. THE FOREIGN BACKGROUND OF AMERICAN PRAGMATISM. Philosophical pragmatism, the theory that the meaning and truth of a belief depend ultimately upon the use to which it is put, is often described as "America's own philosophy" and as one which owes nothing to European influences. And

to a certain extent this is true. It is clear, for example, that no philosophy has expressed more succinctly the American distrust of intellectual subtlety and the American preoccupation with the concrete and the practical, and none to which more Americans have given their allegiance in some form or another. Moreover, it was America which gave the doctrine its name, formulated its most characteristic principles, and, in general, provided it with its most forceful spokesmen. But this should not be taken to imply either that pragmatism is a purely American phenomenon or that none of its roots are European in origin. The history of the doctrine shows just the contrary. Thus, at the very moment Peirce, James, and Dewey were beginning to develop and expound pragmatism in America, European equivalents of the doctrine were already beginning to emerge in the work of such thinkers as Hans Vaihinger, the German, Henri Bergson, the Frenchman, and F. C. S. Schiller, the Englishman. Moreover, the American leaders of the school both borrowed from and acknowledged their debt to foreign thinkers. Thus Dewey came to pragmatism by way of Hegelianism, having been an Hegelian himself as a younger man, while James came to it through a study of the British empiricists; and both men at the outset were very greatly indebted to Darwin. It is worth noting in this connection that James called pragmatism "a new name for some old ways of thinking," and dedicated his *Pragmatism* to John Stuart Mill, "from whom," he says, "I learned first the pragmatic openness of mind and whom my fancy likes to picture as our leader were he alive today." In other words, American pragmatism did not grow up in a vacuum. Although developed independently and in a most original manner by native American thinkers, suggestions and hints of it are to be found in the European writers whom these thinkers studied. For James and his philosophical background see Woodbridge Riley's *American Thought* (New York. 1922. 438 pp.), Chapter IX; E. A. Burtt's introduction to his anthology, *The English Philosophers From Bacon to Mill* (The Modern

THE RELIGIOUS AND PHILOSOPHIC IMPACT

Library. New York. 1939. 1,041 pp.); Maurice Baum's "The Development of James' Pragmatism prior to 1879" (*Journal of Philosophy*, XXX [1933], pp. 43-51); R. B. Perry's *The Thought and Character of William James* (Boston. 1935. 2 vols.), Chapters XXVI through XXXIII, and LXXVII through LXXIX; and William James' *Pragmatism: A New Name for Some Old Ways of Thinking* (New York. 1907. 309 pp.). For further material on James see: Theodore Flournoy's *The Philosophy of William James* (New York. 1917. 246 pp.); Horace M. Kallen's *William James and Henri Bergson* (Chicago. 1914. 248 pp.); Otto F. Kraushaar's "What James' Philosophical Orientation Owed to Lotze" (*Philosophical Review*, XLVII [1938], pp. 517-526); and F. C. S. Schiller's "William James and the Making of Pragmatism" (*Personalist*, VIII [1927], pp. 81-93). For pragmatism in general see: John Dewey's *Reconstruction in Philosophy* (New York. 1920. 224 pp.) which describes the need for and the inevitability of pragmatism; Morton G. White's *The Origin of Dewey's Instrumentalism* (New York. 1943. 161 pp.) which describes the metamorphosis of Dewey's thought from Hegelianism to instrumentalism; and Arthur O. Lovejoy's "The Thirteen Pragmatisms" (*Journal of Philosophy*, V [1908], pp. 6-12, 29-39) which criticizes pragmatism on the ground of its lack of intellectual rigor.

6. CATHOLICISM AND DEMOCRACY. Unlike most of the Protestant sects, which are democratic both in their ecclesiastical organization and in their theories of church government, the Catholic church is frankly hierarchical in government and authoritarian in spirit. This divergence from the American norm has created certain problems for the Catholics, particularly in adjusting their church to a democratic society. Isaac Hecker's *The Church and the Age* (New York. 1887. 322 pp.) is the effort of a nineteenth-century American convert to show the indebtedness of democracy to the Catholic rather than to the Puritan spirit. The "Americanism" heralded in

Hecker's writings was repudiated by Rome at the end of the nineteenth century, and the protest of American Catholics of modernist tendencies is exemplified in William L. Sullivan's *Letters to His Holiness, Pope Pius X* (Chicago. 1910. 280 pp.). A summary of Catholic modernism by a Protestant, with a plea for it as the basis for Christian unity, is found in Newman Smyth's *Passing Protestantism and Coming Catholicism* (New York. 1908. 209 pp.), pp. 40-131. In general, however, Catholic thought in America has been less concerned with theological speculation than with practical matters of education and administration. Thus the ability of the church to hold the Catholic immigrant is demonstrated in Gerald Shaughnessy's *Has the Immigrant Kept the Faith?* (New York. 1925. 270 pp.), while much has been written by Catholic spokesmen to refute the charge that the political teachings of the church are inconsistent with the democratic ideology: see, for example, the articles by John Ireland and John L. Spaulding, in John A. Ryan's and M. F. X. Millar's *The State and the Church* (New York. 1922. 331 pp.), pp. 282-298 and 299-308. The principles of Catholic education and a sketch of the conflicts with proponents of public secular education in the nineteenth century are to be found in James A. Burns' *The Growth and Development of the Catholic School System in the United States* (New York. 1912. 421 pp.), pp. 217-273, while a general survey of the entire range of social adjustments confronting American Catholics from a critical Protestant viewpoint is undertaken by Winfred E. Garrison's *Catholicism and the American Mind* (Chicago. 1928. 267 pp.).

7. RELIGIOUS HUMANISM. Religious humanism in America first appeared within the liberal wing of Protestant Christianity in the late nineteenth century. The theological situation out of which the new humanism grew is sketched in Count Goblet d'Alviella's *The Contemporary Evolution of Religious Thought* (New York. 1886. 344 pp.), pp. 183-207.

O. B. Frothingham's *The Religion of Humanity* (New York. 3rd ed. 1875. 338 pp.), a classic of early humanism, still retains a vestige of theism, but concessions to the new spirit in more orthodox circles are noted in George A. Gordon's *Humanism in New England Theology* (Boston. 1920. 105 pp.). In addition, d'Alviella, Frothingham, and Gordon indicate the various movements in European thought which enter into the formation of religious modernism; for example, romanticism, evolutionism, positivism, the higher biblical criticism, and the divergent ethical ideals of the Oriental religions. The humanist movement culminates in Curtis W. Reese whose *Humanist Sermons* (Chicago. 1927. 262 pp.) is an admirable summary of the movement today. The most important offshoot of humanism was the Ethical Culture movement whose purpose and ideals are described by the founder, Felix Adler, in his *New Statement of the Aim of the Ethical Culture Societies* (New York. 1904. 7 pp.), and by Percival Chubb's *Origin and Growth of the Ethical Movement* (n.p. n.d. 8 pp.). A critique of humanism, which also contains a valuable study of organized humanism today, is found in Arthur H. Dakin's *Man the Measure; an Essay on Humanism as Religion* (Princeton. 1939. 284 pp.).

8. TWENTIETH-CENTURY SUPERNATURALISM. In reaction to humanism and optimistic Protestant modernism, a renewed emphasis in recent years has been placed upon Christian supernaturalism. Much of this emphasis stems from the German, Karl Barth, whose theology in relation to the problems of our time is discussed by Wilhelm Pauck, a German immigrant, in his *Karl Barth: Prophet of a new Christianity?* (New York. 1931. 220 pp.). Adolph Keller's *Karl Barth and Christian Unity* (New York. 1933. 320 pp.), pp. 177-206, analyzes the religious situation in the United States from the Barthian viewpoint, while Elmer Homrighausen's "Barth and the American Theological Scene" (*Union Seminary Review* [Virginia], XLVI [July, 1935], pp. 283-301) seeks to discover

why Barthianism has not had greater influence in America and what elements of it would be pertinent here. The most spectacular critic of American life from the point of view of Protestant modernism is Reinhold Niebuhr; see for example, his "Optimism, Pessimism, and Religious Faith" (*Christianity and Power Politics*. New York. 1940. 226 pp.), pp. 177-202. Many of Niebuhr's insights are derived from Paul Tillich, a recent immigrant from Germany, whose *The Interpretation of History* (New York. 1936. 284 pp.), pp. 219-284, attempts to demonstrate that a humanistic philosophy of history is sterile and that a sense of the true depth and meaning of life can be gained only through the union of the humanistic and prophetic approach.